MAXIMIZE YOUR WRITING

4

Maximize Your Writing 4

Pearson Education, Inc., 221 River Street, Hoboken, NJ 07030 USA

Staff credits: The people who made up the **Maximize Your Writing** team are Pietro Alongi, Rhea Banker, Tracey Munz Cataldo, Mindy DePalma, Gina DiLillo, Niki Lee, Amy McCormick, Lindsay Richman, and Paula Van Ells.

Text composition: MPS North America LLC
Design: EMC Design Ltd
Photo credit: Cover, PHOTOCREO Michal Bednarek / Shutterstock

ISBN-13: 978-0-13-466140-7   ISBN-10: 0-13-466140-0

Printed in the United States of America
2   16

pearsonelt.com/maximizeyourwriting

CONTENTS

Writing Level 4 – Advanced

Pre-Test 1

In the timed Pre-Test 1, you will demonstrate how well you understand sentence structure, grammar, punctuation, mechanics, and organization. You have 50 minutes to complete the test.

Grammar

Circle the letter of the correct answer.

1 I have to meet my mother-in-law tonight. If I

   a don't have to meet

   b didn't have to meet

   c will have to meet

her, I

   a can help

   b could help

   c won't be able to help

the group finish the project.

2 The students were very pleased

   a to have met

   b to meeting

   c meeting

the President during their visit to Washington, D.C. last summer.

3 The house had bad insulation before. Until it was fixed, it

   a would

   b had been accustomed to

   c used to

be colder in here than it was outside.

4 The woman was very tired when she got into the accident. She really

   a couldn't drive.

   b wouldn't be driving.

   c shouldn't have been driving.

5 Ellen went straight into her office without talking to anyone. The meeting with the boss

   a could not be going

   b may not have gone

   c might not go

well.

6 It's important to do well the first time you take the CPA exam. You
- **a** may not allow you to take
- **b** might have been allowed to take
- **c** may not be allowed to take

it again.

7 We all stared at the gaping hole in the wall. None of us could imagine what
- **a** has been happening
- **b** had happened
- **c** has happened

to it.

8 My husband still
- **a** hasn't seen
- **b** hasn't been seeing
- **c** hadn't seen

that controversial movie, so I can't discuss it with him yet.

9 Ginger didn't study for the test, and she thought it was really hard. She really
- **a** hopes
- **b** wishes
- **c** had wished

she had.

10 The store sells only local products.
- **a** Most of the
- **b** Most of
- **c** Most

them come from fewer than one hundred miles away.

Choose the correct original quote for the reported speech.

11 The financial advisor asked if we had ever filed for bankruptcy.
- **a** The financial advisor asked, Have you ever filed for bankruptcy?"
- **b** The financial advisor asked, "Have you ever filed for bankruptcy?
- **c** The financial advisor asked, "Have you ever filed for bankruptcy?"
- **d** The financial advisor asked "Have you ever filed for bankruptcy"?

12 Whole Foods
- **a** that began as a small store in Austin,
- **b** , which began as a small store in Austin,
- **c** began as a small store in Austin

is the largest organic grocery store chain in the country.

13 **a** When the tropical storm had been damaging enough,
- **b** As if the tropical storm had not been damaging enough,
- **c** If the tropical storm had been damaging enough

the people who remained had no electricity, food, or water.

14 Their teacher gave them more time to finish the project, but they
    a have got it to do
    b have to get it done
    c have to get it to do
by next week.

15 Technology is advancing rapidly. By the time we get used to Google Glasses, some other company
    a will have invented
    b will be invented
    c will have been inventing
a microchip implant with Internet access.

16 The staff all wonder
    a who will be laid off next.
    b whether will be laid off next.
    c it will lay off next.

17 Choose the correct way to reduce the underlined words.

Every winter, the children who live in nearby towns skate on the frozen lake.
    a who living in nearby towns
    b lived in nearby towns
    c living in nearby towns

18 We stayed in an isolated
    a cabin by us.
    b cabin by ourselves.
    c cabin by we.

19 It has been suggested
    a that she finish the medical trial
    b finish the medical trial
    c that she finishes the medical trial
before trying another treatment.

Punctuation and Mechanics

Circle the letter of the correct answer.

1 Which sentence is correct?
    a I was named after my grandmother, with whom I share a number of qualities persistence honesty and resilience.
    b I was named after my grandmother, with whom I share a number of qualities: honesty, persistence, and resilience.
    c I was named after my grandmother, with whom I share a number of qualities; honesty persistence and resilience.

2 Which sentence is correct?

   a The President of the United States has two homes, the primary residence located in Washington, D.C. is the White House.

   b The President of the United States has two homes. The primary residence located in Washington, D.C. is the White House.

   c The President of the United States has two homes. The primary residence, located in Washington, D.C., is the White House.

3 Which sentence is correct?

   a The pendulum swung back and forth twenty three times before stopping.

   b The pendulum swung back and forth twentythree times before stopping.

   c The pendulum swung back and forth twenty-three times before stopping.

4 Which sentence is correct?

   a The NAACP (National Association for the Advancement of Colored People) was responsible for many of the successes of the Civil Rights Movement.

   b The NAACP; National Association for the Advancement of Colored People; was responsible for many of the successes of the Civil Rights Movement.

   c The NAACP: National Association for the Advancement of Colored People was responsible for many of the successes of the Civil Rights Movement.

5 Which sentence is correct?

   a There is a twist in the essay, The First Day, which is about a little girl's first day of school.

   b There is a twist in the essay *The First Day* which is about a little girl's first day of school.

   c There is a twist in the essay "The First Day," which is about a little girl's first day of school.

6 Which sentence is correct?

   a The door swung wide open; she ran to close it.

   b The door swung wide open, she ran to close it.

   c The door swung wide open she ran to close it.

Sentence Structure

Circle the letter of the correct answer.

1 No one is allowed in the intensive care unit of the hospital unless

   a he or she is a family member

   b they are family members

   c family members

of the patient.

2 She received the most points in the race, so the medal is

   a she.

   b her.

   c hers.

3 Before the cook attempted the recipe, she carefully gathered the rare and hard-to-find ingredients

  a   , truffles, saffron, and ghee,

  b   : truffles, saffron, and ghee.

  c   ; truffles, saffron, and ghee.

4 When the student was caught cheating, the teacher

  a   did

  b   made

  c   took

an example of him by failing him.

5 Please let the college know

  a   when you receive your student aid report.

  b   when do you receive your student aid report.

  c   when receive you your student aid report.

6 The professor wants to get an assistant

  a   however

  b   ; however,

  c   , however,

all of the TAs are taken.

7 Either the short stop or the pitcher

  a   calls

  b   call

  c   is call

a time-out in the game.

8 Helen called the bank <u>so that she could refinance her loan.</u>

  a   Not a clause

  b   Adverb clause

  c   Adjective clause

  d   Noun clause

  e   Independent clause

9 When the alarm went off, everyone proceeded

  a   quick yet quietly

  b   quickly, but quiet

  c   quickly and quietly

to the emergency exit.

10 Khalil Gibran's poetry is both

    a power

    b powerfully

    c powerful

and beautiful.

11 Choose the correct sentence.

    a Tulips are bulbous flowers often grown in gardens and pots because people enjoy their color in the springtime.

    b Tulips are flowers that grow from bulbs and they are often grown in gardens and pots because people enjoy their color in the springtime.

    c Tulips are flowers that grow from bulbs so they are often grown in gardens as well as pots because people enjoy their color in the springtime.

12 Choose the correct sentence.

    a The protesters outside the factory want that they reduce the pollution.

    b The protesters outside want the factory to reduce the pollution.

    c The protesters outside the factory want reducing the pollution.

13 Choose the correct sentence.

    a Unless I'm home; there will be no one to sign for the package.

    b Unless I'm home there will be no one to sign for the package.

    c Unless I'm home, there will be no one to sign for the package.

14 Choose the sentence that is choppy and needs revision.

    a The assignment, due on Friday, is a four-paged, double-spaced argument essay.

    b The assignment, an argument essay, is due Friday. It should be four pages long and double-spaced.

    c The assignment is an argument essay. It is due on Friday. It should be four pages long. It should be double-spaced.

Paragraph and Essay Organization

Cyber-bullying

Phoebe Prince committed suicide in January 2010, after months of being harassed online by youths from her high school in Massachusetts. They sent her cruel messages via text, and they posted rumors and called her names on her Facebook page.

1 a When

    b Before

    c Even after

her death, they continued to say hateful things about her on Facebook. <u>(a) The Prince family was horrified, and others were outraged, by the students' behavior</u>. The police arrested the students, who were convicted of stalking, harassment, and other charges. Cases like Phoebe's, in which a child is humiliated through social media, are proliferating. Cyber-bullying can cause serious long-lasting damage to the targeted child.

2 a Cyber-bullying is a multi-faceted problem and schools, parents, and police are looking for ways to prevent it.

   b There are a number of ways to combat cyber-bullying, a growing problem in the US schools today.

   c Cyber-bulling is caused by a number of factors and can have serious effects on its victims.

For example, bullies can send mean comments or unflattering pictures via text message or post them on Facebook; they can create websites to make fun of a particular person or hack into a person's account in order to send inappropriate emails with that person's name. When researchers ask cyber-bullies why they do it, they will often say that they disliked the victim or that they were angry with him or her. <u>(b) Children do not fully develop emotionally until their early twenties</u>. In addition, research suggests that children bully online because it increases their social status in the eyes of their peers.

A major issue with cyber-bullying is the damage it does to the victim. For instance, pictures and words posted on the Internet stay there indefinitely. A single mean post, furthermore, can be seen or read by hundreds of people. Cyber-bullying victims are up to nine times

3 a not as likely committing suicide

   b more likely to commit suicide than

   c less likely committing suicide than

the average child.

4 a Thus

   b For the reason that

   c Since

many victims feel helpless and embarrassed, they are less likely to go to parents and teachers for help. <u>(c) It is estimated that over twenty-five percent of school-aged children are victims of bullying online</u>. That leaves a huge number of children at risk.

5 a Despite

   b Due to the problem

   c In spite of the fact

growing awareness of the dangers of cyber-bullying, schools often have trouble addressing it because they can't punish students for things they do when they are not on school property. School officials are helpless to do anything to address the frustration of parents, teachers, and the community. Schools that have tried to punish students for cyber-bullying have lost battles in court. Cyber-bullying can be a difficult problem to address

6 a , neither,

   b in addition

   c , yet

some schools in the United States are employing strategies that seem to be working. First, parents are advised to talk to students about online privacy, identity theft, and cyber-bullying. It is recommended that parents have this talk by the time a child is eight years old. Parents should discuss what to do with

7 a a child is getting bullied as well as encourage them
  b their child if he or she is getting bullied; they should also encourage him or her
  c the child is getting bullied as well as encourage the child

to speak up if another child is getting bullied. Second, schools can include anti-bullying statements in their rules and regulations. <u>(d) Some schools have had some success punishing students for cyber-bullying because they had a written policy in place.</u>

8 a Third,
  b The third
  c Next

states can write laws that make the consequences for cyber-bullying more severe. Many states have made online bullying a criminal offense. Fourth, parents and schools should petition the social media sites for greater control over what under-aged patrons can see and post. Once a bully has attacked someone, there should be a process in place for the victim to have hurtful or embarrassing information removed from the social media site.

Cyber-bullying is quickly becoming a common problem for some of our children. It can have lasting effects on the victims, but there isn't enough help in place for families to deal with the problem. Parents, schools, and lawmakers should get together to create a comprehensive solution that reduces bullying and protects victims.

9 The introduction of the essay begins with
  a background information.
  b a story.
  c a factual statement.
  d a quote.
  e a question.

10 Which of the supporting sentences in the essay (labelled a–d) is off-topic or in the wrong place?
  a
  b
  c
  d

11 The conclusion ends with
  a opinions.
  b suggestions.
  c predictions.

Pre-Test 2

Paragraph and Essay Organization

In the timed Pre-Test 2, you will demonstrate how well you can write about a topic. Pay attention to sentence structure, grammar, punctuation, mechanics, organization, and vocabulary. You have 50 minutes to complete the test.

Write a five- or six-paragraph essay comparing and contrasting two places, such as cities and towns, or parks and neighborhoods.

_____

_____

_____

_____

_____

_____

_____

_____

_____

_____

_____

_____

_____

_____

_____

_____

_____

_____

_____

_____

_____

_____

PUNCTUATION AND MECHANICS

Commas

Presentation

Commas

Rules	Examples
Use commas to separate independent clauses in compound sentences.	Bill took the car to the mechanic, **and** his wife picked the children up. My brother went to law school, **and** he quit to become a teacher.
Use commas to separate a conjunctive adverb at the beginning, middle, or end of a clause.	My brother went to law school. **However**, he quit to become a teacher. My brother went to law school. He quit, **however**, to become a teacher. My brother went to law school. He quit to become a teacher, **however**.
Use commas to separate prepositional phrases, time expressions, and other sentence openers.	**Given the cold weather**, we've decided to go to a movie. **Last week**, the couple left for a family trip down the Oregon coast.
Use commas to separate items in a list of three or more.	I have coffee and toast every morning. (no comma—two items only) The Midwest is the biggest producer of **corn, wheat, and soybeans** in the United States.
Use commas to separate non-essential (non-restrictive) adjective clauses, appositives, and participial phrases.	Providence Hospital, **where I was born**, is closing next year. (adjective clause) Carl Sagan, **a famous American scientist**, wrote the novel *Contact*. (appositive) The Sonics, **sold to Oklahoma City**, left Seattle without a basketball team in 2006. (participial phrase)
Use commas to separate a direct quote before or after the reporting phrase.	"Be careful," **Ann said**, "when you go out tonight."
In dates, a comma separates the month and day from the year.	September 17, 2014
In addresses, commas separate the street from the apartment number and the city from the state. If the address is written as one line, commas also separate the street and city.	301 Main St., Apt. 6 Seattle, WA 98103 301 Main St., Apt. 6, Seattle, WA 98103

A comma separates the last from first name. Do not use a comma if the first name comes first.	Smith, Joseph (last name first) Joseph Smith (last name last)
A comma separates the name from a title.	James Phiri, Accountant William Devon, Jr.
In letters, use a comma after the greeting in informal correspondence and after the closing in both formal and informal correspondence.	Dear John, Sincerely, Bill Crumpler

Practice 1

Circle the letter of the sentence that correctly uses commas.

Example:

1 **ⓐ** *Ms. Baker, the English teacher, is preparing her lessons for the week.*
   b *Ms. Baker the English teacher, is preparing her lessons for the week.*
   c *Ms. Baker, the English teacher is preparing her lessons for the week.*

2 **a** To begin she sits at her desk while thinking about what she needs to teach the next day.
   b To begin, she sits at her desk while thinking about what she needs to teach the next day.
   c To begin, she sits at her desk, while thinking about what she needs to teach the next day.

3 **a** Therefore she goes to the kitchen for coffee, puts the water on the stove to boil, and returns to her desk.
   b Therefore, she goes to the kitchen for coffee, puts the water on the stove to boil, and returns to her desk.
   c Therefore, she goes to the kitchen for coffee, puts the water on the stove to boil and returns to her desk.

4 **a** In the meantime she opens her books and starts to plan the lessons.
   b In the meantime, she opens, her books and starts to plan the lessons.
   c In the meantime, she opens her books and starts to plan the lessons.

5 **a** Almost immediately, she starts to daydream about the costume party she went to on Saturday night.
   b Almost immediately she starts to daydream about the costume party she went to on Saturday night.
   c Almost immediately, she starts to daydream about the costume party, she went to on Saturday night.

6 **a** She is interrupted again when the phone rings.
   b She is interrupted again, when the phone rings.
   c She is interrupted, again, when the phone rings.

7 **a** While she is talking on the phone the water on the stove boils.
   b While she, is talking on the phone, the water on the stove boils.
   c While she is talking on the phone, the water on the stove boils.

8 **a** As quickly as possible, she ends the conversation, goes to the kitchen, and prepares the coffee.

b As quickly as possible she ends the conversation, goes to the kitchen and prepares the coffee.

c As quickly as possible she ends the conversation, goes to the kitchen, and prepares the coffee.

9 **a** Carrying the cup of coffee, she returns to her desk, once again.

b Carrying the cup of coffee she returns to her desk once again.

c Carrying the cup of coffee, she returns to her desk once again.

10 **a** She then realizes it is time to watch *General Hospital* her favorite program, on television.

b She then realizes it is time to watch *General Hospital*, her favorite program, on television.

c She then realizes it is time to watch *General Hospital* her favorite program on television.

11 **a** Ms. Baker decides that the lessons, will have to wait until later.

b Ms. Baker decides that, the lessons will have to wait until later.

c Ms. Baker decides that the lessons will have to wait until later.

Practice 2

Circle the letter of the sentence that correctly uses commas.

Example:

1 **a** *Margo convinced that she had no talent for acting, dropped out of her drama class.*

b *Margo convinced that she had no talent for acting dropped out of her drama class.*

(c) *Margo, convinced that she had no talent for acting, dropped out of her drama class.*

2 **a** The new Cupcake Shop is located at 123 Market Street, Philadelphia, Pennsylvania 19122.

b The new Cupcake Shop is located at 123 Market Street Philadelphia Pennsylvania, 19122.

c The new Cupcake Shop is located at 123 Market Street, Philadelphia Pennsylvania 19122.

3 **a** We had planned a two-week trip to France last summer. We stayed, instead, for three weeks.

b We had planned a two-week trip to France last summer. We stayed instead, for three weeks.

c We had planned a two-week trip to France last summer. We stayed instead for three weeks.

4 **a** During my lunch break I made some last-minute changes to my essay, before handing it in to my teacher.

b During my lunch break, I made some last-minute changes to my essay before handing it in to my teacher.

c During my lunch break I made some last-minute changes to my essay before handing it in to my teacher.

5 **a** The "unsinkable" *Titanic* hit an iceberg and sank in the North Atlantic Ocean on April, 15, 1912.

b The "unsinkable" *Titanic* hit an iceberg and sank in the North Atlantic Ocean on April 15, 1912.

c The "unsinkable" *Titanic* hit an iceberg and sank in the North Atlantic Ocean, on April 15 1912.

6 **a** The U.S. Declaration of Independence states that all men are created equal and are entitled to life liberty, and the pursuit of happiness.

    b The U.S. Declaration of Independence states that all men are created equal and are entitled to life, liberty and the pursuit of happiness.

    c The U.S. Declaration of Independence states that all men are created equal and are entitled to life, liberty, and the pursuit of happiness.

7 **a** "We saw the Picasso exhibition last summer," she said, "during our visit to Barcelona."

    b "We saw the Picasso exhibition last summer" she said, "during our visit to Barcelona."

    c "We saw the Picasso exhibition last summer," she said "during our visit to Barcelona."

8 **a** Mr. Cano, who sat next to me at the recital, slept through the entire performance.

    b Mr. Cano who sat next to me at the recital slept through the entire performance.

    c Mr. Cano, who sat next to me at the recital slept through the entire performance.

9 **a** Rebecca M. Stevens M.D., is the featured speaker at next week's conference on childhood obesity.

    b Rebecca M. Stevens M.D. is the featured speaker at next week's conference on childhood obesity.

    c Rebecca M. Stevens, M.D., is the featured speaker at next week's conference on childhood obesity.

10 **a** Matt Simpson, our next-door neighbor, plays tennis with my husband every Saturday morning.

    b Matt Simpson our next-door neighbor, plays tennis with my husband every Saturday morning.

    c Matt Simpson, our next-door neighbor plays tennis with my husband every Saturday morning.

Parentheses

Presentation

Parentheses

Rules	Examples
We often use parentheses when you need to include extra information, suggestions, or additional comments connected to the main idea of the sentence.	Some animals that hibernate **(mainly bears and rodents)** will sleep for months during the winter.
Use parentheses when you use letters or numbers in lists within a sentence.	The priorities for our party's budget are: **(1)** food, **(2)** music, **(3)** decorations, and **(4)** prizes, in that order.
Use parentheses to explain or clarify numbers, acronyms, measurements, and abbreviations when you mention them the first time.	Hiram applied to New York University **(NYU)** and UCLA **(University of California in Los Angeles).** Please read in the textbook from pages 14–400 **(fourteen to four hundred)** for tomorrow.
Use parentheses with in-text citation and page numbers.	The writer suggests that her great-grandmother was an unhappy woman with many disappointments in her life. **(Cisernos, 12)**
Use parentheses to indicate historical time periods for people and events.	One of the heroes of the Civil Rights Movement, Martin Luther King Jr. **(1929–1968)**, received many commendations in his lifetime, including the Nobel Peace Prize.
Put periods and commas outside the parentheses for words and phrases.	Thank you in advance for reviewing my application **(attached),** and please contact me at your earliest convenience.
Put periods and commas inside the parentheses for complete sentences.	Thank you in advance for reviewing my application. **(I have attached it.)**

Practice 1

Underline the word or words that should be in parentheses.

1 The child picked up the box of toys and dumped it on the floor. He was having a temper tantrum.

2 The accountant found almost $1,500 fifteen hundred dollars in tax deductions for the family.

3 Archeologists believe that ancient crocodiles ca. 150 million years ago had a number of features in common with killer whales, including their feeding habits.

4 The average height for an American woman is about 5'4" 5 feet 4 inches.

5 Under the new Homeland Security laws, the CIA Central Intelligence Agency and the FBI were restructured to make communication between the two agencies easier.

6 Students who want to use the campus computers should follow these steps: 1 go to the student computer lab to sign up, and (2) ask the lab assistant for your username.

7 Sophia finally responded after being silent for several minutes that she did not know who had taken the car.

Practice 2

Circle the letter of the sentence that is written correctly.

Example:

1 **(a)** *An essay consists of three parts: (1) an introduction, (2) a body, and (3) a conclusion.*

   b *An essay consists of three parts: 1) an introduction, 2) a body, and 3) a conclusion.*

2 **a** Harry volunteers at the (SPCA) The Society for the Prevention of Cruelty to Animals three days a week because he strongly believes in its mission to promote the safety and welfare of animals.

   b Harry volunteers at The Society for the Prevention of Cruelty to Animals (SPCA) three days a week because he strongly believes in its mission to promote the safety and welfare of animals.

3 **a** Attached is an updated résumé. (I'll send you a list of references in the morning).

   b Attached is an updated résumé. (I'll send you a list of references in the morning.)

4 **a** Sam promised her (although she didn't believe him) that he would remember their anniversary next year.

   b Sam promised her although she didn't believe him (that he would remember their anniversary next year).

5 **a** One way you can protect and keep your home safe is to leave a light on outside (inside, too) all night.

   b One way you can protect and keep your home safe is to leave a light on outside (inside, too.) all night.

6 **a** A recent study has shown that the genes we inherit and the lifestyle we lead are only two of the factors that determine how long we will live. (Ramsay, 107)

   b A recent study, Ramsay 107, has shown that the genes we inherit and the lifestyle we lead are only two of the factors that determine how long we will live.

7 **a** President John F. Kennedy 1917–1963 spoke these historic words at his (1961) inaugural address: "Ask not what your country can do for you; ask what you can do for your country."

   b President John F. Kennedy (1917–1963) spoke these historic words at his 1961 inaugural address: "Ask not what your country can do for you; ask what you can do for your country."

8 **a** After you have had a chance to review the materials (enclosed), I will call you to discuss possible options.

   b After you have had a chance to review the materials (enclosed,) I will call you to discuss possible options.

Semicolons

Presentation

Semicolons

Rules	Examples
Use a semicolon between independent clauses if there is a clear relationship between the two.	Sunrise is usually at about 6 a.m.; sunset is about 6 p.m.
Use a semicolon with a transition word or phrase and a comma to form a compound sentence. The same sentence can also be divided by a period.	There is a huge danger of forest fires in the summer; **as a result**, many parks do not allow camping fires.
	There is a huge danger of forest fires in the summer. **As a result**, many parks do not allow camping fires.
	There is a huge danger of forest fires in the summer. Many parks, **as a result**, do not allow camping fires.
Use semicolons for items in a list that already includes commas.	I need to pick up a few things at Madison Market, which has the best organic vegetables; at the pharmacy where my doctor sent a prescription; and at Mudbay, which has my cat's food.

Practice 1

Circle the letter of the sentence that is punctuated correctly.

Example:

1 **a** *I like to eat sushi for lunch; my husband, on the other hand, prefers a cheeseburger.*
   b *I like to eat sushi for lunch, my husband, on the other hand, prefers a cheeseburger.*
   c *I like to eat sushi for lunch my husband, on the other hand, prefers a cheeseburger.*

2 **a** Paul spends a lot of time outdoors in activities such as; hiking; bicycling; and swimming.
   b Paul spends a lot of time outdoors in activities such as hiking; bicycling; and swimming.
   c Paul spends a lot of time outdoors in activities such as hiking, bicycling, and swimming.

3 **a** Temperatures soared past 100 degrees this past week as a result, many people suffered from heat stroke.
   b Temperatures soared past 100 degrees this past week; as a result, many people suffered from heat stroke.
   c Temperatures soared past 100 degrees this past week; as a result many people suffered from heat stroke.

4 **a** Our teacher decided; however, to postpone the test until next week.
   b Our teacher decided, however, to postpone the test until next week.
   c Our teacher decided, however; to postpone the test until next week.

5 **a** The new officers are Pilar Sanchez, president: Lucy Hamilton, vice president: and Jeffrey Thompson, treasurer.

b The new officers are Pilar Sanchez, president, Lucy Hamilton, vice president, and Jeffrey Thompson, treasurer.

c The new officers are Pilar Sanchez, president; Lucy Hamilton, vice president; and Jeffrey Thompson, treasurer.

6 **a** For her birthday, Lina wanted a blouse, either white or blue; a pair of jeans; and aviator sunglasses.

b For her birthday, Lina wanted a blouse, either white or blue, a pair of jeans, and aviator sunglasses.

c For her birthday, Lina wanted a blouse; either white or blue; a pair of jeans; and aviator sunglasses.

7 **a** John started his science project late, nevertheless, he got it done on time.

b John started his science project late; nevertheless, he got it done on time.

c John started his science project late, nevertheless, he got it done on time.

8 **a** Although my parents thought the house was selling at a fair price, they weren't sure they wanted to buy it.

b Although my parents thought the house was selling at a fair price; they weren't sure they wanted to buy it.

c Although my parents thought; the house was selling at a fair price they weren't sure they wanted to buy it.

9 **a** Grace has decided to hire a personal trainer to help her with balance. It has been unseasonably warm these past few weeks.

b Grace has decided to hire a personal trainer to help her with balance; it has been unseasonably warm these past few weeks.

c Grace has decided to hire a personal trainer to help her with balance: it has been unseasonably warm these past few weeks.

10 **a** Having made what I believe is the best possible decision; I am not going to listen to any more advice.

b Having made what I believe is the best possible decision I am not going to listen to any more advice.

c Having made what I believe is the best possible decision, I am not going to listen to any more advice.

Practice 2

Circle the letter of the sentence that is punctuated correctly.

Example:

1 **(a)** *Our plan is to find a place where we can relax, make the travel arrangements as soon as possible, and then pack our bags!*

b *Our plan is to find a place where we can relax; make the travel arrangements as soon as possible; and then pack our bags!*

c *Our plan is; to find a place where we can relax; make the travel arrangements as soon as possible; and then pack our bags!*

2 a Many colleges offer financial aid, you just have to know how to find it.

b Many colleges offer financial aid; you just have to know how to find it.

c Many colleges offer financial aid you just have to know how to find it.

3 a Lisa bought a new suit for her cousin's wedding; moreover, she bought a new hat and new shoes.

b Lisa bought a new suit for her cousin's wedding, moreover; she bought a new hat and new shoes.

c Lisa bought a new dress for her cousin's wedding; moreover she bought a new hat and new shoes.

4 a Considering the reduced price of the sofa, though, I think we should buy it now.

b Considering the reduced price of the sofa; though, I think we should buy it now.

c Considering the reduced price of the sofa though; I think we should buy it now.

5 a By the time I arrived home from work, my husband had already straightened up the house, cooked dinner, and set the table.

b By the time I arrived home from work; my husband had already cleaned up the house, cooked dinner, and set the table.

c By the time I arrived home from work, my husband had already cleaned up the house; cooked dinner; and set the table.

6 a The stock market has reached historic highs in the past few months; nevertheless, we should not become overly optimistic until the economy makes a full recovery.

b The stock market reached historic highs in the past few months nevertheless; we should not become overly optimistic until the economy makes a full recovery.

c The stock market reached historic highs in the past few months; nevertheless we should not become overly optimistic until the economy makes a full recovery.

7 a Unless you tell me what the problem is; I can't help you with a solution.

b Unless you tell me; what the problem is, I can't help you with a solution.

c Unless you tell me what the problem is, I can't help you with a solution.

8 a Our English class was canceled because of bad weather. Next week, I'll take my car to the repair shop to be fixed.

b My English class was canceled because of bad weather; next week, I'll take my car to the repair shop to be fixed.

c My English class was canceled because of bad weather, next week, I'll take my car to the repair shop to be fixed.

9 a The best cities to vacation in are Paris, France, London, England, and Washington, D.C.

b The best cities to vacation in are Paris France, London England, and Washington, D.C.

c The best cities to vacation in are Paris, France; London, England; and Washington, D.C.

10 a I never pay full price for anything; I always look for a bargain.

b I never pay full price for anything, I always look for a bargain.

c I never pay full price for anything I always look for a bargain.

Colons

Presentation

Colons

Rules	Examples
Use a colon to introduce a series of items.	I have visited many places this year: San Francisco, Philadelphia, New York, and Miami.
Use a colon to separate hours from minutes.	The appointment is at **5:30** p.m. tomorrow.
Use a colon at the end of a formal letter greeting.	Dear Dr. Espinoza:
Use a colon to connect an independent clause that doesn't have a reporting phrase to a direct quotation.	Hiram reflected on his father's favorite saying: "A bird in the hand is worth two in the bush."
Use a colon to split up a longer quotation from the main body in formal writing.	In Jack London's story, "*The White Silence,*" Jack London shows how Ruth honors her duty and accepts her fate. London writes: Ruth had received her husband's last wishes and made no struggle. Poor girl, she had learned the lesson of obedience well. From a child, she had bowed, and seen all women bow, to the lords of creation, and it did not seem in the nature of things for a woman to resist. (London, 14)
Use a colon to emphasize an appositive at the end of a clause.	The applicant has two weaknesses: difficulty working with others and chronic tardiness.
Use a colon to separate a title from a subtitle.	One of my favorite thrillers, *X-Files: I Want to Believe*, came out in 2008.
The information that follows a colon must be connected to a word or phrase before the colon in the sentence.	Correct: I saw many things on my trip: tigers and bears, birds and bees. Incorrect: I saw many things on my trip: I went on a boat, a plane, and a train.
A colon usually follows an independent clause, not a phrase. If you feel you can logically put a period after the clause, then a colon can go there, too. You may also use *the following* or *as follows* before a colon.	He gave apples, oranges, and pears. > He gave the following: apples, oranges, and pears.
	I've been to many places this year: New York, Paris, and Tokyo. > I have been to the following places this year: New York, Paris, and Tokyo.
Use colons to separate directional words, such as *to, from, date, regarding,* from the information they relate to.	From: Donald Remus, CEO To: Staff Re: Company Closure

Practice 1

Circle the letter of the sentence that is punctuated correctly.

Example:

1 **(a)** *Let's meet at the coffee shop at 9:30 tomorrow morning.*
  b *Let's meet at the coffee shop at 9,30 tomorrow morning.*
  c *Let's meet at the coffee shop at 9;30 tomorrow morning.*

2 **a** My plan for the day is: to spend time at the library, to have dinner at the new Chinese restaurant, and to go to an early movie.
  b My plan for the day is to spend time at the library, to have dinner at the new Chinese restaurant, and to go to an early movie.
  c My plan for the day is: to spend time at the library: to have dinner at the new Chinese restaurant: and to go to an early movie.

3 **a** Do you know if the library has a copy of Stephen King's 2012 novel, *The Dark Tower: The Wind Through the Keyhole?*
  b Do you know if the library has a copy of Stephen King's 2012 novel, *The Dark Tower, The Wind Through the Keyhole?*
  c Do you know if the library has a copy of Stephen King's 2012 novel, *The Dark Tower; The Wind Through the Keyhole?*

4 **a** I always think about my father's words: "Life is not always fair, but, sometimes, neither are we."
  b I always think about my father's words, "Life is not always fair, but, sometimes, neither are we."
  c I always think about my father's words "Life is not always fair, but, sometimes, neither are we."

5 **a** Here are two good rules to live by, be happy and act in a way that makes others happy.
  b Here are two good rules to live by; be happy and act in a way that makes others happy.
  c Here are two good rules to live by: Be happy and act in a way that makes others happy.

6 **a** This play is really boring—the plot is uninteresting; the characters, with the exception of one or two, are unbelievable; and the acting is terrible.
  b This play is really boring—the plot is uninteresting: the characters, with the exception of one or two, are unbelievable: and the acting is terrible.
  c This play is really boring—the plot is uninteresting, the characters, with the exception of one or two, are unbelievable, and the acting is terrible.

7 **a** As my grandmother said yesterday: she has traveled extensively throughout her life and now prefers to stay close to home.
  b As my grandmother said yesterday, she has traveled extensively throughout her life and now prefers to stay close to home.
  c As my grandmother said yesterday; she has traveled extensively throughout her life and now prefers to stay close to home.

8 **a** Here's an example of how to punctuate the first line of a memo: *From: Tanya Ramsay, Manager.*
  b Here's an example of how to punctuate the first line of a memo: *From, Tanya Ramsay, Manager.*
  c Here's an example of how to punctuate the first line of a memo: *From; Tanya Ramsay, Manager.*

9 **a** Three attributes account for Dalia's success in school, dedication, discipline, and diligence!
  b Three attributes account for Dalia's success in school; dedication, discipline, and diligence!
  c Three attributes account for Dalia's success in school: dedication, discipline, and diligence!

10 a Follow this example to begin and end a formal letter: *Dear Dr. Espinoza, ... Sincerely yours: ...*

   b Follow this example to begin and end a formal letter: *Dear Dr. Espinoza, ... Sincerely yours, ...*

   c Follow this example to begin and end a formal letter: *Dear Dr. Espinoza: ... Sincerely yours, ...*

Practice 2

Read the memo. Circle the correct punctuation to complete the sentences. The first one is done for you.

MEMORANDUM

1 DATE , / (:) / ; December 20 , / : / ; 2014

2 TO , / : / ; Staff

3 FROM , / : / ; Larry Jobs , / : / ; Human Resources Manager

4 RE , / : / ; Employee Breaks

I have received a lot of questions about compensation and breaks lately, as the new rules for overtime pay will start in January 2015. I hope this memo addresses employee concerns.

CURRENT U.S. EMPLOYMENT LAW

5 Current employment law does not require rest breaks at all. The U.S. Department of Labor website states the law very clearly , / : / ;

... when employers do offer short breaks (usually lasting about 5 to 20 minutes), federal law considers the breaks as compensable work hours ... meal periods (typically lasting at least 30 minutes) serve a different purpose than breaks and, thus, are not work time.

BREAK POLICY

6 Employees can take a 15-minute break after every two hours of work , / : / ; in addition, after four hours of work, employees are required to clock out for a 45-minute lunch or dinner break. A common example of a break schedule for a shift starting at 7 , / : / ; 00 A.M. might include breaks at the following times , / : / ; 9 A.M., 11 , / : / ; 15 A.M., and 2 P.M.

7 Employees are not required to clock out for the shorter 15-minute break. Shorter breaks are a part of your hours and counted as work time , / : / ; whereas breaks for mealtimes are not considered part of your hours. They are not used when we calculate overtime.

Hyphens

Hyphens

Rules	Examples
Use a hyphen to connect two or more words to form one word. (**Not** all compound words use hyphens.)	With compound adjectives in front of nouns: **Chinese-American** *man*, **ink-black** *sky*. Compound noun that is not a number: *father-in-law* With any prefix used with a proper noun *non-Christian, un-American* After single-letter prefixes *U-turn, e-mail*
Use a hyphen in simple fractions, ranges of numbers, and number words.	Simple fractions: *two-thirds, three-fourths* To express a range of numbers: *21–99* Numbers as words: *thirty-five, seventy-six*
Use a hyphen to divide words at the end of the line of writing: Divide between syllables (Don't divide words with 1 syllable); Divide where there is already a hyphen; Don't divide contractions or names;	We can see the *signif-icance* Angela is my *sister-in-law.*

Practice 1

Underline the phrases that should be hyphenated. Some sentences may need more than one hyphen.

Example:

1 *My daughter is the only <u>left handed</u> person in our family.*

2 My sister in law is studying for a Ph.D in Literature. Her dissertation deals with postmodern poetry.

3 Being praised in front of others can increase a child's self esteem.

4 My brother and his ex wife still talk to each other almost every day.

5 Burning the flag is considered to be an un American act.

6 Doctors and dentists advise pregnant women not to have X rays taken.

7 My cousin was six feet tall by the time he turned twenty one.

8 Because of the snowy climate, they bought a two door car with four wheel drive.

9 The cake recipe calls for two thirds of a cup of butter.

10 Tanvi felt odd being the only Indian American student in her class.

11 The teacher gave the students a five minute warning before instructing them to put down their pencils and hand in their exam papers.

Practice 2

Underline the phrases that should be hyphenated in the following sentences. Ten hyphens total are needed.

1 They have a good tempered, sweet dog who isn't unfriendly to anyone.

2 Ulla is looking for a part time job while she is finishing her physics degree.

3 As long as an American remains in Canada for twenty four hours, he or she can bring back duty free goods.

4 Only two thirds of the class received at least seventy five points on the last project.

5 Dana's ex boyfriend is the most selfish person I know.

6 Georgette is a happy go lucky person; she rarely has a care in the world.

7 The contractor is looking for strong, able bodied construction workers for his upcoming project.

8 The manager sent her employees an e mail about the new vacation policy.

Underlining and Italics

Underlining and Italics

Rules	Examples
We underline to indicate something should be italicized. Underline when you need to italicize your handwritten work. Use italics when typing.	
Underline/Italicize titles of complete works that can be published on their own (long poems, books, newspapers, journals, plays, albums, films, novels, websites). Individual works in a larger work receive quotation marks.	I love the song "Something to Believe In" by The Steve Miller Band. It's on **The Joker** album.
Underline/Italicize famous paintings, sculptures, ships, airplanes, trains, etc.	Picasso's most controversial painting is perhaps *Guernica*, a gruesome painting about war. The *Titanic* sank in 1912.
Underline/Italicize foreign words unless they are used so commonly in English that you can expect a general understanding.	His mother and father named him **Nabil**, which in English means "noble." What does *Sehnsucht* mean in German? I like pasta and Champagne. (no italics because you can expect most readers to understand what they mean)
Underline/Italicize Latin scientific names.	Saffron comes from the stigmas of the *crocus sativas*, a small but beautiful bulbous flower.
When you want to identify a word, letter, or number as itself, italicize or underline it.	You should really mind your *p's* and *q's*. Please define *copacetic* for me. I saw the figure *8* in blue on a silver car.
Italicize software programs.	*Excel, Microsoft Encarta*

Practice 1

Read the sentences below. Underline the ten words and phrases that should be set in italics.

1 Herman Melville wrote the novel Moby Dick and the short story "Bartelby the Scrivener."

2 Every Christmas, the ballet The Nutcracker, by Peter Illich Tchaikovsky, is broadcast on TV.

3 The common ladybug, or coccinella septempunctata, eats common garden pests like aphids.

4 Many Japanese and Korean students have trouble pronouncing r and l sounds in English.

5 The word and is used too often in your writing.

6 Qigong, or life energy cultivation, is an ancient Chinese practice that has been proven to lower blood pressure and quiet the mind.

7 One of the most famous historical speeches is Lincoln's Gettysburg Address.

8 The first time I saw the painting The Mona Lisa, by Leonardo da Vinci, I was surprised that it was so small.

9 Americans are fond of self-help books. One of the earliest and most famous books is How to Win Friends and Influence People, by Dale Carnegie.

Practice 2

Circle the letter of the sentence with the correctly formatted phrases.

1 a The most popular newspaper in the United States is USA Today.

  b The most popular newspaper in the United States is *USA Today*.

  c The most popular newspaper in the United States is "USA Today".

2 a One of the largest passenger ships ever built, "the Queen Mary," was purchased in 1967 by the city of Long Beach, California, where it is a popular tourist attraction.

  b One of the largest passenger ships ever built, the Queen Mary, was purchased in 1967 by the city of *Long Beach, California*, where it is a popular tourist attraction.

  c One of the largest passenger ships ever built, the *Queen Mary*, was purchased in 1967 by the city of Long Beach, California, where it is a popular tourist attraction.

3 a Many English poets during the Romantic Period (mid- to late-18th century) cultivated a lifestyle that followed the motto Carpe Diem, which means *seize the day*.

  b Many English poets during the Romantic Period (mid- to late-18th century) cultivated a lifestyle that followed the motto *carpe diem*, which means "seize the day."

  c Many English poets during the Romantic Period (mid- to late-18th century) cultivated a lifestyle that followed the motto "carpe diem", which means "seize the day".

4 a The most profitable movie ever made was Titanic, which won eleven Academy Awards in 1998.

  b The most profitable movie ever made was "Titanic," which won eleven Academy Awards in 1998.

  c The most profitable movie ever made was *Titanic*, which won eleven Academy Awards in 1998.

5 a As part of the wedding reception, the groom took the microphone and sang "You Are the Sunshine of My Life," his new bride's favorite song.

  b As part of the wedding reception, the groom took the microphone and sang *You Are the Sunshine of My Life*, his new bride's favorite song.

  c As part of the wedding reception, the groom took the microphone and sang You Are the Sunshine of My Life, his new bride's favorite song.

6 **a** American children learn rhymes like i before e except after c in order to remember English spelling rules.

b American children learn rhymes like "i" before "e" except after "c" in order to remember English spelling rules.

c American children learn rhymes like "i before e, except after c" in order to remember English spelling rules.

7 **a** The current issue of *National Geographic* online has an article called "Inside the Tornado" about a man who chases tornadoes to collect scientific data.

b The current issue of *National Geographic* online has an article called *Inside the Tornado* about a man who chases tornadoes to collect scientific data.

c The current issue of "National Geographic" online has an article called "Inside the Tornado" about a man who chases tornadoes to collect scientific data.

Abbreviations

Abbreviations

Rules	Examples
Use abbreviations for words that are familiar to American and Canadian readers in academic writing.	Personal and professional titles with names (**Dr**. Gupta or Allan Gupta, **MD**) Dates 21 **BCE**, 25 **CE**) Familiar corporations, organizations, government bodies, products, tests, etc. (**IBM**, **IRS**, **TOEFL**, **CD**) Acronyms pronounced as words (**AIDS**, **CASAS**) Addresses in letters: Jane Smith, Manager 1001 Salter **St**. New Orleans, **LA** 70118
Do not use certain abbreviations in academic writing.	Measurements (e.g., *Add three tablespoons* not *tbs.*) Names for geographical places (*We live in the United States* not *the US* or *the USA*) Days of the week: (*Today is Monday* not *Mon.*) Months or holidays (*My vacation starts in January* not *Jan.*) Unfamiliar names for schools, businesses, etc. (*University of Virginia* not *UVA*)
Don't use periods or spaces with abbreviations that use all capital letters. Use periods but no space with abbreviations that have a lowercase letter (especially at the end).	USA Ph.D
In academic writing, you can use certain Latin abbreviations.	ca. = "around or approximately" e.g. = "for example" et al. = "and others" etc. = "and so on" i.e. = "that is" NB = " note well" vs. = "versus" or "against" BCE = "before common era" CE = "common era"

Country names should be spelled out. State names in the Untied States can be abbreviated.	Oakland, CA, in the United States.
If you intend to abbreviate an institution, spell it out the first time you mention it. Then put the acronym in brackets.	The Central Intelligence Agency (CIA) is active in covert operations. The CIA also has many agents.
Be consistent. Don't mix the abbreviated form of a term with its long form.	That movie is rated R; **that is,** people under the age of 17 must be accompanied by an adult.

Practice 1

Underline the seven mistakes with abbreviations. Assume that the sentences are using academic writing style.

1 I need to see D.r. Thorvath today.

2 November 11ᵗʰ, Veteran's Day, is a national holiday in the US.

3 In the fall, she will be attending Johns Hopkins Univ. in Baltimore, MD, where she plans to major in French lit.

4 It will cost CA. $2 million to build a new wing on the Y.M.C.A. building.

5 M.s. Estee Lauder, who was born in 1908, founded the famous cosmetics corp. of the same name during the Great Depression.

Practice 2

Read each sentence. Then circle the letter of the answer that uses the correct form of the word or phrase. Assume that the sentences are using academic writing style.

Example:

1 *The sun is about 150 million _____ from the earth.*

   a *k.m.*

   b *km*

   c *KM*

2 Several senators had to wait two days for an _____ with the _____ .

   a APPT; PRES

   b appointment; president

   c appt.; pres.

3 _____ , was the _____ to President George W. Bush.

   a Condoleezza Rice, Ph.D; National Security Advisor (NSA)

   b Dr Condoleezza Rice, PhD; national security advisor

   c Dr Condoleezza Rice; National Security Advisor NSA

4 During the early days of _____ , the European Allied forces fighting against Germany consisted of _____ .

   a WWII; the U.K. and France

   b World War II; the United Kingdom and France

   c World War Two (WWII); the UK and France

5 My name is Soo-Jung Park, and I come from _____ . This year I am studying English in _____ .

   a Ka.; Los Angeles, California in the United States

   b KOREA; LA, CA in the US

   c Korea; Los Angeles, CA, in the United States

6 By 2002, almost 25 million people had died of _____ .

   a A.I.D.S.

   b AIDS

   c aids

7 In our house we have _____ . My daughter rarely uses any of them; she would rather read a book.

   a a television, a VCR, a CD player, a DVD player, and three comps.

   b a TV, a VCR, a CD PLAYER, a DVD PLAYER, and three COMP

   c a TV, a VCR, a CD player, a DVD player, and three computers

Numbers

Presentation

Numbers

Rules	Examples
Use a word not the numeral when the number is only one to two words.	thirty-seven one hundred
Use a numeral if the word would be three or more words.	104 310
Use a word at the beginning of the sentence. Put very large numbers somewhere other than the beginning of the sentence.	**Thirty-one thousand** people were injured in the earthquake. The war led to the deaths of **100 milion people**.
Use a word with ages and simple fractions.	Ninety-eight years old two-fifths
With two separate numbers, write one as a word	six 10 dollar bills
Use numerals and words for numbers one million or larger.	4.5 billion
Use numerals with addresses, times, decimals, years, mixed numbers (whole numbers and fractions), exact amounts of money, statistics	8 Main Street 8:45 8.8 $4.78 the year 2008

Practice 1

Read the paragraph. Underline the seven mistakes with numbers. Assume that the sentences are written in an academic style.

The *Soviet Luna III* was the 3rd probe to be sent to the moon. It was launched in nineteen fifty-nine by Russia. The probe was about 130 centimeters by 1,20 cm. It first approached the south pole of the moon at about 6,200 kilometers before traveling to the far side, which had never been seen at that time. The probe began to capture the first photographic images of the dark side of the moon at six-thirty A.M. on October 7, 1959, from a distance of 63,500 kilometers. 9 pictures were taken in all; the images detailed about 70% of the surface of the far side of the moon. Before the probe was lost, it transmitted some of the pictures to Earth. The 7 pictures recovered were the 1st pictures of the far side of the moon ever seen. It is believed that the probe burned up in the Earth's atmosphere in March 1960.

Practice 2

Read the sentences. Then circle the letter of the answer with correctly formatted numbers. Assume that the sentences are written in an academic style. (All statistics are from *Guinness World Records*, http://www.guinnessworldrecords.com.)

Example:

1 *There are* _____ *feet in a kilometer.*
   (a) *328*
   b *three hundred and twenty eight*
   c *three hundred and twenty-eight*

2 The most successful pop singing group in history is The Beatles. They have sold more than _____ records worldwide.
   a 1 million
   b one million
   c 1,000,000

3 _____ different species of birds were spotted.
   a Thirty-seven
   b 37
   c thirty seven

4 My two dogs have given birth to _____ puppies each.
   a 23
   b twenty-three
   c twenty three

5 The country with the largest population is China, with almost _____ people.
   a one billion three hundred thousand
   b 1,300,000,000
   c 1.3 billion

6 The world's deepest lake is Lake Baikal in Russia. It contains _____ of the world's fresh water.
   a 1/5
   b one fifth
   c one-fifth

7 The average Japanese man lives for more than _____ years, while the average woman lives for nearly _____ years.
   a seventy-seven, eighty-four
   b seventy seven, eighty four
   c 77, 84

8 His new address is _____ Freemont Avenue.
   a twenty seven
   b twenty-seven
   c 27

9 All _____ _____ are in the Himalayas.

    a fourteen, 8,000-meter mountain peaks

    b 14, eight thousand meter mountain peaks

    c four-teen, 8-thousand-meter mountain peaks

10 The world's largest train station is Grand Central Terminal in New York City, built between _____ .

    a nineteen-o-three and nineteen-thirteen

    b 1903 and 1913

    c 19 o-three and 19 thirteen

Capitalization

Presentation

Capitalization

Rules	Examples
Capitalize the first word of a sentence.	**D**o not swim here.
Capitalize proper nouns, months, days of the week, holidays, languages, religions, geographical areas, many physical structures, and historical events.	My brother Larry lives in **T**aiwan.
	I was born in **N**ovember.
	My children are fluent in both **E**nglish and **P**olish.
	World **W**ar II ended in 1945.
Capitalize the most important words of titles. Do not capitalize articles and prepositions in titles unless they begin the title.	Is *Of Mice and Men* a good novel?
	Here's a fascinating article: *The Therapeutic Misconception and Bioethical Frameworks*.
Capitalize the first word in direct quotations anywhere in a sentence.	My mother said, "**C**lean your room."
Capitalize personal and professional titles when they are part of a person's name.	The dinner was hosted by **V**ice **P**resident Anderson.
	Mr. Frank Welfin, **S**upervisor
Capitalize greetings and closings in letters, personal titles, abbreviations suggesting something is enclosed, and names.	**D**ear David, This is Mr. Smith writing. Mrs. Smith and I would like to have you to dinner. **S**incerely, Mr. Smith
Capitalize the first-person singular pronoun (*I*).	**I** believe **I** am qualified because **I** am committed.
Capitalize cardinal directions when naming a region or identifying where something is.	He's from the **S**outh.
Do not capitalize *north, south, east,* and *west* when indicating what direction to go. Capitalize them in addresses and as a part of the name of a place.	Go south for two blocks; then turn left. Go to South America and see Chile.

Capitalize organizations and the names within your own organization, but not names outside your organization.	Sue works in our **Personnel Department.** Send your resume to the personnel department at Microsoft.
Do not capitalize *black* and *white* when they refer to skin color.	The black and white populations lived on opposite sides of the river.
Do not capitalize the word *god* in non-monotheistic religions.	Ganesh is one god among many.
Do not capitalize the names of the seasons.	winter, summer, spring, fall / autumn
Do not capitalize school subjects or fields of study unless it is a class name.	mathematics, history, political science **Physics** 101

Practice 1

Rewrite the sentences with the appropriate capitalization.

Example:

1 *olga is from poland, but she speaks german and english fluently.*

   Olga is from Poland, but she speaks German and English fluently.

2 i had over 300 messages in my e-mail account by the time i returned home from vacation in prague.

   _____

3 after william completes a master's degree in Political Science, he plans to move to washington, d.c. and work for the democratic party.

   _____

4 fanny price is the famous heroine of the novel *mansfield park.*

   _____

5 the declaration of independence was signed on july 4, 1776.

   _____

6 benjamin franklin reportedly said, "we must all hang together, or most assuredly we shall all hang separately."

   _____

Practice 2

Underline the words that should be capitalized in the cover letter below.

september 23, 2015

camilla frantz
1234 devon rd.
denver, co 81102

dear dr. frantz:

i am writing to apply for a position as a research intern at your lab.

i am a fourth year student at the university of colorado. i expect to graduate in june 2016 with a bachelor's degree in organic chemistry. i plan to apply to the cu medical school and eventually become a doctor. i am interested in this position because i am excited about the work you are doing at the cancer center, and i believe i could be a real asset to the lab.

i have attached a copy of my résumé with this cover letter. please feel free to contact me at judith.eglos@uc.edu or call me at (333) 555-2345. thanks in advance for your consideration.

sincerely,

judith eglos

Quotation Marks

Quotation Marks

Rules	Examples
Use quotations to write the exact words from a source (a lecture, book, or radio program).	Barack Obama coined the famous saying "Yes, we can" in his speech at Knox College on June 4, 2005.
Use quotations for titles of songs, poems, speeches, or works that are found in compilations or complete works. Use italics for complete works. (Underline if you write the text by hand.)	I love the song "Something to Believe In" by The Steve Miller Band. It's on *The Joker* album.
	One of my favorite short stories is "Speech Sounds" from *Bloodchild and Other Stories*, a book by Octavia Butler.
Use quotations to emphasize words with an unusual meaning, to provide a translation of a foreign word, or to suggest irony or sarcasm.	That's not a view, that's a "vista." The boys spent the entire day at the beach building "**castles**" of sand. His mother and father named him *Nabil*, which in English means "**noble**."
To write direct quotations, use a subject + reporting verb phrase either before, in the middle, or after the quote. Commas go within the quotation marks if the reporting phrase comes after the quotation. The comma is outside the quotation marks if the reporting phrase come before the quotation	Tan said, "I'm sure I passed my test." "I'm sure I passed my test," Tan said. "I'm sure," Tan said, "that I passed my test."
Put commas, periods, and question marks inside a closed quote.	"I'm sure I passed my test," Tan said.
It's possible to use other phrases without a reporting verb to introduce a quote.	My student Tan is optimistic. **In his words**, "I'm sure I passed my test."

Practice 1

Circle the letter of the sentence that is written correctly.

Example:

1 a *Albert Einstein defined insanity as doing the same thing over and over again and expecting different results.*

   (**b**) *Albert Einstein defined insanity as "doing the same thing over and over again and expecting different results."*

2 **a** Melinda knows all the lyrics to the song "New York, New York."

   b Melinda knows all the lyrics to the song *New York, New York*.

3 **a** A *siesta*, which means *nap* in English, is refreshing in any language!

   b A *siesta*, which means "nap" in English, is refreshing in any language!

4 **a** "What a great party," exclaimed Marcy. "I'm so happy to be here."

   b "What a great party", exclaimed Marcy. "I'm so happy to be here."

5 **a** Maité asked, "What time does the show start"?

   b Maité asked, "What time does the show start?"

6 **a** For his encore, the pianist played Rimsky-Korsakov's dazzling musical piece entitled *Flight of the Bumblebee*.

   b For his encore, the pianist played Rimsky-Korsakov's dazzling musical piece entitled "Flight of the Bumblebee."

7 **a** The big "bargain" turned out to be quite expensive.

   b The big *bargain* turned out to be quite expensive.

8 **a** Robert Frost's poem entitled *The Road Not Taken* is one of my favorites in this book.

   b Robert Frost's poem entitled "The Road Not Taken" is one of my favorites in this book.

9 **a** Did you read the article in *The Washington Post* about employment trends in the United States?

   b Did you read the article in "The Washington Post" about employment trends in the United States?

10 **a** Dana told everyone that "she is getting married next month."

   b Dana told everyone that she is getting married next month.

Practice 2

Circle the letter of the sentence that is written correctly.

Example:

1 **a** *Our teacher noted that "everyone in the class did well on the exam."*

   (b) *Our teacher noted that everyone in the class did well on the exam.*

2 **a** "Crazy in Love" is one of my favorite Beyoncé songs.

   b *Crazy in Love* is one of my favorite Beyoncé songs.

3 **a** Are you familiar with the meanings of these words: *champagne, gourmet,* and *coup d'état*?

   b Are you familiar with the meanings of these words: "champagne," "gourmet," and "coup d'état"?

4 **a** Dana's mother asked her, "Where are you going at this hour?"

   b Dana's mother asked her, "Where are you going at this hour"?

5 **a** Barack Obama coined the famous expression *Yes, we can* in the speech he gave at Knox College on June 4, 2005.

   b Barack Obama coined the famous expression "Yes, we can" in the speech he gave at Knox College on June 4, 2005.

6 a Have you read the mystery "The Murders in the Rue Morgue" from Edgar Allan Poe's collection of short stories?

b Have you read the mystery *The Murders in the Rue Morgue* from Edgar Allan Poe's collection of short stories?

7 a I *love* it when people are rude for no reason.

b I "love" it when people are rude for no reason.

8 a *Charlotte's Web*, a children's novel written by E.B. White in 1952, continues to be a favorite for people of all ages.

b "Charlotte's Web," a children's novel written by E.B. White in 1952, continues to be a favorite for people of all ages.

9 a "That", she said, "was the funniest joke I have ever heard".

b "That," she said, "was the funniest joke I have ever heard."

10 a *The New York Daily News* had an interesting article yesterday about the future of computing.

b "The New York Daily News" had an interesting article yesterday about the future of computing.

GRAMMAR

Complex Sentences

ADJECTIVE CLAUSES

Adjective Clauses

An **adjective clause** is a group of words that functions as an adjective to modify a noun or pronoun. It answers the questions *what kind?*, *how many?*, or *which one?* An adjective clause has its own subject and verb and begins with either a relative pronoun (*who, whom, whose, that*, or *which*) or a relative adverb (*when, where*, or *why*).

There are two types of adjectives clauses: restrictive and non-restrictive.

A restrictive adjective clause limits the possible meaning of the subject that comes before it. This type of clause cannot be removed from the sentence without changing the main idea of the sentence. Restrictive clauses usually begin with *that* and are not punctuated with commas.

Example:

The movie **that my boyfriend and I saw last night** was very violent.

The adjective clause in the example identifies exactly which *movie* (the subject of the main clause) was violent.

A non-restrictive adjective clause provides additional information about the subject that comes before it. This type of clause can be removed from the sentence without changing the main idea of the sentence. Non-restrictive clauses usually begin with *which* and are set off from the rest of the sentence with commas.

Example:

The teams, **which come from rival towns**, met on the hot turf.

The adjective clause in the example provides more information about the teams, but does not change the meaning of the sentence. It is offset with commas because it can be removed without altering the main idea.

Functions	Rules	Examples
Subject	Use *who* or *that* for people in subject positions.	The man **who / that** fixed my computer lives next door. *(restrictive)*
		I visited Mike, **who** has been in the hospital. *(non-restrictive)*
	Use *which* or *that* for things in subject positions.	The car **which / that** we've just bought was cheap. *(restrictive)*
		We visited the Taj Mahal, **which** is in India. *(non-restrictive)*
	(*That* can be used only in restrictive clauses. Do not use *that* in non-restrictive clauses.)	The house, which we painted red, is now for sale. **NOT** The house, that we painted red, is now for sale.
Object	Use *whom* or *that* for people in object positions.	The man **whom/that** you met last night is my brother's best friend. *(restrictive)*
		The manager called Louise, **whom** she had just given a job. *(non-restrictive)*
	Use *which* or *that* for things in object positions.	The house **which / that** they bought needs a lot of work. *(restrictive)*
	Do not use *that* in non-restrictive clauses.	<u>Correct</u>: Linguistics, **which** is not a very popular major, is the study of language. *(non-restrictive)*
		<u>Incorrect</u>: Linguistics, **that** is not a very popular major, is the study of language. *(non-restrictive)*
	The relative pronoun can be omitted in restrictive clauses.	The man (that) you met last night is my brother's best friend. *(You can omit the relative pronoun in a restrictive clause.)*

Possessive	*Whose* is the possessive form of *who*. Use it to indicate belonging or possession with regard to people and things.	The woman **whose** daughter got sick last night is very worried. *(restrictive)*
		My cousin George, **whose** brother lives in Paris, spent two months in Europe. *(non-restrictive)*
		They climbed the mountain **whose** top was covered in snow. *(restrictive)*
		Mount Blanc, **whose** top is always covered in snow, is a difficult mountain to climb. *(non-restrictive)*
	Use of *which* for things in place of *whose*.	They climbed the mountain, the top **of which** was covered in snow.
With prepositions	*Whom* comes after a preposition, **not** *who*. It is possible to use *that* or no relative pronoun for both people and things.	The driver **with whom** she collided didn't have insurance. The man *from whom* I received the call is my father. The driver **(that)** she collided **with** didn't have insurance.
With quantifiers	Use of *whom* for people. (non-essential only) Use of *which* for things. This structure is used only in non-restrictive adjective clauses.	The Johnsons have four boys, **the oldest of whom** is at Harvard University. Soybean crops, **most of which** are genetically modified to resist herbicides, are widely grown because of their versatility.
Describing locations	Use *where* in adjective clauses that describe locations.	The house **where** I lived as a child has been sold.
Describing time	Use *when* in adjective clauses that tell when events happened.	The decade **when** the computer was invented was marked by radical technological change.

Practice 1

Circle the correct adjective clause type. Then circle "yes" or "no."

Example:

1 *The Hershey company which makes candy is opening a new factory.* [**non-restrictive**/
restrictive]
Add commas? [**yes**/ *no*]

2 Many U.S. universities which have a large population of international students have programs to help students adjust to a new life. [**non-restrictive** / **restrictive**]
Add commas? [**yes** / **no**]

3 Children who have dyslexia struggle with reading and writing. [**non-restrictive** / **restrictive**]
Add commas? [**yes** / **no**]

4 My cousin Bella who has curly hair looks just like her mother. [**non-restrictive** / **restrictive**]
Add commas? [**yes** / **no**]

5 The researchers asked everyone who was participating in the study to sign the consent forms.
[**non-restrictive** / **restrictive**]
Add commas? [**yes** / **no**]

6 New York's Financial District which was founded by the Dutch in 1626 is the oldest district in
New York. [**non-restrictive** / **restrictive**]
Add commas? [**yes** / **no**]

7 Abraham Lincoln whose Emancipation Proclamation freed African-American slaves in the
southern United States successfully ended the Civil War in 1865. [**non-restrictive** / **restrictive**]
Add commas? [**yes** / **no**]

8 The man whom you met last night is my brother's best friend. [**non-restrictive** / **restrictive**]
Add commas? [**yes** / **no**]

9 During the Great Depression of the 1930s when one in four Americans was out of work many
families left their hometowns to find jobs in the cities. [**non-restrictive** / **restrictive**]
Add commas? [**yes** / **no**]

10 My cat Emily who is getting old loves to lie in the sun. [**non-restrictive** / **restrictive**]
Add commas? [**yes** / **no**]

Practice 2

Use the information in parentheses to write an adjective clause for the underlined noun.

Example:

1 *Mrs. Jones* , who was upset with her daughter, *refused to let her take the car. (She was upset
with her daughter. non-restrictive clause)*

2 The documents _____ contained an unknown fairytale by Hans
Christian Anderson. (The documents were recently discovered in Denmark. restrictive clause)

3 The Tenderloin, a district in San Francisco _____ has always been infamous for gambling and wild nightlife. (Many famous jazz musicians began their careers in the Tenderloin. restrictive clause)

4 The directions to the film shoot _____ were confusing to me. (The director wrote the directions down. restrictive clause)

5 The teacher discussed the theft of classroom equipment with the students

_____ . (All of the students suspected Agnes. non-restrictive clause)

6 Writers often explain abstract ideas with metaphors or analogies

_____ . (Both metaphors and analogies compare the topic to a more common idea. non-restrictive clause)

7 Groundhog Day is an American tradition _____ . (The tradition began in 1857. restrictive clause)

8 The specialist _____ was the best in his field. (Hiram was referred to the specialist. restrictive clause)

9 The person _____ has posted his secret to Facebook for everyone to see. (Gary confided in the person. restrictive clause)

10 The human body turns the protein _____ into amino acids. (We eat protein. restrictive clause)

11 The curtain _____ barely let the light shine through it. (The curtain was thick with dust and grime. non-restrictive clause)

ADVERB CLAUSES

Presentation

Adverb Clauses

An **adverb clause** is a dependent clause that modifies the verb in the main clause. It usually tells about *how, when,* or *why* something happened. It can also introduce a contrast. Like all other clauses, it has its own subject and verb.

An adverb clause is connected to an independent, or main, clause with a subordinating conjunction.

Adverb clauses of time are introduced by the conjunctions *after, before, until, while, when, whenever, since, as, as soon as, once, by the time (that), so long as, every time (that),* and *the first/last/next time (that).*

Adverb clauses of cause or purpose are introduced by *because, now that, so that,* and *since.*

Adverb clauses of condition are introduced by *in order to, even if, only if, unless, whether or not, in case,* and *in the event that.*

Adverb clauses of contrast are introduced by *whether, though, although, even though, while,* and *whereas.*

Adverb clauses of place are introduced by *where, wherever, everywhere,* and *anywhere.*

The adverb clause can come before or after the independent clause. If it comes first, a comma separates it from the independent clause.

Examples:

Josh didn't call Claire **because he is shy**. (adverb clause answers *why*)

Because Josh is shy, he didn't call Claire. (adverb clause answers *why*)

Types	Examples
Place	The little puppy followed her owner **wherever she went.**
Time	**After the fruit is ripe,** the farmer harvests it immediately.
Cause	I left my home city **because I wanted to go to a better school**.
Purpose	Ivan took a computer course **so that he could apply for a better job.**
Concession	**Although the air was hot,** the ocean was freezing cold.
Condition	**If you are wise with your money,** you will be able to afford a vacation.

Practice 1

Circle the letter of the best subordinating conjunction to complete the sentences.

Example:

1 _____ the lock was rusty, the door opened with one turn of the key.

  a Although   **b** While   **c** Since

2 There are many forms of plant life in the Arctic region that survive, _____ they are covered in snow and ice for most of the year.

  a as though   **b** so that   **c** even though

3 My language partner and I meet _____ we can find coffee, wireless Internet, and some quiet.

  a in order that   **b** wherever   **c** as

4 One of soccer's greatest players, Pelé, was born in Brazil, _____ another of soccer's greats, Diego Maradona, was born in Argentina.

  a whereas   **b** since   **c** such that

5 Puerto Rico has maintained a rich cultural identity _____ it is a territory of the United States.

  a even though   **b** until   **c** as

6 _____ some countries have little access to clean drinking water, many people get sick and die every day.

  a Anywhere   **b** Since   **c** Only if

7 The committee hasn't been meeting _____ they would have preferred.

    a as often as   **b** as though   **c** as if

8 The United States did not actively take part in World War II _____ the Japanese bombed Pearl Harbor.

    a unless   **b** anywhere   **c** until

9 The couple will be able to leave for the theater _____ the babysitter arrives.

    a as soon as   **b** until   **c** while

10 _____ there were very few submissions, the deadline for the literary essay contest has been extended.

    a As though   **b** Since   **c** Unless

11 We will know that the cancer treatment was a success _____ the data show at least a five percent decrease in size.

    a unless   **b** in order that   **c** if

Practice 2

Combine the two sentences using the subordinating conjunction in parentheses. If the conjunction has a capital letter, use it in the beginning of the sentence. Be sure to check your punctuation.

Example:

1 *She plans to accept the marriage proposal. Her father approves. (if)*

    She plans to accept the marriage proposal if her father approves.

2 To prevent identity theft, experts advise researching websites you want to do business with. You can be sure the website is legitimate. (so that)

    _____

3 The lecturer brings her family with her. She travels around the country to speak. (everywhere)

    _____

4 Fossil fuels are not renewable. Researchers have been developing alternative renewable energy sources. (Since)

    _____

5 Adrian is working longer hours. He can save money to pay off his credit card. (so that)

    _____

6 Pistol shrimp snap their claws. The resulting sound paralyzes their prey. (Whenever)

    _____

7 Space travel became possible. The first rockets were developed by German scientists in the 1940s. (only after)

    _____

8 Jacob went back to school. He could apply for a better-paying job. (so that)

_____

9 She is careful with the antique vase. It can be preserved for future generations. (so that)

_____

10 It has been passed down for generations in her family. The china still looks new. (Although)

_____

11 Capital punishment still remains legal in some U.S. states. Canada has banned the practice altogether. (While)

_____

PARTICIPIAL PHRASES

Presentation

Participial Phrases

Participial phrases are groups of words that **a**) begin with a verb form called a participle and **b**) function as adjectives to modify a noun or a pronoun. A participial phrase may begin with a present participle, which is a verb form that ends in -_ing_.

Example:

Singing at the top of her voice, my niece got a standing ovation.

A participial phrase may also start with a past participle, which often ends in -_ed_ or -_en_.

Example:

Covered with mud, my dog ran into the room.

or

Broken by the wind, the tree limb dangled dangerously over the sidewalk.

A participial phrase includes all the words that modify the participle or that act as complements (direct objects, indirect objects, etc.) to it. So, for example, _Singing_ is the participle and _Singing at the top of her voice_ is the complete participial phrase.

Important Points about Participial Phrases

1. A participle or participial phases must be placed as close as possible to the noun or pronoun it modifies. When a participial phrase begins a sentence, it **_must_** modify the subject of the sentence. If it modifies any other word, it is called a dangling participle.

Correct: _Flying to the top of the tree, the bird grasped a worm in its beak._

Dangling participle: _Flying to the top of the tree, a worm was grasped in the bird's beak._

2. When a participial phrase begins a sentence, it must be set off from the rest of the sentence by a comma. When a participial phrase ends a sentence, it is set off by a comma only if it does not immediately follow the word it modifies

Comma: We saw a bird with a worm grasped in its beak, flying to the top of the tree.

No Comma: We saw a bird flying to the top of the tree.

3. When a participial phrase interrupts a sentence, it is set off by commas if it is nonrestrictive (not essential to the meaning of the sentence).

Restrictive: The bird flying to the top of the tree had a worm in its beak.

Nonrestrictive: The bird, holding a worm in its beak, flew to the top of the tree.

Rule	Examples
Reduce adjective clauses to participial phrases when the relative pronoun is the subject: 1. Delete the relative pronoun (*who, which, that*) 2. Change the verb to the correct participle. 3. Use the same comma rules for restrictive and non-restrictive adjective clauses.	The researchers **who worked in the lab all night** went home exhausted in the morning.
	Is reduced to:
	The researchers **working in the lab all night** went home exhausted in the morning.
	The Sonics, **who were sold to Oklahoma City**, left Seattle without a basketball team in 2006.
	The Sonics, **sold to Oklahoma City**, left Seattle without a basketball team in 2006.
Reduce time and reason adverb clauses if the subject or the adverb are continued in the main clause: 1. Delete the subordinator in an adverb clause of reason (*because, since, as*). 2. Keep the subordinator in an adverb clause about time (*after, before, since, while, when*). 3. Delete the subject and change the verb to the correct participle. 4. Use the same comma rules for adverb clauses.	**After she arrives in her hometown,** she plans to visit her grandparents in the country.
	Is reduced to:
	After arriving in her hometown, she plans to visit her grandparents in the country. (active meaning)
	Because he hadn't been read his rights, the criminal could not be charged with the crime.
	Having not been read his rights, the criminal could not be charged with the crime.

Practice 1

Decide whether each sentence requires a comma and where it should go.

Example:

1 *Visiting her brother Joann met her new niece for the first time.*

  (a) *comma after brother*

  b *comma after niece*

  c *no comma*

2 The Arctic tern having flown more than 20,000 miles lives in Antarctica during that continent's summer.

   a commas after *tern* and *flown*

   b commas after *tern* and *miles*

   c no commas

3 Eating only eucalyptus leaves the koala is one of the world's pickiest eaters.

   a comma after *Eating*

   b comma after *leaves*

   c no comma

4 Mississippi called the Magnolia State has many beautiful public gardens.

   a commas after *Mississippi* and *State*

   b comma after *called*

   c no commas

5 For many years Berlin had a wall dividing the city into east and west.

   a comma after *Berlin*

   b comma after *wall*

   c comma after *years*

6 Called the queen of the underworld Persephone was the wife of Hades in Greek mythology.

   a comma after *queen*

   b comma after *underworld*

   c no comma

7 Having invented the flying trapeze Jules Leotard went on to invent the tights we call leotards.

   a comma after *trapeze*

   b comma after *tights*

   c no comma

Practice 2

Determine whether the participial phrase modifies the subject of the sentence, or if it is a dangling participle.

Example:

1 *Frightened of water, Mrs. Alvarez never went swimming with her children.*

   (a) *correct*

   b *dangling*

2 Working at home one day, a radio station called telling me I had won $10,000 in a contest.

   a correct

   b dangling

3 Having small bones, some fish can be tricky to eat safely.

   a correct

   b dangling

4 Tired of washing dishes, my thoughts wandered to the beautiful weather outside.

   a correct

   b dangling

5 Wishing to practice law in the United States, he studied hard for the bar exam.

   a correct

   b dangling

6 Having bright eyes and a glossy coat, I was sure the dog was healthy.

   a correct

   b dangling

7 Broken into a dozen pieces, I picked up the vase I had dropped.

   a correct

   b dangling

8 Polished to a high shine, the floor was beautiful but dangerous.

   a correct

   b dangling

9 Flying quickly from flower to flower, my sister tried to photograph the bee.

   a correct

   b dangling

10 Looking for a spot in the sun, the cat moved up the stairs.

   a correct

   b dangling

Causatives

Copyright © 2017 by Pearson Education, Inc. Duplication is not permitted.

Presentation

Causative Verbs

Causative verbs are used to show that the subject causes or arranges for an action to be done in some way. The subject doesn't actually carry out the action but starts the process. For example, "She had her car repaired." She didn't actually repair it herself, but she called the garage and brought her car there for it to be repaired. The three main causative verbs are *have*, *get*, and *make*. There are many others, including *let*, *help*, *allow*, and *force*.

Active Causative Verbs

Causative verbs in the active voice follow this pattern: "Gary **had** his brother clean the garage." The subject caused another person (his brother) to do something (clean the garage). In the active voice, a causative verb is usually followed by the main form of a verb, in this case *clean*. But the verbs *got*, *allow*, and *force* and certain other verbs are followed by the infinitive form of the verb. "Gary **got** his brother to clean the garage."

Passive Causative Verbs

Causative verbs in the passive voice follow the pattern seen in this example: "Luann **got** her eyes tested" or "Luann **got** her eyes tested by an eye doctor."

The subject caused something to be done to an object (eyes) by someone else (eye doctor), who may or may not be named. In the passive voice, a causative verb is followed by the past participle of a verb, in this case *tested*.

Causative	Form and Use	Examples
Make	*make* + object + base form of the verb Meanings: to compel; to have an effect on	The teacher never answers questions. She always **makes** the students **find** the information themselves. The pollution from the factory **made** the city look dark and dreary.
Have	*have* + object + base form of the verb Meaning: to influence an action by having someone else do it.	The report has some mistakes, so the manager **will have** the assistant **edit** it.
Get	*get* + object + infinitive Meaning: to cause someone or people to make a certain choice or take a certain action	The charity auction will be amazing if we can **get** a lot of people **to buy** tickets.
Let	*let* + object + base form of the verb Meaning: to allow	The mechanic was doubtful, but he **let** his apprentice **work on** the car anyway.

Help	*help* + object + base form of the verb or the infinitive Meaning: to assist	I am already finished with my work, so I **am going to help** you **finish** your project. Hal **has been helping** his friend to **recover** from surgery.
Passive Voice	*have / get* + object + past participle Meaning: to have someone or something take action	Before the family left for vacation, they **had** the house **winterized**. I am going to **have** the horse **pull** this load.

Practice 1

Circle the letter of the word or phrase that is a correct causative verb.

1 The social worker comes to Peter's house and _____ his bills every month.
  a helps him pay
  b pays

2 I _____ by a stylist every six weeks.
  a cut my hair
  b get my hair cut

3 The assistant _____ by keeping the whole crew there all night.
  a got the project finished
  b finished the project

4 Until recently, Karen's parents have not _____ .
  a let her drive
  b driven her

5 Your friends won't be able to leave unless you _____ car.
  a move the neighbors'
  b get the neighbors to move their

6 Will your boss _____ to the conference?
  a let you go
  b send you

7 Joanie _____ at a salon when she has an important meeting.
  a manicures her nails
  b has her nails manicured

8 Ken ordered online and _____ his house.
  a had the tickets sent to
  b received the tickets at

9 Mark _____ in white and shades of blue. He did it himself.
  a decorated his new house
  b had his new house decorated

10 Digital cameras are great because you don't have to _____ at the local store.

  a develop any film

  b get any film developed

Practice 2

Circle the letter of the correct verb form after the causative verb (base, infinitive, or past participle).

Laura and Henry were married a week ago. They had a simple, inexpensive, and very beautiful wedding.

Example:

1 *Laura did not hire a professional dressmaker. Instead, she had her aunt _____ her dress.*

  (a) *sew*   **b** *to sew*

2 Henry's little nephew wanted to be in the wedding, so they let him _____ the ring-bearer.

  a be   **b** to be

3 Laura and Henry did not need to hire a caterer. They got their friends and relatives _____ all the food.

  a prepare   **b** to prepare

4 On the day before the wedding, Laura and Henry bought the flowers themselves. Then they had them _____ by one of Henry's aunts.

  a arrange   **b** arranged

5 They got the church _____ by a group of their friends.

  a decorated   **b** to decorate

6 On the day of the wedding, Laura did not get her hair _____ . Her sister did it for her.

  a do   **b** done

7 On the afternoon of the wedding, Laura's mother got her _____ a nap.

  a take   **b** to take

8 The couple had Laura's grandfather, a minister, _____ the marriage ceremony.

  a perform   **b** performed

9 But Laura and Henry decided to have their wedding pictures _____ by a professional photographer.

  a take   **b** taken

10 At the reception, they had the food _____ by professional waiters.

  a serve   **b** served

11 They wanted to let their guests _____ themselves.

  a enjoy   **b** to enjoy

Conditionals

REAL AND UNREAL CONDITIONAL SENTENCES

Presentation

Conditional Sentences

Conditional sentences always have two clauses. One of the clauses begins with *if* and states a condition. For example, *If it rains...* . The other clause states a result of that condition. For example, *the fans at the ball game will get wet*. **Real** conditional sentences are about possible conditions and their results. **Unreal** conditional sentences are about very unlikely or impossible conditions.

Real Conditional Sentences

The verb of the **condition** clause in a real conditional sentence is always in the present tense and the verb of the **result** clause is almost always in the future tense.

Example:

> If I hear from Jon, I will let you know.
>
> I will let you know if I hear from Jon.

But there are a few exceptions to this rule.

In some cases, a real conditional sentence states a **fact**.

Example:

> If a meteor enters the earth's atmosphere, it burns.

In that case, the result clause may be in either the future or the present tense.

In some cases, a real conditional sentence may describe a **habitual activity**.

Example:

> If my cat is cornered, he attacks.

In that case, the result clause may also be in either the future or the present tense. In both these cases, the word *if* is sometimes replaced by *when* or *whenever*.

Unreal Conditional Sentences

The verb of the **condition** clause in an unreal conditional sentence is in the past tense, with two big exceptions.

If the verb is *be*, then it is always *were*. The result clause uses the auxiliary verb *would* (sometimes *could* or *might*).

Example:

> If I were king, I would have cake every day.

An unreal condition clause may refer to something that could have happened in the past but didn't. In that case, the condition clause uses a past perfect verb.

Example:

If I had remembered his name...

The result clause uses the auxiliary verb *would* (or *could* or *might*).

Rules	Examples
Use the present real conditional to talk about what happens under a certain condition or conditions.	**If** it has been raining for more than three days [condition], the streets flood [result].
Use the present real conditional to explain a general truth about an event.	Elizabeth passes her classes [surprising result] **even if** she doesn't study [condition]. Students can't leave [result] **unless** the teacher hasn't come in the first fifteen minutes [only under this condition].
Use the present real conditional to discuss or explain a habitual action based on a condition.	**When** my daughters aren't feeling well, their father stays home to take care of them.
When the conditional clause comes first in the sentence, use a comma to separate it from the result clause. Do not use a comma if the result clause comes first.	The streets flood **if** it has been raining for more than three days. **If** it has been raining for more than three days, the streets flood.

Practice 1

Circle whether each sentence is a real conditional or an unreal conditional.

1 If you see the play, you will enjoy it a lot.
   a real conditional
   b unreal conditional

2 When birds land in the birdbath, they splash out a lot of water.
   a real conditional
   b unreal conditional

3 If Karla had pitched, we would have won the game.
   a real conditional
   b unreal conditional

4 A young tree will die if it's not watered properly.
   a real conditional
   b unreal conditional

5 If Pat doesn't make it to the yoga class this week, our teacher will be disappointed.
   a real conditional
   b unreal conditional

6 If Betty were a foot taller, she would be a very good basketball player.

    a real conditional

    b unreal conditional

7 That will work better if you use pliers.

    a real conditional

    b unreal conditional

8 I would be more careful if I were you.

    a real conditional

    b unreal conditional

9 If the mail doesn't get here soon, I'll go crazy!

    a real conditional

    b unreal conditional

10 If George hadn't spilled the dye, Maria would still have a white dress.

    a real conditional

    b unreal conditional

Practice 2

Circle the letter of the correct verb form to complete each sentence.

1 If the pipes freeze, what _____ ?

    a will happen

    b would happen

2 If their son _____ classes, the teacher will call to let them know.

    a skipped

    b skips

3 If flowers bloomed in winter, they _____ lovely in the snow.

    a will look

    b would look

4 If the car _____ a strange clunking sound, it is probably time to get it serviced.

    a makes

    b would make

5 When you buy a lottery ticket, you _____ not usually expect to win.

    a did

    b do

Hope vs. Wish

Hope vs. Wish

We use *hope* to express possible situations that we desire in the past, present, or future. *Hope* takes the helping verb *will* or *can*, or the infinitive *to be*.

*I **hope** I can finish the project by the end of the week.* (This is possible.)

We use *wish* to express situations that we desire in the present or future that are not possible. We also use *wish* to express regrets about the past, or complain about something in the present.

*She **wished** she had more money so she could buy a new car.* (not possible)

*I **wish** I had gone to bed earlier last night.* (regret)

*I **wish** my sister would help me clean our room.* (complaint)

Rules	Examples
We can use **hope** to talk about present and future situations that are probable or possible. The verb *hope* can take the present tense. That which is hoped for is in the present or the future tense.	They **hope** (that) the IRS refund will come soon. **I hope** it **stays** sunny today.
Use present or future tenses or the modals **will** and **can** in the noun clause.	I **hope** you **have** a great time at the party. (about a future event) It's so dirty in here. We **hope** we **can clean up** the mess. (about a present desire) She called to say she **hopes** you **will get** the job tomorrow. (about the future)
Use **wish** to talk about past, present, and future situations that are improbable. The verb *to be* takes the subjunctive again and changes to *were* for all nouns and pronouns.	Don't you **wish** you **didn't have to work** for a living? He **wishes** he **were** in Venice.
Use past tenses (simple past, past perfect, etc.) or the modals **would, could** in the noun clause. The verb *to be* takes the subjunctive again and changes to *were* for all nouns and pronouns.	After she got into trouble, the teenager **wished** she **had** just **told** the truth. (about the past) All the people at this meeting **wish** they **weren't** here. (about the present) I **wish** I **could come** with you tonight. (about present ability) The teacher **wishes** more of her students **would come** to class. (about a present desire)

Practice 1

Circle the letter of the best verb tense and form to complete each sentence.

Example:

1 *The committee hopes that Jan _____ to be treasurer.*
   a *will agree*
   b *agreed*
   c *would agree*

2 Angie can't visit until next Christmas. She _____ her parents aren't angry.
   a wishes
   b wished
   c hopes

3 John thinks the interview went pretty well. He hopes they _____ him the job.
   a could call and give
   b will call and give
   c called and gave

4 Katie's husband got so upset about the accident that she _____ she hadn't told him.
   a hoped
   b hopes
   c wished

5 The engineers surveyed the bridge, but they made a few mistakes. They wished they _____ the work.
   a couldn't have to redo
   b don't have to redo
   c didn't have to redo

6 I wish I _____ that dress. It's hideous.
   a don't buy
   b hadn't bought
   c am not buying

7 The teacher _____ her students come to class on time.
   a wishes
   b wished
   c hopes

8 Many illnesses are preventable. Doctors _____ they can encourage their patients to take better care of themselves.
   a hope
   b hoped
   c wish

9 The defense attorney hopes that the judge _____ the evidence.
   a throws out
   b will throw out
   c threw out

10 Arlene really liked Hiram, but he stopped calling. She wishes she _____ him off.

    a scares

    b haven't scared

    c hadn't scared

11 I really want to see that movie with you. I wish I _____ to babysit my nieces.

    a won't have

    b didn't have

    c don't have

Practice 2

Complete the sentences with the correct form of the verbs *hope* or *wish*.

Example:

1 *We hope that the results of the test are posted soon. We can't stand waiting.*

2 We _____ we are able to afford to go on the trip.

3 I _____ my son didn't play video games.

4 I _____ I could focus on this lecture, but it is impossible today.

5 I _____ that you have a wonderful anniversary.

6 Don't you _____ your children would stay young forever?

7 Kyle can't come on the trip, but he wants us to know how much he _____ we have a good time.

8 Parents _____ they will make good decisions in the future.

9 My aunt wrote, "I'm having a great time. I _____ you were here."

10 I _____ the weather had been warmer.

11 They can't wait to invite people to the new apartment. They _____ everyone will like it.

The Future

FUTURE PERFECT VS. FUTURE PERFECT PROGRESSIVE

Presentation

Future Perfect vs. Future Perfect Progressive

We use the **future perfect** tense to talk about an event that will be finished by a particular, stated time in the future. This tense usually takes *will have* + the past participle of the verb.

Example:

*By the year 2017, I **will have lived** in San Francisco for ten years.* (The stated event is the year 2017. It is unclear whether or not the person will continue living there past this time.)

We use the **future perfect progressive** to talk about an event in the future that will continue past a stated time in the future. This tense usually takes *will have been* + verb + *-ing*.

Example:

*By the year 2017, I **will have been living** in San Francisco for ten years.* (This implies that the person will still be living there past the year 2017.)

Rules **Future Perfect**	Examples
To form affirmative statements with the future perfect, use subject + *will have* + past participle. To form negative statements, use subject + *will not have / won't have* + past participle.	He **will have graduated** by the end of the year.
	They **won't have finished** the book when the discussion starts.
To form questions, use *wh-* word or *how* + *will* + subject + *have* + past participle.	How many times **will** you **have** visited India in the next two years?
	When will you **have finished** your homework?
Use the future perfect to talk about a future event that happens before another future event.	There is still time to go to the grocery store for eggs. The children **won't have gotten up** before you return.
Use the future perfect to state how how many times a future event happens before another future event. ***NOTE:** Dependent clauses for future time use present tenses.	By the time we get the new *Shrek 3* video, my niece **will have watched** *Shrek 2* at least a million times.
Use signal words such as *by the time* or *before* with the future perfect.	**Before** you are a old, you will have seen much of the world.

Future Perfect Progressive	
To form affirmative statements with the future perfect progressive, use subject + *will have been* + verb + *-ing*. To form negative statements, use subject + *will not have been / won't have been* + verb + *-ing*.	He **will have been studying** English a long time by the time he can speak fluently.
	They **won't have been watching** the movie long when she arrives.
To form questions, use *wh-* word or *how* + *will* + subject + *have been* + verb + *-ing*.	How long **will** you **have been** working at that job at the end of the year?
Use the future perfect progressive to state how long a future event is happening before another future event.	We should call the plumber before we go to bed. By tomorrow morning, the faucet **will have been dripping** for 10 hours.
	By the time they save enough for a house, the couple **will have been living** in their apartment for five years.
Use signal word *for* with the future perfect progressive.	**For** how long will we have been complaining about our neighbors before we finally do something about them?

Practice 1

Circle the letter of the correct verb to complete the sentences about future events.

Example:

1 *Ms. Tanaka began teaching English in 1995. By 2025, she* _____
  for 25 years.
  a *will have taught*
  ⓑ *will have been teaching*

2 James is on a diet. He has been losing about 2 pounds (1 kilo) per week. By the end of the
  month, he _____ about 8 pounds.
  a will have lost
  b will have been losing

3 Judy and Joe were married in 1984. By 2019, they _____
  married for 35 years.
  a will have been
  b will have been being

4 Thomas started studying at 7 P.M. It is now 8 P.M. By 10 P.M.,
  he _____ for three hours.
  a will have studied
  b will have been studying

5 Why does it take you so long to get ready in the morning? By the time we leave,
  we _____ our bus.
  a will have missed
  b will have been missing

6 Science and technology continue to advance rapidly. By the year 2020,

   a Scientists _____ to produce cloned humans.
      a will have been able
      b will have been being able

   b More nations _____ to solar energy from of oil.
      a will have switched
      b will have been switching

   c Doctors _____ cancer using gene therapy.
      a will have cured
      b will have been curing

   d Lung cancer _____ more people than any disease, including HIV.
      a will have killed
      b will have been killing

   e Space shuttles _____ to and from Earth for almost 40 years.
      a will have traveled
      b will have been traveling

   f The world's population _____ to 7.5 billion.
      a will have grown
      b will have been growing

Practice 2

Complete each sentence with the correct verb form and tense. Pay attention to subject-verb agreement, tense, and spelling.

Example:

They are staying out late tonight. By the time they come home, their oldest daughter

<u>will have fallen asleep</u> (1) *(fall asleep).*

It's important for college students to be more aware of future job trends. That way, by the time they graduate, they _____ (2) (research) the possible changes to their chosen field thoroughly.

There are probably a number of industries that _____ (3) (change) by the time the current students are ready to leave school. For example, the service industry _____ (4) (deliver) services faster and cheaper using advances in robotics; cashiers, salesclerks, and other service jobs may not be necessary.

Some industries _____ (5) (not become) obsolete, though. For instance, it is doubtful that people _____ (6) (lost) their need for entertainment. People in countries such as China and India _____ (7) (earn) more money due to outsourcing from other countries, and consumers in those countries _____ (8) (demand) products that were previously unattainable. Consumers will be happy to note that many industries _____ (9) (produce) safer and more reliable products because of changes to the global market.

FUTURE PROGRESSIVE

Presentation

Future Progressive

We use the future progressive to talk about an action that will happen in the future over a period of time. The future progressive is formed with *will* + *be* + verb + *ing*. It is used in these situations:

Some event or action happens while the future progressive action is going on.

Example:

I **will be driving** home when the sun sets.

The future progressive action is going on when a particular date or time occurs.

Example:

On January 15th, I **will be driving** across the country.

Another way to express the future progressive is with the phrase *going to be*.

Example:

I **am going to be driving** home when the sun sets.

The signal words *by the time*, *when*, *while*, and *at that time* are often used with the future progressive.

Example:

By the time she is sixteen, she **will be speaking** Italian fluently.

Rules	Examples
To form affirmative statements with the future progressive, use subject + *will* + verb + *-ing*. To form negative statements, use subject + *will not* / *won't* + verb + *-ing*.	Adrienne **will be** walk**ing** in the park at 8 pm tonight. She **won't be** work**ing** on her final paper.
To form yes / no questions, use *will* + subject + *be* + verb + *-ing*. To form *wh-* questions, use *wh-* word + *will* + subject + *be* + verb + *-ing*.	**Will you be going** to Sarah's party? **What will you be doing** while they are at dinner?
Use the future progressive to talk about an event that is happening in the future, often when another event occurs.	Tomorrow morning, the couple **will be waiting** to pick up their daughter from soccer practice. I **will be finishing** the presentation when she arrives at the conference.
Use signal words *when*, *while*, *by the time*, *at that time* with the future progressive.	**By the time** you arrive, I will be packing my bags. **At that time**, the president was running for a second term.

Practice 1

Circle whether each underlined verb phrase is in the simple future tense or the future progressive.

Example:

1 *In the morning, we <u>will be driving</u> to Yellowstone for our annual camping trip.*
  ⓐ *future progressive*
  b *future simple*

2 I <u>will be hiking</u> the Appalachian Trail on my birthday.
  a future simple
  b future progressive

3 Next Friday night, we <u>will go</u> to a lecture about Buddhism.
  a future simple
  b future progressive

4 Where <u>will you be living</u> at this time next year?
  a future simple
  b future progressive

5 Look at those clouds. I'm afraid we <u>will be walking</u> home when it starts raining.
  a future simple
  b future progressive

6 We <u>will arrive</u> at the airport before noon because our flight leaves at 2:00.
  a future simple
  b future progressive

7 She <u>will still be working</u> when we leave for the movies.
  a future simple
  b future progressive

8 I <u>will clean</u> the house this afternoon because of the party here at 5 o'clock.
  a future simple
  b future progressive

9 I'm <u>going to be listening</u> to the radio when your show starts.
  a future simple
  b future progressive

10 I'll <u>meet</u> you at the library if you want to do homework together.
  a future simple
  b future progressive

11 By next June, Barry <u>will be swimming</u> like a champion.
  a future simple
  b future progressive

Practice 2

Complete each sentence with the future progressive or future simple.

Example:

1 By the end of June, I <u>will be running</u> 2 miles a day.

2 Ken _____ (work) at the zoo when the new antelope habitat is finished.

3 Paul's afraid we _____ (run out) of energy by the time campaign is half done.

4 The casserole _____ (still cook) when you finish the salad.

5 You know Graham _____ (sleep) by the time Will gets home.

6 At 3 o'clock, I _____ (walk) home from class.

7 I'm afraid Kayla _____ (sit) alone by the time we get there.

8 The play opens in June, so the actors _____ (still rehearse) on May 25th.

9 It is going to be a great party. People _____ (dance) all night.

10 Neil _____ (fix) the car this afternoon when you drop by.

Present Perfect vs. Present Perfect Progressive

Presentation

Present Perfect vs. Present Perfect Progressive

We use the present perfect to indicate an action that has happened at or during an unspecified time in the past. The present perfect is not used with specific time expressions, such as *yesterday*, *last week*, etc. It is used to talk about:

actions, events, or changes that have happened over a period of time and may still influence or be relevant in the present:

> You **have grown** since the last time I saw you.

highly significant events in the past:

> Twelve men **have walked** on the moon.
> Scientists **have discovered** a cure for the disease.

an uncompleted event or action:

> He **has not arrived** yet.

multiple actions before now:

> The dog **has run away** four times in the past five months.

We use the present perfect progressive to indicate an action that started in the past and has continued up until now. This tense puts emphasis on the **duration of an action**.

> The dog **has been barking** for a long time now.
> We **have been working** all afternoon.

Rules **Present Perfect**	Examples
To form affirmative statements with the present perfect, use subject + *have / has* + past participle. To form negative statements, use subject + *have not / haven't / has not / hasn't* + past participle.	Cerise **has found** a new doctor. However, she **hasn't seen** him yet.
To form yes / no questions, use *have / has* + subject + past participle. To form *wh-* questions, use *wh-* words + *have / has* + subject + past participle.	**Have you finished** your homework yet? **What has she done** about her high blood pressure?
Use the present perfect to talk about events that began before and may still be true now.	She **has visited** her grandmother every summer since she was 11 years old. (It started in the past, but it is unclear if it just stopped or if it is still continuing.)

Use the present perfect to talk about events that just finished very recently.	**A:** Are you too tired to work in the garden? **B:** No, I've just **taken** a nap.
Use the present perfect to talk about how much has been achieved or reached until now.	The family **has driven** 200 miles to the coast. (They started driving in the past, and they completed this amount now.)
Present Perfect Progressive	
To form affirmative statements with the present perfect progressive, use subject + *have / has been* + verb + *-ing*. To form negative statements, use subject + *have not / haven't / has not / hasn't been* + verb + *-ing*.	Cerise **has been seeing** that doctor every week for months. However, she **hasn't been following** his directions.
To form yes / no questions, use *have / has* + subject + *been* + verb + *-ing*. To form *wh-* questions, use *wh-* words + *have / has* + subject + *been* + verb + *-ing*.	**Have you been following** your doctor's directions? **What has she been doing** about her high blood pressure?
Use signal words *just, recently, ever, never, yet, already,* and other adverbs of frequency with the present perfect and the present perfect progressive. Use *since* with a specific time to indicate when the event began. Use *for* with a duration of time.	I have been coming here **since 1998**. I have been coming here **for twenty years**.

Practice 1

Circle whether each sentence uses the present perfect tense or the present perfect progressive.

1 Jun Li has visited his parents in Korea twice this year.
   a present perfect
   b present perfect progressive

2 The student has been studying all day.
   a present perfect
   b present perfect progressive

3 Guillermo and his sister haven't seen their parents in many years.
   a present perfect
   b present perfect progressive

4 Her roommate has been traveling a lot lately.
   a present perfect
   b present perfect progressive

5 Berhane has already finished a draft of her research paper.

  a present perfect

  b present perfect progressive

6 She has worked with two or three different partners on the job.

  a present perfect

  b present perfect progressive

7 Andrew and his wife have gone to a number of plays in the park in previous years.

  a present perfect

  b present perfect progressive

8 This year we haven't been going to the beach much.

  a present perfect

  b present perfect progressive

9 John Legend has been playing the piano since he was four years old.

  a present perfect

  b present perfect progressive

10 Legend has received nine Grammy awards since he released his first album, *Get Lifted* in 2004.

  a present perfect

  b present perfect progressive

Practice 2

Complete each sentence with present perfect or present perfect progressive.

Example:

1 *That truck engine* _____ *for an hour.*

  ⓐ *has been running*

  b *has run*

2 Ron's stained shirt _____ since yesterday.

  a has been soaking

  b has soaked

3 The community garden _____ our neighborhood together for two years.

  a has brought

  b has been bringing

4 Amanda _____ art history this semester.

  a has studied

  b has been studying

5 Ina _____ grape jelly again! I can smell it.

  a has been making

  b has made

6 My friend Marilyn _____ dogs for about ten years.
 a has rescued
 b has been rescuing

7 Jim _____ algebra to work out some of the measurements on the room he is building.
 a has been using
 b has used

8 I can't find Leo right now, but I know he _____ this lab lately.
 a has been using
 b has used

9 Luis _____ guacamole for the party all afternoon.
 a has made
 b has been making

10 I _____ Shakespeare's plays and I'm halfway through.
 a have been reading
 b have read

The Past

SIMPLE PAST VS. PAST PERFECT

Presentation

Simple Past vs. Past Perfect

Simple Past

We use the simple past to talk about events that happened in the past. To form the simple past of regular verbs, add –*ed* to the base verb. To form the simple past of irregular verbs, you will have to look up the correct form in a dictionary. Most people learn the irregular verb forms the same way they learn vocabulary, by reading and listening.

Regular

> I **visited** my uncle once.
>
> He **never visited** his uncle.
>
> She **visited** her uncle many times.

Irregular

> I **broke** my hairbrush.
>
> He **brought** his lunch in brown bag.
>
> We **spoke** together often.

Past Perfect

The past perfect is used to talk about an action that happened before a certain time or before another action in the past. To form the past perfect, use *had* + past participle.

> I **had eaten** before the roof collapsed.
>
> We **had known** her long before we met her brother.

Rules	Examples
Simple Past	
To form affirmative statements with the simple past, use subject + verb + -*ed* for regular verbs. Some verbs have irregular past forms. You need to memorize them. To form negative statements, use subject + *did not / didn't* + verb.	Helen **washed** her clothes late last night. We **went** to Paris last September. (The infinitive verb is *go*. The simple past is irregular.) Joe **didn't wash** his clothes last night. We **didn't go** to Madrid.
To form yes / no questions, use *did* + subject + verb. To form *wh-* questions, use *wh-* word + *did* + subject + verb.	**Did you see** a movie last night? **What** movie **did you see**?
Use the simple past to talk about a completed event or situation.	They **arrived** at the Grand Central station this morning. Did you pick them up?
Use the simple past with time expressions like *before* and *after* where the order of events is already clear.	Amy's mother **went** to the dry cleaners before she **picked up** Amy and her friends.

Past Perfect	
To form affirmative statements with the past perfect, use subject + *had* + past participle. To form negative statements, use subject + *had not / hadn't* + past participle.	He **had graduated** before he took the job. They **hadn't finished** the book when the discussion started.
To form yes / no questions, use *had* + subject + past participle. To form *wh*-questions, use *wh*- word + *had* + subject + past participle.	**Had you visited** your family before you asked them for money? **How many times had you visited** your family before you had a child?
Use the past perfect to talk about something that happens before another event in the past.	The Sounders game **had finished** by the time they **got** to the stadium. (First, the game finished. Then they arrived.)
Use the past perfect as the past tense of the present perfect.	"Someone has robbed the bank," shouted the security guard. The security guard shouted that someone had just **robbed** the bank.
Use signal words *just, by the time, when, until, as soon as* with the past perfect.	

Practice 1

Complete each sentence with verbs in simple past or past perfect tense. Pay attention to subject-verb agreement, tense, and spelling.

Example:

1 She <u>ate</u> (eat) a huge dinner because she <u>had missed</u> (miss) lunch.

2 I _____ (just wash) my car when it _____ (begin) to rain.

3 Before I _____ (see) the movie, I _____ (read) the reviews.

4 By the time Sonia _____ (start) college, she already _____ (have) several part-time jobs. She _____ (work) as a waitress, a store clerk, and a babysitter, all before the age of 18.

Practice 2

Complete each sentence with verbs in simple past or past perfect tense. Pay attention to subject-verb agreement, tense, and spelling.

Jackie _____ (live) in the United States for almost six months when her father _____ (come) for a visit. She _____ (not receive) many letters from home, so she _____ (be) eager to hear news about her family. Her father _____ (tell) her that her mother _____ (not be) well for several weeks during the summer, but she _____ (recover) completely by the time he _____ (leave) for the United States. She _____ (ask) him why her mother _____ (be) so ill, and he _____ (say) that she _____ (have) the flu.

PAST PROGRESSIVE

Presentation

Past Progressive

The past progressive is used to express a continuing action at some point in the past. It can be used to express an incomplete action and indicates limited duration of the action. In other words, something took place while the other action was happening.

For example:

> I **was sleeping** on the couch when the phone rang. (The phone interrupted the sleep.)

> She **was studying** for her test while her brother watched TV. (The studying was taking place at the same time that her brother watched TV.)

To form the past progressive, use the past form of the verb *be* + the present participle (or verb + *-ing*).

Rules	Examples
To form affirmative statements with the past progressive, use subject + *was / were* + verb + *-ing*. To form negative statements, use subject + *was not / were not / wasn't / weren't* + verb + *-ing*.	Adrienne **was walking** in the park at 8 pm last night. She **wasn't working** on her final paper.
To form yes / no questions, use *was / were* + subject + verb + *-ing*. To form *wh-* questions, use *wh-* word + *was / were* + subject + verb + *-ing*.	**Were you working** last night? **What were you doing** when it happened?
Use the past progressive to talk about a situation happening over time in the past. The action is progressive and describes a process, not a one-time event.	At 7 a.m., she **was getting** ready for work. (She was in the process of preparing for work.)
Use the past progressive to talk about an event that continues for a period of time in the past.	I **was watching** that movie for three hours last night.
Use the past progressive to talk about two past events that happen at the same time.	Jack **was watching** T.V. while Jill **was learning** the dance.
Use the past progressive to talk about a past event that begins and continues when another event happens.	The string on my guitar broke while I **was playing**. (I played the guitar. As I played, the string broke.)
Use signal words *when, while, for a period of time, as long as,* and *at that time* with the past progressive.	

Practice 1

Circle whether the underlined verb phrase in each sentence is the past progressive or some other tense.

Example:

1 Stephen <u>was thinking</u> about a new haircut, but I didn't think it was a good idea.
   a *simple past*
   (b) *past progressive*

2 Richard <u>wore</u> a tuxedo when he gave his recital.
   a simple past
   b past progressive

3 Kari <u>was painting</u> a landscape while Hanna read her book.
   a past perfect
   b past progressive

4 My brother <u>had been selling</u> real estate until 1995.
   a past perfect progressive
   b past progressive

5 When I got back to the table, my dog <u>was looking</u> hungrily at my dinner.
   a past perfect
   b past progressive

6 Kathryn <u>had grown</u> the most beautiful roses before she moved to an apartment.
   a past perfect
   b past progressive

7 A wonderful owl <u>was living</u> in the woods near my house until the developer cut down the trees.
   a simple past
   b past progressive

8 When Jennifer arrived, I <u>was finishing</u> dinner.
   a past perfect
   b past progressive

9 We <u>were growing</u> pumpkins for awhile, but they got stolen.
   a past perfect progressive
   b past progressive

10 Liz <u>had been cooking</u> for the church all day.
   a past perfect progressive
   b past progressive

Practice 2

Complete each sentence with the past progressive form of the verb in the parentheses.

1 Aaron _____ (write) his first book when I met him.

2 His cat _____ (fight) with a bottle cap for about an hour.

3 She _____ (look) out the car window when a man ran out of the bank carrying a bag.

4 When I got to the park, Marcello _____ (already sit) on our favorite bench.

5 That song came on the radio and suddenly Aliza _____ (play) air guitar like crazy.

6 Gayle _____ (audition) for the orchestra while I tried out for the play.

7 The wolf pack _____ (howl) yesterday because it had lost one of its members.

8 Lynnette _____ (wait) outside her son's school when her car was hit from behind.

9 Chebon _____ (play) football for our school the year we won the championship.

10 I suddenly realized I _____ (worry) about nothing.

Reflexive Pronouns

Reflexive Pronouns

We use reflexive pronouns to emphasize who received the action in a sentence. Reflexive pronouns are not the same as subject or object pronouns. They are used when the subject and object are the same. For example: *He watched **himself** on television.* This means a man watched his own image on television. *He watched him on television* means he watched someone else, not his own image, on television.

Reflexive pronouns can also be used to emphasize the subject:

I *myself* don't like bananas.

Reflexive pronouns end in *–self* or *–selves*.

Singular Reflexive Pronouns

> I enjoy **myself** at parties.
>
> You enjoy **yourself** at parties.
>
> He/she enjoys **himself/herself** at parties.
>
> The dog (it) enjoys itself at parties.
>
> One enjoys **oneself** at parties. (Use for a more academic style)

Plural Reflexive Pronouns

> We enjoy **ourselves** at parties.
>
> You (all) enjoy **yourselves** at parties.
>
> They enjoy **themselves** at parties.

Rules	Examples
Use a reflexive pronoun when the subject receives the action of the verb.	The teacher told her students very sternly, "**You** behave **yourselves** while I am gone."
Use as an appositive to emphasize the noun or pronoun. The reflexive pronoun intensifies the subject.	The teenagers destroyed the frame of the painting, but they managed not to ruin the **painting itself**.
Use a reflexive pronoun with certain idiomatic expressions and phrases.	The family went on vacation, but the daughter stayed **by herself**. (all alone)
	I refused to use the manual. I wanted to build the bookshelf **by myself**. (without assistance)
	When Matt goes on dates, he tries to **be himself**. (act as he always does, not in a special way)

Practice 1

Circle the letter of the correct subject, object, or reflexive pronoun. Some sentences may not need a pronoun.

Example:

1 *My cat spends hours each day licking* _____ .
   a *hisself*
   (b) *herself*
   c *It*

2 A: What happened to you? Your face is bleeding.
   B: It's nothing. I cut _____ shaving.
   a myself
   b me
   c no pronoun

3 Did you get dressed _____ yet? We need to leave soon.
   a yourself
   b yourselves
   c no pronoun

4 Yesterday morning, I got _____ up early to go for a run.
   a myself
   b me
   c no pronoun

5 At what age will you allow your son to stay home by _____ ?
   a hisself
   b himself
   c Him

6 The boys and _____ went to the store.
   a I
   b themselves
   c myself

7 Linda and Tom cannot afford to hire a gardener, so they take care of their garden _____ .
   a they
   b theirself
   c themselves

8 When you leave, take the dirty clothes with _____ .
   a you
   b yourself
   c yourselves

9 Do you like my hair? I cut it _____ .

    a I

    b me

    c myself

10 My daughter is teaching _____ how to ride a bike.

    a himself

    b herself

    c no pronoun

11 Our English class is going to have a Halloween party next week. The students and I will decorate the room and make all the food _____ .

    a us

    b ourself

    c ourselves

Practice 2

Complete the sentences with an object, subject, or reflexive pronoun.

When I was a child, both my parents worked outside the house, so my four siblings and I sometimes stayed home by <u>ourselves</u>. Our parents always encouraged us to be independent. It was not a problem for _____ to be alone because my oldest brother took care of us _____ . We all knew we could depend on _____ to drop us off and pick us up from school. He was very strict, so we usually behaved _____ around _____ . He didn't know how to cook, though, so my oldest sister had to prepare the meals by _____ . As a result, from a young age, I learned to solve problems by _____ . Today, I am a father, too, and I also encourage my children to do as many things as possible for _____ .

Noun Clauses

Presentation

Noun Clauses

Noun clauses are dependent clauses that perform the same functions as regular nouns. This means they can be the subjects, objects, or complements.

Rules	Examples
The word *that* can be used to introduce a noun clause. It can be omitted when it introduces a noun clause that is an object. It cannot be omitted when it introduces a noun clause that is a subject.	Scientists believe **(that) the pistol shrimp uses sonic waves to paralyze its prey**. (object) **That the students re-take the exam** is out of the question. (subject)
Noun clauses can be introduced by question words. The phrases introduced by question words are called embedded questions. An embedded question is a part of a sentence that would be a question if on its own, but is not a question in the sentence. Noun phrases introduced by question words can be both objects and subjects. A noun clause subject takes a singular verb. Use statement word order, not question word order, in embedded questions.	They asked, "When did the game start?" They would like to know **when the game started**. (object, embedded question) **When the game started** isn't clear. <u>Correct</u>: I'm wondering what he's going to do. <u>Incorrect</u>: I'm wondering what is he going to do.
When you change a yes / no question into an embedded question, use *if* or *whether (or not)* to introduce the noun clause. *Whether* and *if* have the same meaning. *If* cannot be used in a noun clause in the subject position.	"Was anyone hurt in the accident?" I wonder **whether / if** anyone was hurt in the accident. <u>Correct</u>: Whether anyone was hurt in the accident isn't clear. <u>Incorrect</u>: If anyone was hurt in the accident isn't clear.
Whether ... or not can replace *whether* in all noun clauses. *If ... or not* can replace *whether* in all noun clauses except in noun clauses in the subject position.	I'd like to know **whether** Ms. Smith is coming to the meeting. I'd like to know **whether / if** Ms. Smith is coming to the meeting **or not**.

Practice 1

Find and underline the 11 noun clauses in the paragraph.

Example:

Our English teacher announced that we would have a vocabulary test on Friday.

Ms. Angela White is one of the most respected teachers in our school for several reasons. First, she takes the time to find out who her students are. She wants to know what her students are interested in, and she tries to connect her lessons *to* what her students want to learn. Second, her students say that she is very fair. She makes sure that every person in her class gets an equal chance to participate, and she never plays favorites. Next, Ms. White always gives clear instructions so that students understand exactly what they are supposed to do. In addition, she is sensitive *to them.* If they make mistakes, she knows how to correct them so that students do not feel ashamed. One last thing that makes Ms. White such a good teacher is her nice voice. Her students always mention how much they enjoy listening to her.

Practice 2

Change the sentence or question in parentheses to a noun clause. Pay attention to meaning, capital letters, punctuation, and spelling.

Example:

1 *My parents decided* that I should become a businessman *(I should become a businessman), without asking me* what I wanted to do *(What did I want to do?) with my life.*

2 No one remembers _____ .
(What is the homework for Monday?)

3 A: I'm trying to find the post office. Can you tell me _____ ?
(How can I get there?)

B: Sure. It's at the corner of Olympic Boulevard and First Street. Do you know
_____ ? (Where is that?)

A: No, I don't. I'm concerned _____ . (I won't find it.)

B: I wonder _____ . (Do you have GPS on your phone?)

A: I think I do, but I have never used it.

B: I can show you _____ . (How does it work?)

A: Thanks.

4 I don't know _____ .
(Who directed the movie *Titanic*?)

5 If we want to get good seats for the concert, it's essential _____
_____ . (We are at the auditorium no later than 7 P.M.)

6 Excuse me, can you tell me _____ ? (What time is it?)

The Subjunctive

Presentation

The Subjunctive

The subjunctive is a grammatical mood, like the indicative (e.g. *Jack likes cheese.*) or imperative (e.g. *Do your homework!*), not a tense. The subjunctive verb forms express many things, such as desire, emotion, necessity, advisability, possibility, and states of unreality. The subjunctive is used mostly in dependent clauses and is often preceded by *that*. Sometimes, *that* is implied.

Examples:

It is important that you **speak** loud.

I wish it **were** summer.

Rules	Examples
The subjunctive is used after certain verbs: advise (that) ask (that) command (that) demand (that) desire (that) insist (that) propose (that) recommend (that) request (that) suggest (that) urge (that)	He recommended (that) I see a doctor soon. I urged (that) Mark complete his work by Friday.
The subjunctive is used after certain expressions: It is best (that) It is crucial (that) It is desirable (that) It is essential (that) It is imperative (that) It is important (that) It is recommended (that) It is urgent (that) It is vital (that) It is a good idea (that) It is a bad idea (that)	It is essential (that) Frank come to the meeting. It is a good idea that we arrive 15 minutes ahead of time.
Use the base form of the verb in the subjunctive.	The doctor advised (that) the child **stay** home for a week. It is important (that) Donna **take** a few days off.

You can use the subjunctive in a negative, passive, and progressive form.	It is **necessary** (that) children **not miss** too much school in their early education. (negative)
	The doctor urged (that) the baby **be sent** to the hospital immediately. (passive)
	I suggest (that) we **be waiting** for Clara at her apartment when she comes home. (progressive)
You can use an infinitive or gerund phrase instead of the subjunctive in statements that emphasize the importance of something.	It is desirable **for you to finish** the application before interviewing for the job.
	We recommend **taking** the exam after the workshop.
You can use *should* instead of the subjunctive in statements of advisability.	We suggest that patients who need emergency appointments **should not call** but **should** just **come in**.
The subjunctive form of *to be* is irregular. It is either *be* or *were*. *Were* indicates an unreal condition.	I suggest the children *be* taken to school now.
	If I *were* she, I would not wear that dress.

Practice 1

Write the correct verb form. Use subjunctive or present/future tense. Use contractions wherever possible.

Example:

1 *I suggest that you <u>make</u> (make) an appointment with the visa counselor.*

2 Everyone knows that Ms. Gates _____ (be) a very strict teacher. For one thing, she insists that students _____ (not turn in) their homework late. She believes that a student _____ (learn) anything if he or she doesn't practice.

3 In addition, she requires that everyone _____ (be) in the classroom at 9:00 A.M. sharp.

4 Moreover, whenever she gives a homework assignment, she insists that we _____ (follow) directions precisely. She says that most mistakes _____ (not happen) if students read directions.

5 On the other hand, Ms. Gates is very generous and helpful. For example, if a student is having a problem with English, she often recommends that he _____ (study) a certain section of the book and _____ (discuss) it with her the next day. She cares that every student _____ (understand).

6 One time I was totally confused about the proper way to use the past perfect tense. Ms. Gates offered to help me and proposed that I _____ (meet) her after school.

Practice 2

Write the correct subjunctive noun clause or phrase using the sentence in parentheses. Remember to use contractions and check punctuation, spelling, and verb form.

Example:

1 *If you have a question about your visa, I suggest* <u>that you make an appointment with the visa counselor</u> . *(You (need to) make an appointment with the visa counselor.)*

2 It is essential _____ .
(You (should) see your dentist twice a year.)

3 It is necessary _____ .
(You (must) pay your phone bill on time.)

4 The Surgeon General advises _____
because they cause cancer. (Everyone (shouldn't) smoke cigarettes.)

5 It is urgent _____ .
(We (should) call the fire department if we smell gas.)

6 It is vital _____ .
(American workers (must) pay their income taxes by April 15.)

7 My mother suggested _____ .
(I (shouldn't) procrastinate on my college applications.)

8 It is advisable _____
if a person hits her head. (A person (should) see a doctor.)

9 We would strongly urge _____
before the trip. (You (must) get your brakes checked.)

10 It is important _____ .
(I (must not) wait to buy my textbooks.)

11 The manager recommends _____
to balance the budget. (A few workers (must) be laid off.)

Gerunds and Infinitives

Practice 1

Complete the sentences with the correct gerund or infinitive form.

Example:

1 *Stop watching television. You need <u>to study</u> (study) for your history test tomorrow.*

2 I need _____ (have) some water to quench my thirst.

3 It was kind of him _____ (carry) that heavy box for me.

4 Yesterday a boy in my class was caught _____ (cheat) during a test. At first he denied _____ (do) it, but after the teacher showed him the two nearly identical test papers, he admitted to _____ (copy) a few answers. The teacher told him that she wouldn't allow him _____ (get away with) it. She threatened _____ (give) him ten extra hours of homework as punishment. She also recommended _____ (study) harder in the future.

5 Do you think a 12-year-old is responsible enough _____ (babysit)?

6 I plan on _____ (meet) my parents for dinner tonight.

Practice 2

Complete the sentence with the correct gerund or infinitive form. Use past, present, progressive, and passive forms, if necessary. Add prepositions to gerunds if needed.

Example:

1 *Stop watching television and finish <u>studying</u> (study) for your history test tomorrow.*

2 Newborn babies need _____ (pick up) and _____ (hold) in order to develop normally.

3 I'm going to put off the house _____ (clean) until tomorrow.

4 **Sarah:** Robbie invited me ＿＿＿＿＿＿ (go) to a party with him on Saturday night.

   Mother: Alone? No, Sarah. You are too young ＿＿＿＿ (go out) alone with boys.

5 Last night, the people next door had a party. The music was so loud that I couldn't concentrate on ＿＿＿＿ (study). The laughing and talking prevented me from ＿＿＿＿ (be) able to focus on my work. At midnight I finally went over there and asked them to quiet down. They apologized for ＿＿＿＿ (make) so much noise.

6 It is very important for travelers ＿＿＿＿ (learn) about local customs in different countries.

7 It is foolish ＿＿＿＿ (offer) a bribe to a police officer in many countries.

8 Can you teach me ＿＿＿＿ (tune) a guitar?

Direct and Indirect Speech

Direct and Indirect Speech

Direct speech uses quotation marks to report speech in its original form. The quotation marks indicate that the speech is from the speaker and not reported by someone else.

"I love cheese," said Sam.

We use reported speech to paraphrase what others say, write, or think. You may have to change pronouns, possessives, time and location words, and verb tenses in the paraphrase.

Sam said he loved cheese.

Practice 1

Change the quoted speech into reported speech. Pay attention to verb tense, pronouns, time expressions, and location phrases.

Example:

1 *"I don't feel well."*
   She said that <u>she didn't feel well</u> .

2 "I must finish the project tonight."
   Simret told us that _____ .

3 "Are the researchers presenting here at the conference?"
   Narayan wanted to know _____ .

4 "Don't turn the table over until all of the table legs have been screwed in."
   The table assembly manual informed us _____ until all of the
   table legs _____ .

5 "Yawning can be very contagious."
   The teacher asserts that _____ . That's why we
   should cover our mouths.

6 "How can I find a study group for this class?"
   Marcus, a new student, inquired _____ .

7 "There is a higher likelihood that a marriage will last if the couple has a similar background."
   Researchers believe that there _____
   a similar background.

8 "Collect your things and go to the nearest exit ."
   The announcement on the intercom told them _____
   to the nearest exit.

9 "Workers have been taking too many breaks."

The manager claimed _____ .

10 "Drivers shouldn't talk on the phone."

The law says that _____ .

11 "I'll pick up the children from soccer practice."

My husband promised that _____ .

Practice 2

Read the dialogue. Then complete the paragraph with the correct use of reported speech.
Pay attention to verb tense, pronouns, time expressions, and location phrases.

ELLEN: "I met a cool guy last night."

NANCY: "Where did you meet him?"

ELLEN: "I met him at the supermarket last night."

NANCY: "Really?"

ELLEN: "Yeah, we were standing in line, and he introduced himself."

NANCY: "Was he attractive?"

ELLEN: "He was nice-looking and very charming."

NANCY: "Did you exchange phone numbers?"

ELLEN: "He gave me his number and asked me to call him tomorrow."

NANCY: "Are you going to go out with him?"

ELLEN: "I wish I could, but I can't."

NANCY: "Why not?"

ELLEN: "Hiram and I have decided to get back together."

Ellen and Nancy met for coffee last week to catch up and hang out. Ellen told Nancy that (1) _she_
had met a cool guy the night before. Nancy wanted to know (2) _____ ,
so Ellen reported that (3) _____ at the supermarket, and the guy
had introduced himself. Nancy wondered (4) _____ , to which
Ellen replied that (5) _____ and very charming. Nancy asked
(6) _____ phone numbers. Ellen said that (7) _____
to call him (8) _____ . Nancy wanted to know (9) _____
_____ with him. Ellen maintained that she (10) _____ .
After Nancy asked her why not, she explained that her old boyfriend Hiram and (11) _____
_____ to get back together.

Modals

ABILITY AND POSSIBILITY

Practice 1

Complete each sentence with the correct form of *can, could, be able to, may, might,* or *must*. Pay attention to tense and meaning. Use contractions when possible.

Example:

1 A: <u>Can you play</u> *(you, play) chess?*

  B: *Of course, we play every Sunday afternoon.*

2 Angel _____ (not come) to the choir because she has no babysitter for her daughter.

3 Gabriel _____ (not join) us at the party because his mother is sick in the hospital.

4 Walking down the street, you pass a woman who looks just like your sister. However, your sister is in San Francisco. You say, "That _____ (be) her."

5 She _____ (be) on a diet. She's lost a little weight.

6 The students _____ (think) they will pass now. They were caught cheating.

7 In a movie theater, the person in front of you is wearing a tall hat. You say to the person, "Excuse me. I _____ (not see) the screen. Would you mind removing your hat? Thank you."

8 It's been a long and cold winter. There _____ (still be) a lot of snow in the mountains.

9 You are in a cafeteria. There are no free tables. At one table, a woman is eating by herself. You approach her and ask, "Is this chair empty? _____ (I, sit) here?"

10 People believe that the government cutbacks _____ (weaken) the economy further.

11 A long time ago, girls in U.S. public schools _____ (wear) skirts or dresses. Nowadays they are allowed to wear pants.

Practice 2

Complete each sentence with the correct form of *can, could, be able to, may, might,* or *must.* Pay attention to tense and meaning. Use contractions when possible.

Example:

According to the research study, monarch butterflies in Minnesota <u>might not survive</u> (not survive) because of deforestation.

Switzerland is a very small country, but it has four official languages: German (70%) , French (20%), Italian (4%), and Romansch (1%). Every school child _____ (learn) at least one second language in school. Furthermore, many children _____ (pick up) a third or fourth language. Swiss people value multilingualism.

As English is becoming increasingly popular in Switzerland, more Swiss people _____ (choose) to study English instead of one of the official languages. Thousands of tourists visit Switzerland each year, and most of them _____ (not speak) any of the country's official languages. Almost all of them _____ (speak) English, however.

Some Swiss people are worried about the growing use of English in their country. They ask: "What effect _____ (English, have) on the relationships between the different linguistic groups in the country?" These people are afraid that English _____ (take) over as the principal method of communication in the country and that this _____ (cause) the minor languages to die out. They say that the Swiss people _____ (not allow) this to happen because multilingualism is an essential feature of Swiss history, culture, and identity.

NECESSITY AND ADVISABILITY

Presentation

Modals: Necessity and Advisability

We use modals to give more information about a verb. They *modify* the meaning of a verb. Modals tell us about ability, necessity, possibility, or advisability. Modals can indicate degree and time. The modals we use for **necessity** are *have to, have got to,* and *must.* The modals we use for **advisability** are *should, ought to,* and *had better.*

Practice 1

Complete each sentence with the correct form of *have (got) to, must, should, ought to,* or *had better.* Pay attention to tense and meaning. Use contractions when possible.

Example:

1 *Ran has been diagnosed with diabetes. <u>Should she have</u> (have) a piece of cake?*

2 If you want to study in the United States, you _____ (receive) a student visa.

3 You _____ (not be) a U.S. citizen to get a driver's license, however.

4 Adrian passed the NCLEX test for nursing, so she _____ (not study) anymore. She can find a job.

5 The Voting Rights law asserts that states _____ (not change) voting practices without the permission of the federal government.

6 He _____ (help) his parents with money right now. It's the right thing to do.

7. We _____ (cancel) our vacation next week if we don't find a cat sitter soon.

8 Karen is really angry. She says, "Those kids _____ (stop) throwing eggs at her car."

9 There is a new "driving while texting" law. You _____ (not text) and drive. The ticket is really expensive.

10 I know you have been having money trouble. _____ (you, declare) bankruptcy?

11 The counselor told the couple that they _____ (not get married) until they sought counseling.

Practice 2

Complete each sentence with the correct form of *have (got) to, must, should, ought to,* or *had better*. Some sentences are either necessity or advisability. Pay attention to tense and meaning. Contractions are possible.

Example:

Jennifer <u>has to wear</u> (wear) a hat when she works in the garden.

Family Estate Planning Pamphlet

Have you thought about what would happen to your estate if you became disabled or died? Many people don't, but they _____ (consider) it carefully.

If you want to save your family from a headache and extra taxes, you _____ (protect) your estate with a legal plan of some sort.

Here are three good reasons to have a legal plan:

After you die, the courts _____ (follow) state law if there is no legal plan. Your family _____ (complete) a legal process called probate to receive your property and possessions. During the probate process, the court can take about five percent of the estate.

So, what _____ (you, do)? There are three ways to protect your family in the event that you are disabled or die.

Most importantly, you _____ (set up) a trust for assets like bank accounts, houses, and cars. If there is a trust, your family _____ (not go) to court. You can use a kit to set up a trust. All you _____ (do) is choose a person called a trustee to be in charge of your trust after you die.

Additionally, you _____ (designate) or choose a beneficiary for your retirement and IRA accounts. You _____ (not include) these accounts in your trust. It's not allowed.

Finally, don't forget to write a will for special possessions and instructions. Examples of special possessions are jewelry, clothing, and funeral arrangements.

PAST HABITUAL ACTIVITY

Presentation

Modals: Past Habitual Activity

We use the modal *would* to talk about willingness and refusal to do something, as well as repeated past actions. We use *used to* and *be used to* in order to talk about habits, and familiarity with something in the past tense.

Practice 1

Write the correct use of *would, used to,* or *be/get used to* in order to complete the sentence.

become used to	would get	would work
used to get	you use to go	wouldn't help

1 *When I went to the bank without my ID, the teller* <u>wouldn't help</u> *me.*

2 The man _____ a lot of parking tickets, but now he checks the signs before he parks.

3 Jeremy and I _____ together for breakfast once a week.

4 Before she had surgery, the manager _____ until late in the evening every night.

5 You look familiar. Did _____ to Ridgemount High School?

6 The workers have _____ taking lunch early.

Would you listen	Are you used to	wouldn't have
didn't use to have	used to staying up	

1 When we were children, my sister _____ a bath in the evening.

2 Now that school is starting, the boys are going to have to go to bed on time. They have been quite _____ late.

3 She is always late now. She _____ this problem.

4 _____ to your parents as a child?

5 How is your class? _____ that new teacher yet?

Practice 2

Complete the sentence with the correct use of *would, used to*, or *be/get used to*. Pay attention to meaning, form, and tense. Use contractions when possible.

Example:

<u>Did you use to daydream</u> *(daydream) in school when you were little?*

When I was seven years old, I _____ (not go) near the water because I _____ (be afraid). My mother _____ _____ (bring) my brothers to the pool for swimming lessons every Saturday. In the beginning, she _____ (not require) me to come. But after a while, she _____ (make) me come because she wanted me to learn. My brothers _____ (get) in the water right away. They loved swimming. By that time, they had been swimming for over a year. However, I _____ _____ (start) crying when we got there. Eventually, though, I _____ _____ the water. The teacher was very patient. She _____ _____ (hold) my hand and walk me down the stairs into the shallow end of the pool. Because of her, I'm not afraid anymore.

PERFECT FORMS

Presentation

Modals: Perfect Forms

We use modals in perfect tense to express opportunity, possibility, impossibility, regret, blame, disappointment, suggestion, or preferences in the past. The general form of a perfect modal is: subject + modal + *have* + past participle. We use the perfect form to talk about things that did not happen, or that we are not sure about, in the past. We use it when we speculate about what possibly happened, or imagine about how things could have been different.

Practice 1

Complete the sentences with a perfect modal (*could, can, might, may, must, should, ought to, would rather, would*). Pay attention to meaning and past participle spelling.

Example:

1 *Helen came in late this morning. She <u>might have been out</u> (be out) late last night.*

2 You had enough money for two pairs of inexpensive shoes or one pair of expensive ones. You bought the inexpensive ones, and they wore out after two months. Looking back, you _____ (buy) the expensive ones.

3 Last night, Max ate three hamburgers, a large bag of french fries, and a double ice cream cone. Afterward, he didn't like how he felt. He _____ (not eat) so much.

4 On Friday night, Jenny and her boyfriend went to see a movie. It was terrible. Afterward, both of them agreed that they _____ (stay) home.

5 Ching's library book was due yesterday, but she still hasn't returned it. She _____ _____ (not finish) reading it yet.

6 Jorge _____ (not go) to college without the financial support of his family.

7 I called Steve at 8:00 P.M. last night, but he didn't answer the phone. He _____ _____ (be) studying or taking a shower.

8 I _____ (not make) that mistake if I had been paying attention.

9 Elaine forgot to pay her water bill, so the city turned off her water. She _____ _____ (pay) her water bill.

10 Mayumi was late to her English class this morning. She _____ (oversleep).

11 My boss is in a very bad mood this morning. He _____ (have) a fight with his wife.

Practice 2

Complete the conversation with a perfect modal (*could, can, might, may, must, should, ought to, would rather, would*). Pay attention to meaning and past participle spelling. Use contractions when possible.

Example:

WIFE: *I had the worst day today. This morning, the car would not start, so I had to find a different way to get to work.*

HUSBAND: *What did you do?*

WIFE: *Well, I* <u>would have taken</u> *(take) the bus, but the bus station is too far to walk.* I guess I _____ (call) a taxi, but I was worried about money. Taxis are very expensive, and I know we don't have much money right now. In the end, I called in sick again.

HUSBAND: Oh no, what _____ (happen)?

WIFE: It _____ (not be) the gas. I just filled the tank. It _____ (be) the battery. That's the only other thing I can think of.

HUSBAND: I thought you replaced it when you went to the mechanic last week. You _____ _____ (get) the battery replaced when you had the chance.

WIFE: I know, but I _____ (not replace) it last week. I hadn't been paid yet.

HUSBAND: You _____ (not wait). I know you don't want to bother me, but _____ _____ (ask) me for the money? I _____ (help) than risk your missing any more work.

WIFE: I had no idea you _____ (give) me the money. You are right. I _____ _____ (tell) you what was happening.

PROGRESSIVE FORMS

Modals: Progressive Forms

We use the modals in progressive tense to talk about activities in progress in the present, past, or future. These are activities that are going on, or were, or would be already going on. The basic form is: modal + a form of *be* + verb ending in *–ing*. The modals modify the verb by indicating possibility, necessity, suggestion, or preference. The action described in the sentence may or may not be happening.

He **will be working** *now.* (The action is taking place.)

He **should have been working**, *but he was not.* (The action is not taking place.)

Practice 1

Complete the conversation with a progressive modal (*could, can't, might, may, must, should, ought to, had better, would, would rather*). Pay attention to meaning and past participle spelling. Some modals may be in the perfect tense.

Example:

1 *If you work hard, you* <u>could be running</u> *(run) this company in a few years.*

2 I _____ (fly) to Las Vegas with my friends if I hadn't decided to change my plans.

3 They _____ (celebrate) their 25th anniversary, but they got a divorce last year.

4 She isn't able to attend the lecture right now because she _____ (work).

5 A: I have finished the filing. What _____ (I, do) right now?
B: You _____ (call) our clients right now.

6 They _____ (not sleep) while we were gone. Now they aren't ready, and we _____ (leave) for the bus station soon.

7 A: Where is Andrew? What _____ (do)?
B: He _____ (not watch) the movie downstairs. He hates that movie.
A: He _____ (play) soccer outside.

Practice 2

Complete the conversation with a progressive or perfect progressive modal (*could, can't, might, may, must, should, ought to, had better, would, would rather*). Pay attention to meaning and past participle spelling. Do not use contractions.

1 A: *Do you hear the noise upstairs?*

B: *The children* <u>must be playing</u> *(play) those video games again.*

A: They _____ (not *possibly* study) for their test with all of that noise.

2 She really _____ (ski) instead of being at home all weekend.

3 You _____ (not work) at a job you like if you had stayed in school.

4 A: Dan didn't deliver the proposal on time. I wonder what _____ (prevent) him from finishing. It's not like him to be irresponsible.

B: He _____ (visit) his wife in the hospital. She got into an accident. Otherwise, he _____ (feel) well. He's been under a lot of stress lately.

5 When the foreman returns, the factory workers _____ (start up) the assembly line again. There will be layoffs if they don't meet their quota this week.

6 A: How did Peter break his arm? It looks as though he is in pain.

B: I'm not sure. He _____ (ride) his bike. He likes to do that.

A: I don't think so. He _____ (not ride) his bike. It's in the shop. He had to have it repaired.

B: Hmm… we should probably ask him what happened then.

The Passive Voice

The Passive Voice

We use passive voice to emphasize what happened. That is, we emphasize the action **not** the actor (agent). We use it when it is not important or not known who or what is performing the action. We can also use it if we don't want to name the agent of an action. In the passive voice, the object of an active sentence becomes the subject of the passive one. The subject of the active becomes the object of the passive or is dropped. See the **Appendix** for regular and irregular past participles.

The basic form of the passive voice is:

Subject + form of *be* + past participle

Active voice:

The cat broke the vase. (*cat* = actor/subject; *broke* = verb; *vase* = thing that received the action)

Passive voice:

The vase was broken. (agent is not named; *was broken* = passive form of *to break*; *vase* = thing that received the action/subject)

If the agent needs to be mentioned in the passive sentence, use *by* + noun/pronoun.

Examples:

   The cat broke the vase. (active)

   The vase was broken by the cat. (passive)

Practice 1

Read the sentence in the active voice. Then complete the next sentence using the passive voice.

1 *The judge adjourns the trial at 5 P.M. every day.*
   The trial is adjourned at 5 P.M. every day.

2 They were tailoring the wedding dress all afternoon.
   The wedding dress _____ all afternoon.

3 By the time I arrived, the workers had fixed the refrigerator.
   By the time I arrived, _____ .

4 The teacher may ask the students to revise their papers carefully.
   The students _____ their papers carefully.

5 Jack is an amazing worker, and his boss is going to promote him.
   Jack is an amazing worker, and he _____ .

6 The office manager hired an interior decorator to plan and manage the work.

An interior decorator _____ the work.

7 Many people feel that capital punishment is murder by the state.

It _____ capital punishment is murder by the state.

8 Volunteers have been reading books to children at the center.

Children _____ at the center.

9 Customers detest clerks serving them last.

Customers detest _____ last.

10 They are going to write the proposal this weekend.

The proposal _____ this weekend.

11 The team tolerated the coach having yelled at them.

The team tolerated _____ .

Practice 2

Circle the letter of the correct verb form using the active or passive voice.

1 Phyllis _____ pinch pots at the pottery school today.

  a made   **b** was made

2 Consuelo _____ in a performance at the concert in El Paso last week.

  a saw   **b** was seen

3 Lauran _____ blood at the blood center today.

  a donated   **b** was donated

4 Bob _____ a snack before he picked up his daughter at gym.

  a ate   **b** was eaten

5 The play _____ by the Ash Grove Theater.

  a presented   **b** was presented

6 Ben _____ at his new baby brother for a long time.

  a was being looked   **b** was looking

7 Kelly's hair _____ by an expert, and it looks like it.

  a cut   **b** was cut

8 The camel _____ across the desert sands.

  a walked   **b** was walked

9 The doctor _____ Jane's eyes carefully.

  a examined   **b** was examined

10 That sculpture _____ by one of our town's finest artists.

  a created   **b** was created

Quantifiers

Practice 1

Underline the correct quantifier to complete the sentence.

Example:

1 *There were [several, any, much] mistakes in Jane's paper.*

2 [A number of / The number of] international students in the United States has grown since the recession.

3 When her son was diagnosed with mild autism, she could find [any / hardly any / some] medical research to help him. [Most / Most of / Most of the] articles she did find were about very extreme cases.

4 [Each / Each of] the cadets is expected to rise early and be ready for morning warm-ups.

5 There are [a great deal of / several] excellent museums in New York. In fact, you can spend [a large amount of / plenty of] your stay visiting them.

6 In [a lot / a lot of / a lot of the] major cities such as Seattle, housing prices have been rising because there are [enough / plenty of] people buying and there isn't [many / much] housing. Thus, not [many / much] people can afford to buy a home.

Practice 2

Underline the words in brackets that complete the sentence correctly.

Example:

1 *The teacher wants you to redo your essay. She says there is [any / not much / several] content.*

2 You still have [a few / a little / few / little] time to submit your taxes, but you must hurry! There are [a few / a little / few / little] days left before April 15.

3 [One / One of / One of the] my favorite cities in the United Kingdom to visit is London.

4 You will need [a number of / the number of] days to see London because it has so [many / much] places to visit.

5 It's easy to get there because there are [a great deal of / enough / many] airports around London, [a large amount / and every one of / some of] them is quite busy.

6 London is wonderful. There are [most of / plenty of / some] museums, theaters, and famous sights to visit.

7 However, [some / some of / some of the] people complain about the weather. There's [any / enough / not enough / plenty of] sunshine. In fact, half of the days of the year are cloudy and overcast.

Articles

> ## Presentation
>
> ### Articles: Indefinite and Definite
>
> Articles come before nouns. We use them to show whether the noun is indefinite (*a*, *an*) or definite (*the*).

Practice 1

Underline the words in brackets that complete the paragraph correctly.

(1) [A / An / Ø / The] Library of Congress, (2) [a / an / Ø / the] national library of the United States, is located near (3) [a / an / Ø / the] Capitol building in Washington, D.C. Its main purpose is to serve (4) [a / an / Ø / the] Congressional members, but it is also open as (5) [a / an / Ø / the] reference library. It contains (6) [a / an / Ø / the] original copy of every book published in the United States. There are also collections of (7) [a / an / Ø / the] musical instruments and (8) [a / an / Ø / the] other documents. One of (9) [a / an / Ø / the] most famous documents is (10) [a / an / Ø / the] first draft of (11) [a / an / Ø / the] speech by Abraham Lincoln.

Practice 2

Underline the words in brackets that complete the sentence correctly.

1 [A / An / Ø / The] drunk driver hit my car while I was stopped for [a / an / Ø / the] red light. Fortunately, I was not hurt, but unfortunately, he did not have [a / an / Ø / the] car insurance.

2 [A / An / Ø / The] telephone was invented by Alexander Graham Bell.

3 My daughter has asked for [a / an / Ø / the] mobile phone for her 12th birthday.

4 Since [a / an / Ø / the] 1920s, [a / an / Ø / the] cars have been made mainly of steel. Nowadays, however, more and more car parts are made of [a / an / Ø / the] plastic. [A / An / Ø / The] Daimler Chrysler Company, for example, is planning to manufacture [a / an / Ø / the] unusual car body made entirely of [a / an / Ø / the] durable plastic.

SENTENCE STRUCTURE

Agreement
PRONOUNS

Presentation

Agreement: Pronouns

Pronouns are used to replace nouns in sentences. They must agree with the person, gender, and number of the noun that they refer to.

Examples:

José and Alicia are in my English class. **They** are from Guatemala.

I'm reading an interesting **book** about U.S. presidents. I'll lend **it** to you when I finish.

Rules	Examples
Use the correct subject or object pronoun in plural phrases.	**She and I** went to the movies. (Use subject pronouns.) George decided to come with **her and me**. (Use object pronouns.)
Use the correct subject or object pronoun with comparative phrases.	Jan is faster than **me**. (informal, grammatically incorrect) Jan is faster than **I**. (formal, grammatically correct) We are not as rich as them. (informal, grammatically incorrect) We are not as rich as **they (are)**. (Include the verb to check whether the pronoun is a subject pronoun.)
Certain words (*all, none, most, some*) use singular and/or plural pronouns. It depends on the prepositional phrase following them.	All of the **popcorn** is gone. The kids ate **it** fast. (non-count noun = singular pronoun) We know all of **those people**. **They** go to our school. (plural noun = plural pronoun)
Use plural pronouns with collective nouns to refer to individual members.	The **faculty** is on strike because **they** want better working conditions. My **family** goes on vacation every year. **We** all drive to the coast together.
Use the correct pronoun with non-human nouns.	The **computer** wouldn't work. **It** just went blank. We need to fix **it**. (singular) We need to repair the **buildings** and remodel **them**. **They** are falling apart. (plural)

Practice 1

Read the sentences. Circle the letter of the correct (formal) pronouns to replace the underlined words.

1 After months of searching, we finally found the perfect house!
   a it   **b** she   **c** her

2 My oldest daughter Olivia is more athletic than my son.
   a it   **b** he   **c** him

3 By the time we got to the party, most of the food was gone!
   a they   **b** them   **c** it

4 Jane and I went to the movies last night and saw a great film.
   a Me and her   **b** Her and I   **c** She and I

5 Do you want to go to dinner with Tom or Mary tomorrow evening?
   a he or she   **b** him or her   **c** them or they

6 The hospital staff worked hard to keep their patients safe during the tornado.
   a They   **b** We   **c** It

7 I study English many more hours than my friends.
   a they   **b** her   **c** them

8 Luckily, I closed all of the windows before the rain started.
   a them   **b** it   **c** they

9 The committee took its responsibility seriously and came up with a positive solution.
   a They   **b** Them   **c** It

10 The newspaper had an interesting article this morning about travel in the United States.
   a It   **b** Them   **c** She

Practice 2

Circle the correct pronouns in brackets to complete the paragraph.

Bill Gates was born on October 28, 1955, in Seattle, Washington. His interest in software began at an early age. By 13, Gates had already begun programming computers, and by 20 (1) [he, they, him] had co-founded Microsoft with his childhood friend, Paul Allen. Together, (2) [them, they, we] began developing software for personal computers.

On January 1, 1994, Gates married Melinda French, and the couple had two children. Later, (3) [they, it, them] founded the Bill & Melinda Gates Foundation. A person of great financial means (Forbes magazine has ranked (4) [them, he, him] as the richest person in the world 15 times), Gates has made philanthropy an important part of his life. (5) [She, He, Him] and Melinda have endowed their foundation with more than $21 billion to support initiatives in global health and learning. Gates believes that ". . . if you show people the problems and you show (6) [them, her, we] the solutions, (7) [them, it, they] will be moved to act." And (8) [they, he, him] uses his vast fortune to bring solutions to people most in need.

Gates also believes that personal computers have revolutionized how people communicate and interact worldwide. To (9) [him, he, we] ". . . personal computers have become the most empowering tool we've ever created. (10) [It's, He's, They're] tools of communication, they're tools of creativity, and (11) [they, it, he] can be shaped by their users"—that is, by people like (12) [us, them, you] and (13) [him, me, I].

Although one of the wealthiest and most influential people in the world, Gates is, in many ways, just like the rest of (14) [us, we, they]—he worries about his children and their future, and he complains about spam mail! As he says, "Like almost everyone who uses email, (15) [she, it, I] receive a ton of spam every day. Much of (16) [they, it, them] offers to help (17) [me, they, I] get out of debt or get rich quick. It would be funny if (18) [I, we, it] weren't so irritating."

POSSESSIVE ADJECTIVES AND PRONOUNS

Presentation

Agreement: Possessive Adjectives and Pronouns

Possessive adjectives and pronouns express who or what owns the noun. When a possessive is in front of the noun, it acts like an adjective (***my*** *dog*). When a possessive is by itself, it acts like pronoun (*the dog is* ***mine***). Both possessive adjectives and pronouns must agree with person, gender, and number. Review the form and meaning of possessive adjectives and pronouns in the chart.

	Possessive Adjectives	Possessive Pronouns
1st person singular	There's **my** book.	That book is **mine**.
2nd person	There's **your** book.	That book is **yours**.
3rd person (female)	There's **her** book.	That book is **hers**.
3rd person (male)	There's **his** book.	That book is **his**.
3rd person (non-human)	The car is a mess. **Its** floors are so dirty.	The snake and I stared at each other. My eyes were on it, and **its** were on me.
3rd person plural	There's **their** book.	That book is **theirs**.
1st person plural	There's **our** book.	That book is **ours**.
Relative and Interrogative	**Whose** books are these? Mary, **whose** books I borrowed, wants them back.	

Practice 1

Circle the correct possessive adjective or pronoun in brackets.

When (1) [our, ours, theirs] ESL writing teacher walked into the room on the first day, she said, "Welcome to class! (2) [Hers, My, Mine] name is Ms. Barton, but you can call me Jamie."

She greeted every student individually and asked each one, "What is your name?"

Then, she marked each student's name in (3) [her, hers, yours] attendance book. After that, she distributed (4) [our, ours, theirs] syllabus. We reviewed (5) [ours, its, mine,] policies and rules.

Next, she told us that many of the students last quarter came to see her often before they wrote (6) [their, theirs, our] papers. (7) "[Yours, Its, Your] papers can be as good as (8) [ours, theirs, their]," she said. "The office next to (9) [ours, our, hers] classroom is (10) [mine, my, hers]. Come and see me anytime."

Practice 2

Circle the correct possessive adjective or pronoun in brackets.

This afternoon, when Sandra and (1) [her, hers, ours] family came home, they noticed a very bad smell coming from the kitchen.

"Phew," she said, "What is that smell?"

"It has to be the trash, Mom," (2) [his, her, hers,] son, Michael, said. "Ugh, I can't stand that smell."

As Sandra's husband came in the door, carrying (3) [hers, his, her] briefcase, he wrinkled (4) [its, his, ours] nose. (5) "[Who's, Whose, ours] turn is it to take out the trash?" he boomed.

"It's not (6) [my, ours, its] turn," Sandra replied. "Is it (7) [your, yours, my], Michael?"

Michael replied, "No, it's not (8) [mine, your, his]."

Sandra commented, "Did you ask (9) [mine, your, yours] sister, Andrea? Maybe it's (10) [her, hers, theirs]."

"It's (11) [our, ours, its] problem if it is," Michael said, "She is never home now that she has a new boyfriend."

INDEFINITE PRONOUNS

Agreement: Indefinite Pronouns

Indefinite pronouns are words that do not refer to a specific person, thing, or amount. Most indefinite pronouns are either singular or plural, but there are a few that can be either, depending on the context. Singular pronouns will take a singular verb. Plural pronouns will take a plural verb.

Can **anyone** answer this question? (*anyone* is singular)

I'm sure that **others** have tried before us. (*others* is plural)

Here is **some**. (*some* is singular)

Some have arrived. (*some* is plural)

Meaning	-one	-body	-thing	Others
all people or things	everyone	everybody	everything	one
a person or thing not specified	someone	somebody	something	each
it doesn't matter which	anyone	anybody	anything	either
no person or thing	no one	nobody	nothing	neither

Practice 1

Circle the letter of the correct indefinite pronoun.

Example:

1 _____ on the committee is voting to fund the children's program. We love the idea!
   a *No one*
   b *Anyone*
   c *Everyone*

2 We should ask Andy to pick up _____ for dinner.
   a anyone
   b something
   c nothing

3 Mom can't cook, and there isn't _____ left from last night.
   a anything
   b everything
   c several

4 Where's Andy? We can do _____ without him.
   a nothing
   b everything
   c none

5 Has _____ talked to him?

   a any

   b anyone

   c others

6 I don't know where he is. He didn't tell me _____ .

   a some

   b everything

   c anything

7 Maybe _____ can call him.

   a everybody

   b anybody

   c somebody

8 I can't find him _____ !

   a everthing

   b anywhere

   c no one

9 We will have to eat jam or cheese sandwiches. _____ is very good, unfortunately.

   a Neither

   b Each

   c One

Practice 2

Underline the eight singular indefinite pronouns in the paragraph.

In the United States, anyone who wants to be a teacher must have a college education. No one is given a class to teach unless he or she also completes at least one year of supervised teaching. Many colleges offer five-year programs that give students more time in the classroom. Each new teacher is also required to pass tests to get a teaching certificate from his or her state. Several states require more than one test, while others have a video evaluation. Everything new teachers have to go through is worth it, though. Each time a child learns something new, one forgets about everything else. For most teachers, nothing else is better that.

Collocations

Presentation

Collocations

Collocations are words that are commonly found together. Using collocations in your writing makes your writing easier to read. If you read and listen carefully, you can see and hear patterns of words that are often found together. Some dictionaries also list collocations. Common collocation patterns include:

Noun-verb collocations

*My niece jumped back in fright when she heard the **lion roar**.*

The phrase *lion roar* is a collocation because *roar* is used with *lion* and other similar words, such as *grumble* or *shout*, are not. Therefore, we can say that *lion roar* is a strong collocation.

Adjective-noun collocations

*When the couple first married, they had a **difficult relationship**.*

The phrase *difficult relationship* is a collocation because *difficult* is used more often with *relationship* than many similar words, such as *tough* or *hard*. Therefore, we can say that *difficult relationship* is a strong collocation.

Adverb-adjective collocations

*Many people feel that it is **fundamentally wrong** to cut funds to social programs during an economic crisis.*

The phrase *fundamentally wrong* is a collocation because *fundamentally* is used more often with *wrong* than many similar words, such as *deeply* or *primarily*. Therefore, we can say that *fundamentally wrong* is a strong collocation.

Adverb-verb collocations

*I **reluctantly agreed** to let my friend borrow my car.*

The phrase *reluctantly agreed* is a collocation because *reluctantly* is used more often with *agreed* than many similar words, such as *hesitantly* or *unenthusiastically*. Therefore, we can say that *reluctantly agreed* is a strong collocation.

Verb-noun collocations

*I always **do my homework** after dinner and before I go to bed.*

The phrase *do my homework* is a collocation because *do* is used more often with *homework* than many similar words, such as *perform* or *carry out* are not. Therefore, we can say that *do homework* is a strong collocation.

Practice 1

Read the sentence. Circle the letter of the word that makes sense in the sentence and forms a collocation with the underlined word(s).

Example:

1 *I tried to _____ advice to Don, but he wouldn't listen.*

   a *do*

   (b) *give*

   c *make*

2 Could you please _____ me a favor and close the window.

   a do

   b fix

   c take

3 At three years old, Marco is not capable of sitting quietly and not _____ a sound.

   a taking

   b uttering

   c bringing

4 When I spoke to Marta today, she said she was feeling _____ .

   a better

   b recovery

   c medicine

5 Everyone _____ the atmosphere at the party last night.

   a took

   b enjoyed

   c danced

6 On our drive to the Grand Canyon, we stopped several times to _____ the view.

   a admire

   b make

   c visit

7 Susana is a trustworthy friend who can _____ a secret.

   a take

   b keep

   c write

8 If you park in front of the fire hydrant, you will have to _____ a fine.

   a pay

   b tow

   c buy

9 It was _____ cold when I left the house, so I went back inside to get my hat and gloves.

   a funnily

   b bitterly

   c famously

Practice 2

Read the sentence. Circle the letter of the word that correctly completes each sentence and forms a collocation with the underlined word(s).

Example:

1 *Susan was* _____ *sorry for the confusion she caused yesterday.*

   (a) *extremely*   **b** *happily*   **c** *forcefully*

2 Although he has been in the United States for seven years, Antonio still speaks English with a _____ Spanish accent.

   a good   **b** minor   **c** thin

3 The new film was released last week to _____ acclaim. Everyone loved it!

   a ordinary   **b** tragic   **c** critical

4 In his recommendation, your professor gave a glowing _____ of your wonderful academic achievements.

   a account   **b** excuse   **c** lights

5 The _____ consumption of junk food in this country is responsible for several health issues, such as obesity and diabetes.

   a minimal   **b** widespread   **c** lacking

6 When Tim heard the tragic news, he _____ tears.

   a felt   **b** burst into   **c** cried

7 Unfortunately, Jack caused the _____ accident that hurt many people.

   a dreadful   **b** minor   **c** silly

8 My niece's newly adopted baby was _____ welcomed by our entire family.

   a grudgingly   **b** wholeheartedly   **c** sadly

9 Because of the _____ rain, we decided to postpone our meeting until next week.

   a heavy   **b** deep   **c** medium

10 The twin brothers are very close and share _____ affection.

   a superficial   **b** careless   **c** deep

Correlative Conjunctions

Presentation

Correlative Conjunctions

Correlative (or paired) conjunctions connect two equal grammatical items, such as words, phrases, and clauses. The five correlative conjunctions are *both . . . and, not only . . . but also, neither . . . nor, either . . . or,* and *whether . . . or.*

Rules	Examples
To add information, use *both . . . and* and *not only . . . but also.*	The book was so good that I **both** laughed **and** cried. **We not only** saw dolphins, **but also** caught sight of whales. (The additional information suggests surprise.)
To express a choice, use *either . . . or, neither . . . nor,* or *whether . . . or.*	We can **either** take a break or try to finish early. (positive choices) For the math test, you can use neither a calculator nor scratch paper. (negative choices) They don't know **whether** to travel in the morning **or** travel by night. (A decision has to be made as to the best choice.)
To express contrast, use *not . . . but.*	**Not** Elijah **but** Sara will come with me to the bank.
Use parallel structure with correlative conjunctions. That is, you must make sure you have equal grammatical units after both parts of the conjunction.	The woman is **neither** *ugly* **nor** *beautiful.* (parallel adjectives) In my free time, I enjoy **both** *reading a good book* **and** *spending time with friends.* (parallel verb phrases) She hasn't decided **whether** *she should go to the library,* **or** *she should study at home.* (parallel clauses)
Use plural verb forms with *both . . . and,* but for all other paired conjunctions, the verb should agree with the noun closest to it.	**Both** the driver **and** the passengers **were** uninjured in the accident. **Either** our next-door neighbors **or** the **young man** down the street **is** planning to house sit for us. **Either** the young man down the street **or** our **next-door neighbors are** planning to house sit for us. **Not** Maria **but** the **girls plan** to come to the party.
Use inverted word order, the kind you find in a question, in clauses with the negative words *not only, neither,* and *nor.*	**Neither** *would* the naughty child *clean* his room **nor** *would* he do his chores. **Not only** *is* Helen furious, **but also** she *is planning* to write a letter to complain.

Practice 1

Read the sentences. Circle the letter of the sentence that is written correctly.

Example:

1 **(a)** *Both Ana and her brother are coming to the celebration next week.*

   b *Both Ana and her brother is coming to the celebration next week.*

2 **a** To be healthy, not only do we need to eat right, but we also need to exercise regularly.

   b To be healthy, not only we do need to eat right, but we also need to exercise regularly.

3 **a** Would you rather go to a movie or watch TV tonight?

   b Would you rather go to a movie, or watching TV tonight?

4 **a** We haven't decided whether we will go the beach or to the mountains.

   b We haven't decided whether we will go the beach or we should go to the mountains.

5 **a** Rafael is not very athletic; he neither runs or swims.

   b Rafael is not very athletic; he neither runs nor swims.

6 **a** Either Joan or her brothers are in the school cafeteria.

   b Either Joan or her brothers is in the school cafeteria.

7 **a** Neither my children nor my husband have any idea where we should go for vacation next year.

   b Neither my children nor my husband has any idea where we should go for vacation next year.

8 **a** When I'm on vacation, I enjoy both seeing the sights and to eat in good restaurants.

   b When I'm on vacation, I enjoy both seeing the sights and eating in good restaurants.

9 **a** Neither she would call me, nor she would text me after the disagreement we had last week.

   b Neither would she call me, nor would she text me after the disagreement we had last week.

Practice 2

Write in the correct correlative conjunction to combine the sentences.

Example:

1 *To get to the city center from here, you can catch a streetcar at the corner.*

To get to the city center from here, you can walk two blocks to the subway station.

To get to the city center from here, you can <u>either</u> catch a streetcar at the corner or walk two blocks to the subway station.

2 Harry Potter is popular with children.

Harry Potter is popular with adults.

Harry Potter is popular _____ with children and with adults.

3 The new law is very popular in the largest county in the state.

It will pass if the counties to the east vote against it.

It will pass if the counties to the west vote against it.

The new law is very popular in the largest county in the state, so it will pass whether the counties to the east _____ the counties to the west vote against it.

4 Many kids today won't eat asparagus.

Many kids today won't eat cauliflower.

Many kids today will eat neither asparagus _____ cauliflower.

5 The likelihood of a car accident increases when a driver is texting.

The likelihood of a car accident increases when a driver is driving too fast.

The likelihood of an accident increases not only when a driver is texting _____ when he or she is driving too fast.

6 She isn't sure if she should eat her lunch now.

She isn't sure if she should eat her lunch later.

She isn't sure _____ she should eat her lunch now or eat it later.

7 The cupcakes are on the front hall table.

The ice cream is on the front hall table.

_____ the cupcakes and the ice cream are on the front hall table.

8 Red is not Allison's favorite color.

Blue is Allison's favorite color.

Not red _____ blue is Allison's favorite color.

9 Chris is planning to write a complaint letter.

Chris is going to attend the board meeting.

_____ is Chris planning to write a complaint letter, but he is also going to attend the board meeting.

Parallel Structure

Parallel Structure

Parallel structure means that each item in a list or in a comparison follows the same grammatical form or pattern. For example, if you are writing a list and the first item in your list is a noun, you write all the other items as nouns. Or if the first item is a conjugated verb or an *-ing* word, you make all the others conjugated verbs or *-ing* words.

Nouns

Incorrect: The qualities you need for this job are responsibility, independence, and **hard-working**. (*Hard-working* is an adjective, not a noun; it doesn't fit with the sequence *responsibility, independence.*)

Correct: The qualities you need for this job are responsibility, independence, and commitment.

Verb Phrases

Incorrect: She picks up the dry-cleaning, stops at the bank, and **dropping** off the mail every Monday morning. (wrong verb form)

Correct: She picks up the dry-cleaning, stops at the bank, and drops off the mail every Monday morning.

Gerunds/Infinitives

Incorrect: In order to avoid another burglary, the police recommend getting a security system, starting a neighborhood watch, and to lock the doors and windows before we leave. (Infinitive doesn't fit with the gerund form.)

Correct: In order to avoid another burglary, the police recommend getting a security system, starting a neighborhood watch, and locking the doors and windows before we leave.

Note: In parallel structure with infinitives, either repeat the word *to* with each verb, or put it only with the first verb and omit with the subsequent verbs.

If you want to be healthy you need **to** eat well, **to** exercise, and **to** get enough sleep.

or

If you want to be healthy you need **to** eat well, exercise, and get enough sleep.

Adjectives/Adverbs

Incorrect: We love our new roommate. She is kind, generous, and **a fun person** to be around. (Noun phrase doesn't fit with the two adjectives.)

Correct: We love our new roommate. She is kind, generous, and fun.

Clauses

Incorrect: They didn't care which country he came from but **his future plans**. (The items should be two parallel noun clauses.)

Correct: They didn't care which country he came from but what his future plans were.

Comparatives

Incorrect: The IT department at Microsoft is the same size as **Google**. (Comparatives should compare similar entities. A department is not equal to the entire company.)

Correct: The IT department at Microsoft is the same size as the IT department at Google.

Practice 1

Read the sentences. Underline the element in each sentence that is not parallel.

Example:

1 *Mai is studying English, looking for an interesting job, and <u>she hopes to make</u> a lot of money.*

2 We will leave on schedule because it is neither raining nor snow.

3 Nowadays, people communicate through email, text messages, and they also use social media.

4 To protect your children from the dangers of the Internet, you might want to periodically monitor their online activity, speak openly with them about their Internet use, and blocking them from accessing any inappropriate sites.

5 Because he has so much work to do, Jim is neither going to the gym nor go to the pool today.

6 Many people exercise regularly to stay healthy, to lose weight, and they also hope to live longer.

7 To plan an exciting vacation, save the money to pay for it, and to enjoy it when the time comes—this is my primary goal for the year!

8 Marcia asked for three things for her birthday: a pair of sunglasses, a pair of jeans, and she also wanted an iPad!

Practice 2

Combine the sentences using parallel structure. Pay attention to word form, agreement, and word order.

Example:

1 *During an earthquake drill, you must stop.*
During an earthquake drill, you must drop.
During an earthquake drill, you must cover yourself.
During an earthquake drill, you must <u>stop</u>, <u>drop</u>, and <u>cover yourself</u>.

2 The gardener opened the shed.
The gardener grabbed his tools.
Then, the gardener headed towards the vegetable patch.

The gardener _____ and _____
before _____ .

3 During George's annual review, he was told that he was doing a good job with his projects.
During George's annual review, he was told that he wasn't working very well with his coworkers.

During George's annual review, he was told that _____ ,
but _____ .

4 A person must have an associate's degree to apply for this job.

A person must have three years of experience to apply for this job.

A person must have two letters of reference to apply for this job.

A person must have _____ , _____ ,

and _____ to apply for this job.

5 The library sign reminds its patrons to keep quiet.

The library sign reminds its patrons to turn off their phones.

The library sign reminds its patrons not only _____ ,

but also _____ .

6 Jun's determination to win has been important to his success.

Jun's willingness to work long hours has been important to his success.

_____ has been just as important to his success

as _____ .

Word Forms

Word Forms

Many English words share a pattern and the same root meaning, but they can take different forms depending on their function in a given sentence. A word will often change form depending on whether it is, for example, a noun, verb, adjective, or adverb.

Examples of Changing Word Forms:

*Can we **devote** some time to the project today?* (verb)

*His **devotion** to helping others is impressive.* (noun)

*Her husband is a loving and **devoted** man.* (adjective)

*My grandmother **devotedly** tends to her garden every day.* (adverb)

How to Learn Word Forms

1. Look up the word in the dictionary and notice any word forms that are listed in the entry.

2. Learn the common endings of words that determine whether they are nouns, verbs, adjectives, or adverbs.

Verb	Noun	Adjective	Adverb
to benefit	benefit	beneficial	beneficially
to coincide	coincidence	coincidental	coincidentally
to minimize	minimum	minimal	minimally

Practice 1

Write the words from the box under the correct headings.

threateningly	measurement	inclusiveness	classify
exceptional	threaten	effect	creatively
demonstrate	demonstrability	modification	classifiable

Verb	Noun	Adjective	Adverb
accelerate	acceleration	accelerative	acceleratingly
broaden	broadness	broad	broadly
_____	classification	_____	classifiably
create	creation	creative	_____
_____	demonstration, _____	demonstrative, demonstrable	demonstratively, demonstrably
_____	effectiveness	effective	effectively
except	exception	_____	exceptionally
include	inclusion, _____	inclusive	inclusively
measure	_____, measurability	measurable	measurably
modify	_____	modifiable	[no adverb form]
_____	threat	threatened, threatening	_____

Practice 2

Complete the sentences on the next page with the correct word form for each root word. Remember the common endings for verbs, adjectives, adverbs, and nouns. You may need to consult a dictionary.

recognition	establish	distinguished	establishment
critically	recognizably	criticizes	innovative
placement	distinguished	innovations	

Place

Example:

1 *Every student needs to take a test for* <u>placement</u> *into English and math at this college.*

Critical

2 It is _____ important that you remember to bring your passport on this trip.

3 In many cultures, new wives and mothers-in-law have trouble getting along, especially when the mother-in-law _____ everything her son's wife does.

Distinguish

4 The mint family of flowering plants is a family _____ by its aromatic leaves and easy propagation.

5 The gentleman looked quite _____ in his suit, tie, and bowler hat.

Establish

6 It is advisable that working mothers _____ a feeding and sleeping schedule with new infants as soon as possible.

7 During the French Revolution, the people sought to overthrow the _____ to create a more egalitarian society.

Innovate

8 Steve Jobs, the man who founded Apple, was known for his _____ ideas in technology and music.

9 New _____ to voter registration have made it easier to change your information before you receive your ballot by mail.

Recognize

10 Even though the Toyota Highlander, a new 2013 hybrid SUV, has added several radical changes to the original SUV design, it is still _____ similar in appearance and performance to other Toyota SUVs.

11 Despite her retirement from public life, the senator continues to receive _____ for her long years of public service.

Appositives

Appositives

An appositive is a noun or noun phrase that renames or describes in more detail the noun or pronoun right beside it. Appositives provide more information about a noun and usually appear after the noun they modify.

Necessary (essential) appositives identify and limit the possible meaning of the noun or pronoun. They tell us something essential about the noun or pronoun. They do not take commas.

Example:

The man **who has blond hair** committed the crime.

Unnecessary (nonessential) appositives provide extra information about the noun or pronoun. We use commas because this is extra, nonessential information.

Example:

Thomas, **the youngest of five brothers**, still lives with his parents.

Appositives that contain lists using commas should be separated from the sentence with dashes (—).

Example:

Everyone in the school district—**teachers, students, and administrators**—was shocked when the superintendent quit.

Practice 1

Circle the letter of the appositive in each sentence.

Example:

1 *Rome, the capital of Italy, is one of the most popular tourist destinations in Europe.*
   a *Rome*
   (b) *the capital of Italy*
   c *is one of the most popular tourist destinations*
   d *in Europe*

2 The city welcomes many visitors—between 10 and 15 million—each year.
   a The city
   b welcomes many visitors
   c between 10 and 15 million
   d each year

3 Rome, with its long history, has been called the Eternal City.

   a Rome

   b with its long history

   c has been called

   d the Eternal City

4 There are so many things to see—churches, palaces, ancient buildings, and monuments—in this historically and culturally rich city.

   a There is much to see

   b churches, palaces, ancient buildings, and monuments

   c in this historically and culturally

   d rich city

5 Vatican City, the spiritual and official center of the Roman Catholic Church, is located in the Eternal City.

   a Vatican City

   b the spiritual and official center of the Roman Catholic Church

   c is located

   d in the Eternal City

6 Several modes of transportation—bus, taxi, car—are available for tourists.

   a Several modes of transportation

   b bus, taxi, car

   c are available

   d for tourists

7 The best and most efficient way to get around the city is by riding the ATAC, Rome's main bus company.

   a The best and most efficient way

   b to get around the city

   c is by riding the ATAC

   d Rome's main bus company

Practice 2

There are 12 appositives in the biography. Find and underline the seven mistakes related to the appositives.

Rosa Parks the mother of the Civil Rights Movement who began the Montgomery Bus Boycott was born Rosa Louise McCauley on February 4, 1913, in Tuskegee a city in the state of Alabama.

She left Tuskegee when her parents got divorced. She moved to a farm in Pine Level, where her grandparents lived. They had been slaves and opposed Jim Crow laws, laws segregating whites and blacks in the South.

Rosa's early experiences with segregation affected her deeply. For example, she went to a segregated school for African Americans. Her school had no money for important resources books, pens, paper, school buses, whereas the white school had supplies and school buses for its children.

Rosa wasn't able to finish school because her grandmother got sick. When she was 19 years old, she married a barber Raymond Parks from Montgomery, another city in Alabama. Raymond Parks was a member of the NAACP, the National Association for the Advancement of Colored People a society dedicated to improving African American lives. He encouraged Rosa to finish school and get involved in the organization. Soon, she became the secretary to E.D. Nixon, the president of the NAACP.

Rosa's involvement in the Civil Rights Movement began on December 1, 1955. She was working as a seamstress a job sewing clothing and rode the bus to and from work. At that time, the law stated that African Americans and whites had to sit separately on buses, so blacks sat in the back of the bus, and whites sat in the front. If the bus got too crowded, blacks were asked to stand. Rosa was tired that day, so when she was asked to stand, she refused. She was arrested and taken to jail.

The people in the NAACP decided to protest her arrest and the law. They started the Montgomery Bus Boycott a city-wide boycott of the bus system. No African Americans in the city took the bus for almost one year. They walked, biked, carpooled, and took taxis. On December 20, 1956, Montgomery changed the law and stopped segregation on public buses. This initial success led to the Civil Rights Movement, a decade-long campaign against segregation in the South.

Simple Sentences

Simple Sentences

A simple English sentence is a complete idea that can stand alone. It also:

- begins with a capital letter.
- ends with punctuation, usually a period, question mark, or exclamation point.
- has a subject. The subject tells who or what the sentence is about.
- has a verb or verb phrase. The verb tells what the subject is or what the subject does.

Example:

She *(subject)* is *(verb)* my mother.

Simple Sentence Patterns

one subject + one verb

Raquel went to the superintendent.

compound subject + one verb

John and Joanna are close friends.

one subject + compound verb (two or more verbs)

The professor lectured for an hour **and gave** an assignment.

compound subject + compound verb

The students and teachers are attending the poetry conference **and going** to the reading afterwards.

Practice 1

Read each sentence. Circle the letter of the subject, verb or verb phrase, and sentence pattern.

Chocolate and avocadoes are highly poisonous foods for dogs.

Example:

1 *Subject of the Sentence:*
   (a) *chocolate and avocados*
   b *poisonous*
   c *dogs*
   d *no subject*

2 Verb or verb phrase:
   a are
   b highly
   c no verb phrase

3 What is the sentence pattern?
   a Compound Subject + Verb
   b Compound Subject + Compound Verb Phrase
   c Not a sentence

The overcast weather in Seattle is very depressing.

4 Subject of the Sentence:

   a overcast

   b weather

   c Seattle

   d no subject

5 Verb or verb phrase:

   a in

   b is very depressing

   c is

   d no verb

6 What is the sentence pattern?

   a Subject + Verb Phrase

   b Compound Subject + Verb Phrase

   c Subject + Compound Verb Phrase

   d Compound Subject + Compound Verb Phrase

   e Not a sentence

My friends and I drove to the coast and stayed in a cabin all weekend.

7 Subject of the Sentence:

   a My friends

   b the coast

   c My friends and I

   d no subject

8 Verb or verb phrase:

   a stayed

   b drove

   c drove and stayed

   d no verb phrase

9 What is the sentence pattern?

   a Subject + Verb Phrase

   b Compound Subject + Verb Phrase

   c Subject + Compound Verb Phrase

   d Compound Subject + Compound Verb Phrase

   e Not a sentence

The diligent students have been studying for their final exams.

10 Subject of the Sentence:

   a students

   b final exams

   c diligent

   d no subject

11 Verb or verb phrase:

   a have

   b studying

   c have been studying

   d no verb phrase

12 What is the sentence pattern?

   a Subject + Verb Phrase

   b Compound Subject + Verb Phrase

   c Subject + Compound Verb Phrase

   d Compound Subject + Compound Verb Phrase

   e Not a sentence

By next week, the police will have found enough evidence to charge the suspect.

13 Subject of the Sentence:

   a police

   b evidence

   c suspect

   d no subject

14 Verb or verb phrase:

   a will

   b will have found

   c charge

   d no verb phrase

15 What is the sentence pattern?

   a Subject + Verb Phrase

   b Compound Subject + Verb Phrase

   c Subject + Compound Verb Phrase

   d Compound Subject + Compound Verb Phrase

   e Not a sentence

Practice 2

Read each sentence and the statement that follows it. Circle the letter for true or false.

Example:

1 *Jorge cooks and cleans at his mother's house on Saturday.*
The subject of the sentence is his mother's house.

   a *true*

   (b) *false*

2 *The commuters catching the bus to work.*
This is not a sentence. It has no verb.

   a true

   b false

3 *Bing and Google are currently the most popular search engines.*
The sentence pattern is Subject + Verb Phrase.

a true
b false

4 *The walls in her house are a little dingy and need to be washed.*
The verbs in the sentence are *are* and *need*.

a true
b false

5 *Hawaii and Alaska were the last two states added to the union.*
The subject of the sentence is Hawaii and Alaska.

a true
b false

6 *Jamie and her husband will be running errands and taking care of their children all afternoon.*
The sentence has a compound subject and a verb phrase.

a true
b false

7 *A hot dog with mustard is Jake's all-time favorite food.*
The subject of the sentence is *hot dog*.

a true
b false

8 *Our four-year-old dog and 12-year-old cat sleep and eat together.*
The sentence has a compound subject and a compound verb.

a true
b false

9 *The teenagers yelled and screamed at the rock concert.*
The verb is *yelled*.

a true
b false

Compound Sentences

Presentation

Compound Sentences

A compound sentence contains two independent clauses that are joined using a conjunction or semicolon. Except for very short compound sentences, a comma always precedes conjunctions. The conscious use of conjunctions changes the relationship between the clauses, since conjunctions have different meanings. See the Appendix for a complete list of conjunctions and conjunctive adverbs used in compound sentences.

Rules	Examples
Use *and* or *nor* to make additions to a sentence. Use *and* to combine similar ideas. *Nor* is used to connect two ideas that are negated.	Gary has lived in Spain, **and** Joanne has lived in Japan. Gary hasn't lived in France, **nor** has Joanne lived in China.
Use *nor* or *neither ... nor* to combine similar ideas that are negated. Do not use a negative verb phrase in the clause that follows *nor*. The clause that follows *nor* takes the same word order as a question.	**Neither** Gary **nor** Joanne has lived in Russia.
Use *both ... and; not only ... but also, besides, furthermore, moreover* to add information. With *furthermore* and *moreover*, use a semicolon and a comma to separate the clauses. You can also use a period and start a new sentence.	Gary has lived in Spain; **furthermore,** Joanne has lived in Japan. Gary has lived in Spain. **Furthermore,** Joanne has lived in Japan.
Use *but* or *yet* to contrast. Use *but* to combine opposite ideas.	I was working a lot, **but** I was still unable to pay the rent.
Use *yet* to combine surprisingly opposite ideas.	I didn't study at all, **yet** I passed the test.
Use *however* or *nevertheless* to contrast. Use a semicolon and a comma to separate the clauses. You can also use a period and start a new sentence.	I didn't study at all; **however,** I passed the test. I didn't study. However, I passed the test.
Use *so* or *for* to indicate cause and effect. In sentences with *so*, the first clause is the cause, and *so* introduces the clause with the effect.	John didn't have any eggs to make an omelet, **so** he went to the store.
In sentences with *for*, the first clause is the result, and *for* introduces the clause with the cause.	I couldn't eat lunch, **for** I had left my wallet at home.

Use *therefore, thus,* or *subsequently* to indicate cause and effect. Use a semicolon and a comma to separate the clauses. You can also use a period and start a new sentence. *Therefore, thus,* and *subsequently* introduce the result of the cause in the main clause.	John didn't have any eggs for breakfast; **therefore,** he went to the store. John didn't have any eggs for breakfast. **Therefore,** he went to the store. The general rallied his troops; **thus,** the battle was won. I ate too much; **subsequently,** I got sick.
Use *or* and *either . . . or* to introduce a choice. The choice in each clause is equally possible.	We can go for a walk, **or** we can drive to my friend's party. After the movie, we can **either** go for a walk **or** we can drive to the party.
Use *otherwise* to introduce a condition. *Otherwise* means that the action in the subsequent clause will happen if the condition isn't met. Use a semicolon and a comma to separate clauses. You can also use a period and start a new sentence.	Going to bed on time is important for me; **otherwise,** I feel cranky and irritated in the morning. Going to bed on time is important for me. **Otherwise,** I feel cranky and irritated in the morning.

Practice 1

Circle the letter of the correct conjunction to join the two clauses in each sentence. Pay attention to the meaning of the conjunction.

Example:

1 *Janet is quite health-conscious* _____ *she rarely eats sweets.*

   a *, for*

   b *, but*

   (c) *; therefore,*

2 Many people believe the myth that bats drink human blood and _____ they are terrified of bats.

   a , but

   b , subsequently,

   c , in fact,

3 In fact, most species of bats do not consume blood _____ do they carry the disease rabies, another common myth.

   a ; furthermore,

   b , for example

   c , nor

4 Seventy percent of the world's bat species eat only insects _____ they are extremely beneficial animals.

   a , so

   b , similarly,

   c , for

5 In the winter, _____ bats migrate to warmer
places _____ they hibernate in caves.

   a either

   b neither

   c , or

   d , nor

6 A small percentage of bats feed on the blood of warm-blooded
animals _____ they are called "vampire" bats.

   a , for

   b , and

   c , but

7 Vampire bats are extremely rare _____ they are the most famous
type of bat.

   a , yet

   b ; in addition,

   c ; for instance,

8 Another myth about bats is that they sometimes fly into people's
hair _____ this is also untrue.

   a ; however,

   b ; subsequently,

   c , so

9 Bats, like humans, are warm-blooded mammals _____ they
have hair and give birth to live young.

   a , but

   b ; however,

   c ; moreover,

10 Most bats are very small, weighing less than 100 grams _____ they
can live as long as 30 years.

   a , but

   b ; for example,

   c , nor

11 Bats are not dangerous _____ they are not aggressive.

   a , and

   b ; on the other hand,

   c , yet

Practice 2

Combine each pair of sentences into one sentence using the most appropriate sentence connector. Write in the conjunction and punctuation if necessary. Pay attention to capital letters, punctuation, and spelling.

Example:

1 *Diabetes is a disease in which blood sugar rises to dangerous levels. There isn't enough insulin to metabolize it.* (nor, or, for)

Diabetes is a disease in which blood sugar rises to dangerous levels ⌐for *there isn't enough insulin to metabolize it.*

2 It is essential that adults and children get enough calcium. It is needed for a number of functions in the body. (for, but, so)

It is essential that adults and children get enough calcium _____ it is needed for a number of functions in the body.

3 Calcium sends signals from the brain to other body parts. It is also necessary to work muscles and move blood throughout the body. (however, both…and, ;)

Calcium sends signals from the brain to other body parts _____ it is also necessary to work muscles and move blood throughout the body.

4 Including foods that contain calcium in our diets is important. The stores of calcium in our bodies become depleted. (thus, otherwise, furthermore)

Including foods that contain calcium in our diets is important _____ the stores of calcium in our bodies become depleted.

5 The largest stores of calcium in the human body are in the bones and teeth. The body will automatically take the calcium it needs from there. (yet, therefore, for)

The largest stores of calcium in the human body are in the bones and teeth _____ the body will automatically take the calcium it needs from there.

6 The amount of calcium you need depends on your age. Young children need about 500 milligrams a day. (for example, similarly, nevertheless)

The amount of calcium you need depends on your age _____ young children need about 500 milligrams a day.

7 Adults need about 1,000 milligrams of calcium daily. Their bones become soft and break easily. (or, therefore, not only…but also)

Adults need about 1,000 milligrams of calcium daily _____ their bones become soft and break easily.

8 The best source of calcium is milk. Many people dislike the taste of milk. (or, and, yet)

The best source of calcium is milk _____ many people dislike the taste of milk.

9 Milk is high in calories. It is hard for some people to digest. (nor, not only…but also, nevertheless)

Milk is _____ high in calories _____ hard for some people to digest.

10 People can get their calcium from protein sources such as salmon and tofu. People can eat vegetables such as kale and broccoli. (otherwise, so, either…or)

_____ people can get their calcium from protein sources such as salmon and tofu _____ they can eat vegetables such as kale and broccoli.

11 It is best to get calcium from the foods you eat. There are a number of calcium supplements available for people who don't get enough from food. (besides, neither…nor, however)

It is best to get calcium from the foods you eat _____ there are a number of calcium supplements available for people who don't get enough from food.

Independent and Dependent Clauses

Presentation

Independent and Dependent Clauses

A clause is a group of words that contains at least a subject and verb or verb phrase. **Independent clauses** express a complete idea and can be used alone in simple sentences, combined in compound sentences, or used as a main clause in a complex sentence. **Dependent clauses** start with a subordinating word and are combined with independent clauses to make complex sentences. They cannot stand alone as sentences.

Rules	Examples
An independent clause has at least one subject and at least one verb phrase. It expresses a complete idea and can be used as a simple sentence.	**Jorge and his friends have been playing soccer.** *(Jorge and his friends = subject; have been playing = verb phrase)*
A dependent clause starts with a subordinating word. It has at least one subject and at least one verb phrase. It must be used with an independent clause to form a complete idea and a legitimate sentence, and it cannot stand alone as a simple sentence.	**Wherever I go,** I bring my asthma medicine with me.
Independent and dependent clauses can be combined to form complex sentences. A dependent clause can come before or after an independent clause. If it begins a sentence, a comma must separate it from the independent clause. Do not use a comma if the independent clause comes first.	**Since I work from home,** my work hours are flexible.
	My hours are flexible **since I work from home**.

Practice 1

Circle the letter of the answer that identifies the underlined part of the sentence.

Example:

1 *After he picked up his daughter, Juan drove to the park to meet friends.*
  a *Independent clause*
  ⓑ *Dependent clause*
  c *Not a clause*

2 The payroll department accountant <u>who gave me my application for benefits</u> helped me fill it out and submit it on time.

   a Independent clause

   b Dependent clause

   c Not a clause

3 <u>The woman took the car to the mechanic</u> when it wouldn't start.

   a Independent clause

   b Dependent clause

   c Not a clause

4 Many people assume <u>that New York's Central Park is the largest in the country.</u>

   a Independent clause

   b Dependent clause

   c Not a clause

5 Although Central Park is probably the most well known, South Mountain Park, <u>located in Phoenix, Arizona,</u> is actually the largest city park in the United States.

   a Independent clause

   b Dependent clause

   c Not a clause

6 In the fall, <u>we harvest vegetables on our farm and sell them at the local market.</u>

   a Independent clause

   b Dependent clause

   c Not a clause

7 The author shows <u>how he felt about his mother</u> in the essay.

   a Independent clause

   b Dependent clause

   c Not a clause

8 <u>Do you know</u> where the nearest gas station is?

   a Independent clause

   b Dependent clause

   c Not a clause

9 <u>When couples divorce,</u> both people might experience a substantial decrease in wealth.

   a Independent clause

   b Dependent clause

   c Not a clause

10 The performance will begin at 8:00 P.M., <u>so we need to leave at 7:00 P.M.</u>

   a Independent clause

   b Dependent clause

   c Not a clause

11 The house <u>where Gaudi lived</u> is now a museum in Parc Güell, a park he designed.

   a Independent clause

   b Dependent clause

   c Not a clause

Practice 2

Find and underline the nine dependent clauses in the text.

Do you know the difference between an alligator and a crocodile? Many people confuse these reptiles because they look so similar and have comparable behaviors. Nevertheless, alligators and crocodiles are different in several ways.

One difference can be seen in the animal's nose, or snout. An alligator has a wide, round snout, whereas the snout of a crocodile is longer and more pointed.

A second difference is where the two animals can be found. Alligators are found in only two places in the world: the United States and China. In contrast, crocodiles are found in 91 countries, which is about 51 percent of all the countries in the world. However, they can live only in warm, wet climates. Therefore, there are no crocodiles in Canada, northern Europe, or Russia.

The wild alligator population in the United States is estimated to number more than 1 million; on the other hand, the Chinese alligator, which is smaller than its American cousin, is nearly extinct. American alligators outnumber American crocodiles by about 1,000 to 1. Since only about 500 wild crocodiles remain on the whole continent, crocodiles are considered a species that is endangered and needs protection by law.

There are many myths about alligators and crocodiles. For example, many people believe that they can live for hundreds of years, but this is only a myth. In fact, though captive alligators and crocodiles may live 60 to 80 years, wild alligators and crocodiles usually only live to be 30 or 40 years old.

Complex Sentences

Complex Sentences

A complex sentence contains one independent (or main) clause and one or more dependent clauses. The dependent clause expresses a subordinate (or minor) detail about an idea in the independent clause. There are three types of dependent clauses: *adverb*, *adjective*, and *noun*.

Adverb Clause

An adverb clause acts like an adverb and tells *where, when, why*, and *how*. Subordinators, such as *when, while, because*, and *although*, introduce adverb clauses.

Adjective Clause

An adjective clause acts like an adjective and describes a noun or pronoun. Relative pronouns such as *who, whom, whose, that*, or *which* introduce adjective clauses. Adjective clauses follow the nouns or pronouns they describe and can be essential or nonessential. (Note: Use commas around an adjective clause if it is nonessential.)

Noun Clause

A noun clause acts like a noun and can be either the subject or the object of the independent clause. A *wh-* question word, *that, whether*, or *if* introduces a noun clause.

Rules	Examples
An **adverb clause** is a clause that functions as an adverb. It usually answers *how, when,* or *why* and can indicate contrast. It does not express a complete thought, but modifies the independent clause. It begins with a subordinating conjunction. It can come before or after the main clause. Use a comma if the adverb clause introduces the sentence.	The students met at the library **after** they finished their test. She's going to the party **because** she wants to dance. I'm not going to talk to her **if** she keeps being so mean to me. **Although** he had just won a prestigious award, he felt sad.
An **adjective clause** begins with a relative pronoun (*who, whose, whom, that,* or *which*) or relative adverb (*when, where,* or *why*) and gives more information about a given noun. It answers *what kind, how many,* or *which one.* Use commas only if the adjective clause provides non-essential information and the noun is already clearly identified. If the information is essential, use *that.* If non-essential, use *which.*	The movie **that** my boyfriend and I saw last night was very violent. (essential information) John, **who** is a student in my class, works at Microsoft. (non-essential information)
A **noun clause** acts the same way a noun or pronoun does. It can be the subject or object of a verb or object of the preposition. Some words that introduce it are (*that, if, whether, who, what, where, when, why, how*). Don't use commas with noun clauses.	It is out of the question **that** the student re-take the exam. I wonder **if** anyone was hurt in the accident. They would also like to know **when** the game started.

Practice 1

Read the sentence. Circle the letter of the choice that tells what type of clause the underlined part of the sentence is.

Example:

1 *That antibiotics have been misused in this country is a widely known fact.*
   - **a** *dependent clause* ⟵ circled
   - **b** *independent clause*

2 Although antibiotics can save lives, <u>the misuse of antibiotics has increased the number of drug-resistant germs.</u>
   - **a** dependent clause
   - **b** independent clause

3 Drug resistance occurs <u>when antibiotics are no longer effective in treating bacteria that cause disease.</u>
   - **a** dependent clause
   - **b** independent clause

4 This is a major problem <u>because many people can and will die from bacteria and germs for which there is no effective antibiotic.</u>
   - **a** dependent clause
   - **b** independent clause

5 Although experts work hard to develop new antibiotics that can treat antibiotic-resistant strains of bacteria, <u>the bacteria adapt quickly to resist the new drugs.</u>
   - **a** dependent clause
   - **b** independent clause

6 Inasmuch as antibiotic-resistant bacteria will continue to be a major health concern, <u>it is important to use antibiotics wisely in order to prevent the spread of the harmful organisms.</u>
   - **a** dependent clause
   - **b** independent clause

7 For example, <u>if antibiotics are used too often for illnesses they cannot treat, such as colds, flu, or other viral infections,</u> they become less effective against the bacteria they are intended to treat.
   - **a** dependent clause
   - **b** independent clause

8 <u>Moreover, not taking the full dosage of antibiotics that a doctor prescribes can also lead to problems</u> because the antibiotics may kill only some of the bacteria.
   - **a** dependent clause
   - **b** independent clause

9 <u>When some of the bacteria survive,</u> they become more resistant and can spread to other people.
   - **a** dependent clause
   - **b** independent clause

Practice 2

Circle the letter of the best revision of the sentences to create a complex sentence that clearly and concisely expresses the writer's meaning.

1 A law must first be sent to Congress as a bill. Then a law can be enacted.

    a Before a law can be enacted, it must first be sent to Congress as a bill.

    b After a law is enacted, it must be sent to Congress as a bill.

2 Anyone can propose an idea for a bill. Only members of Congress can introduce a bill.

    a Because anyone can propose an idea for a bill, only members of Congress can introduce it.

    b Although anyone can propose an idea for a bill, only members of Congress can introduce it.

3 A bill is introduced. It is then referred to a committee. The committee will study the bill and decide if it has a chance to pass.

    a Once a bill is introduced, it is referred to a committee who will study it and decide if it has a chance to pass.

    b Unless a bill is introduced, it is referred to a committee who will study it and decide if it has a chance to pass.

4 A bill is often sent to a subcommittee for hearings. This allows for the views of those who support the bill and those who oppose the bill to be recorded.

    a A bill is often referred to a subcommittee for hearings after it allows for the views of those who support the bill and those who oppose the bill to be recorded.

    b A bill is often referred to a subcommittee for hearings, which allows for the views of those who support the bill and those who oppose the bill to be recorded.

5 The hearings conclude. Then the subcommittee sends the bill back to the full committee.

    a The subcommittee sends the bill back to the full committee once the hearings conclude.

    b Before the hearings conclude, the subcommittee sends the bill back to the full committee.

6 The full committee votes on whether to send the bill to the House or Senate. They do this once they receive the subcommittee's report on the bill.

    a Upon receiving the subcommittee's report on a bill, the full committee votes on whether to send the bill to the House or Senate.

    b Until the full committee votes on whether to send the bill to the House or Senate, the subcommittee does not send a report on the bill.

7 The members of the House or the Senate debate and approve any amendments to the bill. They then vote to pass or defeat the bill.

    a After the House or the Senate debates and approves any amendments to the bill, the members vote to pass or defeat it.

    b Whereas the members of the House or the Senate debate and approve any amendments to the bill, they vote to pass or defeat it.

8 A bill passed in the House or the Senate is sent to the other chamber. There it goes through the same process.

    a After a bill goes through the same process, it is sent to the House or the Senate, where it is passed.

    b A bill that passes in the House or the Senate is sent to the other chamber, where it goes through the same process.

9 Both the House and the Senate approve a bill. The bill is sent to the president.

    a If both the House and the Senate approve a bill, it is sent to the president.

    b After a bill is sent to the president, both the House and the Senate approve it.

10 The president approves and signs a bill. The bill becomes a law.

    a If the president approves and signs a bill, the bill becomes a law.

    b Unless a bill becomes law, the president does not approve or sign it.

Compound-Complex Sentences

> ## Presentation
>
> ### Compound-Complex Sentences
>
> Compound-complex sentences contain at least two independent clauses and one dependent clause.
>
> To form a compound-complex sentence, first combine two independent clauses to form a compound sentence.
>
> > *The team captain jumped for joy.*
> >
> > *The fans cheered.* (two independent clauses)
> >
> > *The team captain jumped for joy, and the fans cheered.* (compound sentence)
>
> Then add a dependent clause to the compound sentence.
>
> > *When we won the game, the team captain jumped for joy, and the fans cheered.* (*When we won the game* = dependent clause)

Practice 1

Read each sentence. Circle the letter for *true* if it is a complex sentence, and circle the letter for *false* if it is not.

1 My sister travels a lot because she works as a sales representative for a pharmaceutical company.

   a true
   b false

2 When John heard about the lay-offs, he decided to take the accounting classes he needed to complete his bachelor's degree so that he could find another job.

   a true
   b false

3 Scientists have predicted that this summer will be unusually hot, so many buildings have been outfitted with new air conditioners.

   a true
   b false

4 Animals have some amazing ways of adapting to the environment; for instance, the bottom-feeding flounder can change its color to match the ocean floor so that it can hunt for prey.

   a true
   b false

5 Some historians doubt that the great pyramids were built by the Egyptians because of their architectural complexity, and they wonder who might have built them.

   a true
   b false

6 Because the home-made split pea soup was cold, I warmed it in the microwave.

   a true

   b false

7 Jason forgot his parents' anniversary, so he sent them a card when he finally remembered.

   a true

   b false

8 Since we weren't around for the performance, we bought a DVD of the play that our friend starred in.

   a true

   b false

9 April wore a fancy dress and she had her hair done for the occasion.

   a true

   b false

Practice 2

Circle the letter for simple, compound, complex, or compound-complex to identify each sentence type.

Example:

1 *My friend invited me to a party this weekend, but I don't think I'll go.*

   a *simple*

   (b) *compound*

   c *complex*

   d *compound-complex*

2 While I like beef, Jane likes pork, and Tim only eats chicken.

   a simple

   b compound

   c complex

   d compound-complex

3 It is not surprising that Henry—who likes stories filled with horror, suspense, and fantasy—has read all of Stephen King's novels.

   a simple

   b compound

   c complex

   d compound-complex

4 Laura needs a new computer and is going to the computer store next week on her day off to buy one.

   a simple

   b compound

   c complex

   d compound-complex

5 Many people loved the movie, but I didn't like it at all.

 a simple

 b compound

 c complex

 d compound-complex

6 We all went hiking last weekend; however, Alicia stayed home because she wasn't feeling well.

 a simple

 b compound

 c complex

 d compound-complex

7 I haven't bought new clothes in more than a month because I don't have time to shop; moreover, I don't have the money!

 a simple

 b compound

 c complex

 d compound-complex

8 In the winter, my friends and I go to the Pocono Mountains in Pennsylvania at least once a month to ski, snowboard, and just have a good time.

 a simple

 b compound

 c complex

 d compound-complex

9 Even though it was a windy day, many people were on the beach; they were flying kites.

 a simple

 b compound

 c complex

 d compound-complex

10 Since I have an English test tomorrow, I will stay home tonight to study.

 a simple

 b compound

 c complex

 d compound-complex

Fragments

Sentences/Fragments

A **sentence** is a complete thought that has a subject and a verb. A **fragment** is an incomplete sentence. It may express an incomplete idea, and it may be missing a subject or verb.

To fix a fragment, you can:

- Add the missing subject.
- Add a verb or verb phrase.
- Add the fragment to the sentence that comes before or after it by combining them.

Solutions	Fragments	Revisions
Add subject	Is nobody in the street.	**There** is nobody in the street.
Add verb or verb phrase	The ship been sailing for twenty days in the Arctic Ocean.	The ship **has** been sailing for twenty days in the Arctic Ocean.
Combine two clauses	I have seasonal allergies. Especially in the spring and the summer.	I have seasonal **allergies**, especially in the spring and the summer.
	When she goes to college. My daughter wants to study graphic design.	When she goes to **college, my** daughter wants to study graphic design.

Practice 1

Circle the letter of the answer that describes the sentence or fragment.

Example:

1 *Some mushrooms are poisonous.*
  (a) *Correct Sentence*
  b *Missing the Subject*
  c *Missing the Verb or Verb Phrase*
  d *Missing the Subject and Verb or Verb Phrase*
  e *Dependent Clause Only*

2 Especially in the early morning.
  a Correct Sentence
  b Missing the Subject
  c Missing the Verb or Verb Phrase
  d Missing the Subject and Verb or Verb Phrase
  e Dependent Clause Only

3 Mountain biking a favorite sport for many young people.

   a Correct Sentence

   b Missing the Subject

   c Missing the Verb or Verb Phrase

   d Missing the Subject and Verb or Verb Phrase

   e Dependent Clause Only

4 Want the city to do something because the traffic is so bad every day.

   a Correct Sentence

   b Missing the Subject

   c Missing the Verb or Verb Phrase

   d Missing the Subject and Verb or Verb Phrase

   e Dependent Clause Only

5 Hand me the phone.

   a Correct Sentence

   b Missing the Subject

   c Missing the Verb or Verb Phrase

   d Missing the Subject and Verb or Verb Phrase

   e Dependent Clause Only

6 Broken down on the side of the road.

   a Correct Sentence

   b Missing the Subject

   c Missing the Verb or Verb Phrase

   d Missing the Subject and Verb or Verb Phrase

   e Dependent Clause Only

7 When it opens.

   a Correct Sentence

   b Missing the Subject

   c Missing the Verb or Verb Phrase

   d Missing the Subject and Verb or Verb Phrase

   e Dependent Clause Only

8 The cat watching the street sitting in the window.

   a Correct Sentence

   b Missing the Subject

   c Missing the Verb or Verb Phrase

   d Missing the Subject and Verb or Verb Phrase

   e Dependent Clause Only

9 The most livable cities.

   a Correct Sentence

   b Missing the Subject

   c Missing the Verb or Verb Phrase

   d Missing the Subject and Verb or Verb Phrase

   e Dependent Clause Only

10 Since they didn't go to the picnic.

    a Correct Sentence

    b Missing the Subject

    c Missing the Verb or Verb Phrase

    d Missing the Subject and Verb or Verb Phrase

    e Dependent Clause Only

11 In the kitchen on the sink is the stack of dishes.

    a Correct Sentence

    b Missing the Subject

    c Missing the Verb or Verb Phrase

    d Missing the Subject and Verb or Verb Phrase

    e Dependent Clause Only

Practice 2

Underline the ten fragments in the paragraph.

The History of Corn

Corn that is a native plant to the Western Hemisphere. The Indians of North and South America growing corn for thousands of years before Columbus arrived in the New World in 1492. Indeed, fossils of ancient corn cobs can be found in museums today. When Columbus and his ships landed in the West Indies. He traded with the natives there. Taking corn back with him to Spain. From there, corn was introduced to other Western European countries. And eventually to the rest of the world. When the first European settlers came to the New World, the Indians given them corn to eat. Thereby saving them from near-certain starvation. During their first harsh winter in America, the Indians called this life-saving food "ma-hiz." Which the settlers pronounced as "maize." Later, the Indians taught the settlers how to plant corn and use it in the preparation of various foods. Corn was very valuable in those days. That was used as a form of money and traded for meat and furs. Today, the United States grows about 80 percent of the world's corn. And the world's largest exporter.

Run-On Sentences and Comma Splices

Presentation

Run-on Sentences and Comma Splices

A **run-on sentence** is two or more clauses that have been incorrectly combined with missing or incorrect punctuation and/or connectors.

Example:

I am in Spain I am happy.

A **comma splice** is two or more clauses combined with a comma and no coordinating conjunction.

Example:

I am in Spain, I am happy.

To correct run-on sentences and comma splices:

- Use appropriate punctuation (check for correct use of periods, semicolons, and commas).
- Use coordinating conjunctions to combine equal, independent clauses.
- Use subordinating conjunctions to combine clauses if one is secondary and dependent.
- Use a transition signal to combine the clauses with a semicolon and comma.
- Use a transition signal, and separate the clauses with a period.

There needs to be a comma between a subordinating clause and an independent clause if the subordinating clause starts the sentence. If the independent clause starts the sentence, no comma is necessary.

Examples:

If it rains, we will not go outside.

We will not go outside if it rains.

Run-on Sentences	Possible Revisions	Solutions
My name is Cristina I am from Brazil.	My name is Cristina, and I am from Brazil.	Add a comma + a coordinating conjunction *and*. (Adding just a comma does not fix the run-on sentence.)
	My name is Cristina. I am from Brazil.	Divide the run-on sentence into two sentences.
I will finish my homework, after I will go to bed.	I will finish my homework, and then I will go to bed.	Write a compound sentence.
	After I finish my homework, I will go to bed.	Write a time clause with *after*.
	I will finish my homework, after which I will go to bed.	Write a time clause with *after*.

I hate my apartment, I'm going to move.	I hate my apartment. I'm going to move.	Replace the comma with a period.
	I hate my apartment, so I'm going to move.	Add a coordinating conjunction.
Comma Splice	**Possible Revisions**	**Solutions**
Lisa came to the game, her roommate went to the library.	Lisa came to the game, but her roommate went to the library.	Use a coordinating conjunction.
	Lisa came to the game although her roommate went to the library	Use a subordinating conjunction.
	Lisa came to the game; however, her roommate went to the library.	Use a transition signal with a semicolon.
	Lisa came to the game. Her roommate, however, went to the library.	Separate clauses with a period, and use a transition signal.

Practice 1

Circle the letter of the answer that correctly describes each sentence.

Example:

1 *Washington, D.C. is the capital of the United States, and it is one of the most visited cities in the world.*
   a *run-on sentence*
   b *comma splice*
   c *correctly written*

2 The city is fun for the entire family it has so many things to see and do.
   a run-on sentence
   b comma splice
   c correctly written

3 A favorite stop is the National Zoo, the giant pandas Mei Xiang and Tian Tian make their home there.
   a run-on sentence
   b comma splice
   c correctly written

4 Because it has a mock cockpit in which they can play pilot, children love the "America by Air" exhibition at the National Air and Space Museum.
   a run-on sentence
   b comma splice
   c correctly written

5 At the National Museum of Natural History, nature lovers can walk among living butterflies in the museum's Butterfly Pavilion, or they can marvel at the life-like dioramas in its Mammal Hall.

   a run-on sentence

   b comma splice

   c correctly written

6 At Friendship Park, Washington's most popular playground, children can roam free and play in the park's huge sandbox it is always full of toys.

   a run-on sentence

   b comma splice

   c correctly written

7 The National Museum of American History is a treasure chest of history, the original "Star-Spangled Banner" flag, which inspired our national anthem, is just one of the many artifacts on display there.

   a run-on sentence

   b comma splice

   c correctly written

8 The National Archives houses the documents that shaped the political evolution of the United States, the Declaration of Independence, the Bill of Rights, and the Constitution have been on display there since 1952.

   a run-on sentence

   b comma splice

   c correctly written

Practice 2

Read each sentence for run-on or comma splice errors. Then rewrite the sentence using one of the connectors provided or by changing the punctuation. Pay attention to meaning and punctuation.

Example:

1 *There is a place where I can get a hot shower I don't want to go camping.* (**unless, because, if**)
<u>Unless there is a place where I can get a hot shower, I</u> *don't want to go camping.*

2 The band didn't sound very good, they were missing their guitarist. (so, subsequently, because)
The band didn't sound very _____ .

3 The air quality in San Pedro is terrible people are getting sick from the fumes. (so…that, as if, similarly)
The air quality in San Pedro _____
are getting sick from the fumes.

4 Hoarding is a form of obsessive-compulsive disorder affecting over 4 million people in the United States, it has detrimental social and financial effects on the individual and his or her family. (but, furthermore, while)
Hoarding is a form of obsessive-compulsive disorder affecting over 4 million people
_____ detrimental social and
financial effects on the individual and his or her family.

5 I completed the online survey, I received an email with an e-certificate for free music downloads then. (yet, in addition, as soon as)

_____ received an email with an e-certificate for free music downloads.

6 While the woman was in the shower the package was delivered. (punctuation change)

_____ was delivered.

7 Every spring, the non-profit has an auction they can get donations from individuals and groups to pay for their expenses. (for, in order to, thus)
Every spring, the non-profit has _____
from individuals and groups to pay for their expenses.

8 Many city-dwellers dread winter because of the snow avid skiers can't wait for that first snow. (but, while, otherwise)
Many city-dwellers dread winter _____
for that first snow.

9 My uncle and his family are coming down from Canada this weekend, we are going to the Tulip Festival in Mount Vernon. (for, as long as, likewise)
My uncle and his family are coming down from Canada _____
the Tulip Festival in Mount Vernon.

10 Whenever the students want to study late they go to the only late-night coffee shop near the university. (punctuation change)

_____ to the only late night coffee shop near the university.

11 My boss sent everyone in the office an urgent memo about emergency procedures, the building next to us had a fire. (and, after, instead)
My boss sent everyone in the office an urgent memo about
_____ next to us had a fire.

Choppy Sentences

Presentation

Choppy Sentences

Short, simple sentences can emphasize an idea with clarity and precision. However, while many of these together may be grammatically correct, they do not result in good style. Academic writers in particular avoid too many short, simple sentences because the relationship between the sentences can break the rhythm and logical flow of a paragraph.

To correct choppy sentences, think about the relationships between ideas:

- Use coordination (coordinating conjunctions, correlative conjunctions, or conjunctive adverbs) to combine equal, independent clauses.

- Use subordination (adverb, adjective, or noun clauses) to combine clauses if one is secondary and dependent.

Example:

The *Coccinella Septempunctata* or the common ladybug is well loved all around the world. Ladybugs got their name from farmers in Europe. The farmers' crops were being destroyed by aphids. The farmers prayed to Mary about their insect problem. Ladybugs came and ate the insects. They thought the beetles were sent by God. The farmers called them "beetles of our Lady." Eventually, the name was shortened to lady beetles or ladybugs.

Revised Paragraph:

Ladybugs got their name from farmers in Europe **when** the farmers' crops were being destroyed by aphids. The farmers prayed to Mary about their insect problem; **meanwhile**, ladybugs came and ate the insects. They thought the beetles were sent by God, **so** the farmers called them "beetles of our Lady," **which** eventually was shortened to lady beetles or ladybugs.

Practice 1

Circle the letter of the best revision of the sentences for clarity and concision. If the sentences do not need to be revised, circle "c" for "Correct as is."

Example:

1 *My neighbor's name is Matt. He is a researcher. He works at the National Institutes of Health.*
  a *My neighbor Matt is a researcher who works at the National Institutes of Health.*
  b *My neighbor works at the National Institutes of Health. His name is Matt.*
  c *Correct as is*

2 The rate of unemployment is still high. This is due to a poor job market. Finding jobs is not easy.
  a Today unemployment is still high because of a poor job market. Therefore, finding a job is not easy.
  b Because of the poor job market, finding a job today is not easy, and unemployment remains high.
  c Correct as is

3 Amy signed up for an art class. She realized that she had no natural talent for drawing. She dropped out.

    a Amy signed up for an art class, and after she realized that she had no natural talent for drawing, she dropped out.

    b Amy dropped out of the art class she had signed up for. The reason is that she realized she had no drawing talent.

    c Correct as is

4 Businesses find and hire workers. Several online sites offer this service. Businesses are becoming increasingly interested in using these sites.

    a Businesses are becoming increasingly interested in using online sites to find and hire workers.

    b Using online sites to find and hire workers is increasing because of the increasing interest of businesses to use these sites.

    c Correct as is

5 Last Saturday was cold. It was also rainy. We didn't go to the beach. We went to the movies.

    a Last Saturday was cold, and it was rainy. We went to the movies instead of going to the beach.

    b Last Saturday was cold and rainy, so we went to the movies instead of the beach.

    c Correct as is

6 After I had cleaned the house and gone shopping in preparation for my friend's visit, he called to say that he had changed his plans.

    a I had cleaned the house and gone shopping in preparation for my friend's visit. My friend called to say that he had changed his plans.

    b I had cleaned the house, and I had gone shopping. I had prepared for my friend's visit. Then he called to say that he had changed his plans.

    c Correct as is

7 Jose woke up this morning with an upset stomach. He woke up with a headache, too. He didn't go to work. He decided to stay in bed.

    a Jose woke up with an upset stomach, and he woke up with a headache, too. He decided not to go to work. He stayed in bed.

    b Because he woke up this morning with an upset stomach and a headache, Jose didn't go to work but decided to stay in bed instead.

    c Correct as is

8 Many people follow the news. They prefer to follow the news by digital means or on TV. They prefer not to read newspapers.

    a Many people prefer to follow the news by digital means or on TV rather than through newspapers.

    b Many people prefer to follow the news by digital means or on TV. Many people don't like to read newspapers.

    c Correct as is

9 John enjoys spending time in his neighbor's beautiful garden. His neighbor is Jim. John has no interest in maintaining his own garden. It takes a lot of time to seed, plant, prune, weed, mow, fertilize, and water the plants and grass.

   a John enjoys spending time in his neighbor Jim's beautiful garden and has no interest in maintaining his own because it takes a lot of time to seed, plant, prune, weed, mow, fertilize, and water the plants and grass.

   b Because John enjoys spending time in his neighbor Jim's beautiful garden, he has no interest in maintaining his own. It requires a lot of hard work to seed, plant, prune, weed, mow, fertilize, and water the plants and grass.

   c Correct as is

10 It was a cool summer evening. Debbie and Gabby took a walk to the park. At the park, they sat on a bench. They had a long chat.

   a Debbie and Gabby went for a walk in the park because of the cool summer evening. In the park, they sat on a bench and had a long chat.

   b It was a cool summer evening, so Debbie and Gabby took a walk to the park where they sat on the bench and had a long chat.

   c Correct as is

Practice 2

Read the sentences. Circle the letter of the sentence that combines them in the way indicated in parentheses, either by subordination or coordination.

Example:

1 *Many people think they know what organic farming is. No universally accepted definition of the term* organic farming *exists. (Subordination)*

   (a) *Although many people think they know what organic framing is, no universally accepted definition of the term exists.*

   b *Many people think they know what organic farming is, and no universally accepted definition of the term exists.*

2 For most people, organic farming is a production system. The production system has a specific goal. (Subordination)

   a For most people, organic farming is a production system, so it has a specified goal.

   b For most people, organic farming is a production system that has a specific goal.

3 The production system aims to avoid the use of synthetic pesticides. It aims to avoid the use of harmful fertilizers. It aims to avoid the use of livestock feed additives. (Coordination)

   a Because the production system aims to avoid the use of synthetic pesticides, it also aims to avoid harmful fertilizers and livestock feed additives.

   b The production system aims to avoid the use of synthetic pesticides, harmful fertilizers, and livestock feed additives.

4 Most organic farming systems use "Alternative Farming Methods." "Alternative Farming Methods" include crop rotation, integration of crops and livestock, and conversion of animal manure into fertilizers. (Subordination)

    a Most organic farming systems use "Alternative Farming Methods," which include crop rotation, integration of crops and livestock, and conversion of animal manure into fertilizers.

    b Most organic farming systems use "Alternative Farming Methods," but they include crop rotation, mechanical cultivation, animal manures, green manure, and integrated pest management.

5 Alternative farming methods help to maintain healthy soil. They help to grow healthy plants. They help to control pests and weeds. (Coordination)

    a Alternative farming methods help to maintain healthy soil, grow healthy plants, and control pests and weeds.

    b Alternative farming methods help to maintain healthy soil because they grow healthy plants and control pests and weeds.

6 Some people believe that organic farming methods should include sustainable farming practices. Other people believe that sustainable farming practices are not essential to organic farming. (Subordination)

    a Some people believe that sustainable farming practices are an essential part of organic farming, but others do not.

    b While some people believe that sustainable farming practices are an essential part of organic farming, others do not.

7 There is disagreement. The disagreement is about the role of sustainable farming practices in organic farming. The disagreement has made it difficult to have a universally accepted definition of organic farming. (Subordination)

    a Because of the disagreement over whether sustainable farming practices should be a part of organic farming, no universally accepted definition of the term has been reached.

    b There is disagreement about the role of sustainable farming practices in organic farming, and there is no universally accepted definition of the term.

Stringy Sentences

Presentation

Stringy Sentences

Writers who write the way they speak often produce long strings of ideas in one sentence. These "stringy" sentences may be grammatically correct, but they are too long. Good academic writing avoids them. They often overuse connecting words, such as *and, or, but, so,* and *because.* For this reason, it can be difficult to identify the main and supporting ideas in a given text.

To correct stringy sentences:

Avoid overuse of *and, or, but, so,* and *because.*

Simplify long clauses using parallel words or phrases, participial phrases, and appositives.

Break long sentences into sentences with two or three clauses.

Use coordination (coordinating conjunctions, correlative conjunctions, or conjunctive adverbs) to combine equal, independent clauses.

Use subordination (adverb, adjective, or noun clauses) to combine clauses if one is secondary and dependent.

Break long sentences into sentences with two or three clauses.

Example:

There are over 5,000 species of *Coccinella Septempunctata* or the common ladybug, but the most common in North America is the seven-spotted ladybug, which has three spots on either side of its body and one spot in the middle. All ladybugs have six legs and red, orange, or yellow coloring with special markings that look like stripes or dots, and they eat aphids and other pests, so many gardeners think they are good luck. They don't have many predators, but frogs and birds like to eat them, and scientists believe that ladybugs have bright colors and special markings to warn these predators that they are not very tasty because they discharge a nasty-tasting liquid if they are threatened.

Revision:

> There are over 5,000 species of *Coccinella Septempunctata*, or the common ladybug. **However**, the most common in North America is the seven-spotted ladybug, which has three spots on either side of its body and one spot in the middle. All ladybugs have six legs **with** red, orange, or yellow coloring **and** special markings that look like stripes or dots. They eat aphids and other pests; **thus**, many gardeners think they are good luck. They don't have many predators, **though** frogs and birds like to eat them. **In fact**, scientists believe that ladybugs have bright colors and special markings to warn these predators that they are not very tasty. **Often**, they will discharge a nasty-tasting liquid if they are threatened.

Practice 1

Circle the letter of the answer that correctly describes each sentence: *Too stringy* (too much coordination and/or subordination) or *Well-written*.

Example:

1 *Barack Obama was born in Honolulu, Hawaii, on August 4, 1961, to an American mother from Fort Leavenworth, Kansas, and an African father from Kolego, a small village in western Kenya.*
   a *Too stringy*
   (b) *Well-written*

2 Obama left Hawaii to attend college and earned a degree from Columbia University, and after that he moved to Chicago where he worked as a community organizer, and then he went to Harvard Law School, where he became editor of the Harvard Law Review.
   a Too stringy
   b Well-written

3 While working as a community organizer and teaching at the University of Chicago, Obama met and married Michelle Robinson in 1992 and had two daughters—Malia Ann, born in 1998; and Natasha (Sasha), born in 2001.
   a Too stringy
   b Well-written

4 Obama was elected to the Illinois state senate in 1996 and served there for eight years; in 2004, he was elected to the U.S. Senate as a Democrat representing the state of Illinois.
   a Too stringy
   b Well-written

5 Obama gained national attention in July 2004 when he delivered the keynote speech at the Democratic Convention in Boston, a speech that not only made him a household name, but also changed his life, and it led to his running for president four years later.

    a Too stringy

    b Well-written

6 In February 2007, Obama announced his candidacy for presidency of the United States, and, after a long and historic campaign against Hillary Rodham Clinton, a U.S. senator from New York and former first lady, he won the Democratic nomination.

    a Too stringy

    b Well-written

7 Obama won the general election against Republican nominee Senator John McCain on November 4, 2008, and he was inaugurated as the 44th president of the United States on January 20, 2009, and indeed he became the first African-American to serve in that office.

    a Too stringy

    b Well-written

8 In April 2011, Obama announced that he would run for re-election in 2012, and on November 6, 2012, he defeated Republican nominee Mitt Romney, thereby winning a second term as the president of the United States.

    a Too stringy

    b Well-written

Practice 2

Read each stringy sentence. Then choose the sentence connector from the word box to revise the sentence using coordination or subordination.

because it	because they	However, he
Unfortunately, he	; in addition, they	

1 *Tran took the placement test for the ESL program, **and** he placed into a high-intermediate class, **but** he couldn't attend the class **because** it meets in the mornings, **and** he works then.*

Revision:

When Tran took the placement test for the ESL program, he placed into a high-intermediate class.
<u>However, he</u> *couldn't attend the class* _____
meets in the mornings. _____
works then.

2 Many students prefer face-to-face learning to online classes **because** they like to work in groups, **and** they feel they learn faster when they can talk to the teacher.

Revision:

Many students prefer face-to-face learning to online classes _____ like to work in groups; _____ feel they learn faster when they can talk to the teacher.

; it is	Furthermore, the	in order to
Nevertheless,	However, the	, so

3 There are 1.3 billion Muslims in the world, **and** the largest Muslim population is not actually in the Middle East, **but** it is in Indonesia, **and** the second-largest population of Muslims is in India.

Revision:

There are 1.3 billion Muslims in the world. _____ largest Muslim population is not actually in the Middle East; _____ in Indonesia. _____ second-largest population of Muslims is in India.

4 Many employees in American companies are required to complete annual reviews of their work performances, **and** look at their strengths and weaknesses, **but** many managers and employees think the review process is meaningless, **and** they don't take the time to do any real evaluation.

Revision:

Many employees in American companies are required to complete annual reviews of their performances _____ look at their strengths and weaknesses. _____ both managers and employees think the review process is meaningless _____ they don't take the time to do any real evaluation.

Paragraphs

TOPIC SENTENCES

Presentation

Topic Sentence

A topic sentence states the main idea of the paragraph. The sentence should control the scope of the paragraph by introducing the general subject and limiting the topic. The topic sentence is usually the first sentence in a paragraph.

Topic sentences have two parts:

Topic = who or what the paragraph is about

Controlling Idea = what the author will say about the topic

Mistakes with Topic Sentences:

A topic sentence that lacks a focused controlling idea introduces a subject that is **too general or broad**. It cannot be adequately supported. An unfocused controlling idea offers too much for one paragraph to handle.

A topic sentence with too much detail and explanation introduces a very limited subject that is **too specific or narrow**. If the topic sentence is too detailed, there will not be enough to say in the paragraph.

An **off-topic** sentence is one that does not relate to the given assignment. For example, if you are asked to write a paragraph about the causes of and solutions to noise pollution, and your topic sentence reads, "Noise pollution has been in existence since the dawn of time," this sentence is off topic. You are asked to discuss causes and solutions, not the history of noise pollution.

Example Topic Sentences

Topic: Noise pollution

There are three main sources of noise pollution in modern society.

The writer plans to classify three sources of noise pollution. This topic sentence is appropriate.

Noise pollution can have a number of serious effects on human health.

The writer plans to explain the health effects of noise pollution. This topic sentence is appropriate.

Noise pollution is any environmental noise that disturbs people and animals.

The writer plans to define noise pollution. This topic sentence is appropriate.

Too much noise can be a problem.

The topic sentence is too broad. It needs to be narrowed to present a manageable topic.

> *Noise pollution is harmful.*
>
> This topic sentence is too broad. The reader does not know what the paragraph is about.
>
> *The main source of noise pollution on the outskirts of cities is traffic because of the noise made near highways, an area where sound is not muffled by trees or houses.*
>
> The writer has given too much detail. There is nothing else to talk about in the paragraph. The topic sentence is too narrow.

Practice 1

Read the writing topic and topic sentence. Circle the letter for *true* if the topic sentence is appropriate and *false* if the topic sentence is not appropriate.

Writing assignment: Write a paragraph that describes the different types of cat behavior and categorizes them by their function.

1 Cats often like to play and pounce.
   a true   **b** false

2 The majority of cat behavior can be divided into the following functions: hunting, grooming, and socializing.
   a true   **b** false

3 Like humans, many animals behave in certain ways in order to get what they need.
   a true   **b** false

4 Dogs and cats behave in similar and different ways.
   a true   **b** false

Writing assignment: William Butler Yeats was one of the great writers of lyric poetry in English. Write a paragraph explaining how the poem "The Lake Isle of Innisfree" fits the definition of a lyric poem.

5 Many lyric poems express strong, personal emotion.
   a true   **b** false

6 In every way, "The Lake Isle of Innisfree" is a classic lyric poem.
   a true   **b** false

7 "The Lake Isle of Innisfree" was used for the lyrics of a song by the Waterboys.
   a true   **b** false

8 All the elements of a lyric poem are clearly present in Yeats's "The Lake Isle of Innisfree."
   a true   **b** false

Writing assignment: Many accountants work as financial advisors who give advice to the public about a variety of topics. Write a paragraph advising how someone should prepare to do his or her taxes.

9 In order to file taxes without problems, a person should start early and follow a few simple steps.

   a true

   b false

10 It's important to seek financial advice before making decisions about your money.

   a true

   b false

11 An essential step to filing taxes is keeping all of your receipts for your business.

   a true

   b false

12 Taxes must be filed by April 15th in the United States.

   a true

   b false

Practice 2

The following paragraphs are missing topic sentences. Circle the letter of the best topic sentence to complete the paragraph.

1 Topic Sentence: _____

This is true even when the sleeper is not exposed to moonlight. Sleepers in a lab took about five minutes longer to go to sleep on the four nights that had a full moon. They slept about 20 minutes less. They also slept less deeply. The reasons for this phenomenon are not clear, but scientists think that our internal clocks may be linked to lunar cycles. Another possibility is that the lab subjects were affected by the greater light at night during the days before they went into the lab. Clearly, there will have to be more research on this subject.

   a There have always been myths and legends about the full moon.

   b Many different forces affect how well we sleep at night.

   c Scientists have recently discovered that people sleep less on nights with a full moon.

2 Topic Sentence: _____

First, the person should consider his or her goals and evaluate the best way to achieve them. Most likely, he or she is already working, and either wants to change jobs or get a promotion. In either case, it is important to be clear about why a person wants to return to college. Once a person is clear about his or her goals, the person ought to research local schools to determine what college would be the best fit. He or she should make an appointment to talk to advisors at local colleges about a given program and ways to pay for it. Finally, before starting a program, a person had better determine whether he or she has the time and energy to balance school, work, and family responsibilities. Going to school while working and taking care of a family can be exhausting, and many students end up failing or quitting if they don't have help.

a Adults planning to return to college should take three important steps before enrolling in a college program.

b Adults who go back to school have a number of reasons for doing so.

c There are a number of colleges with specific programs that can be helpful for adult students returning to school.

3 Topic Sentence: _____

When the great Mexican artist began painting his murals, he was determined to restore the reputation of the ancient civilizations destroyed by the conquistadors. He also wanted to change the attitudes of the Mexican ruling class, which favored European values and looked with scorn on native Mexicans. His murals showed Indian and mestizo peoples as beautiful and proud and taught his viewers about the achievements of their ancestors.

a Diego Rivera was a great Mexican artist who painted murals.

b Diego Rivera's stunning murals helped rewrite Mexican history.

c The ancient civilizations of Mexico were destroyed by Europeans.

SUPPORTING SENTENCES

Presentation

Supporting Sentences

Supporting sentences explain and give evidence to support the main idea in the topic sentence. Supporting details can include reasons, anecdotes, facts, statistics, expert opinions, examples, and personal accounts.

Review the supporting sentences for the paragraph on reducing accidents with traffic tickets.

Topic Sentence:

If the police increased the number of tickets they gave for traffic violations, there would be fewer car accidents.

Supporting Sentences:

An overwhelming 95 percent of car accidents in the United States and Europe are caused by aggressive driving behavior. (gives a statistic)

The National Safety Council characterizes these aggressive driving behaviors as speeding, changing lanes frequently, and running red lights. These are also considered traffic violations and are illegal. (gives an expert opinion)

The current fines have not decreased traffic violations because police do not give them often enough. (introduces a sub-topic)

If drivers were more likely to be fined for infractions, they would drive more carefully. (gives a reason or explanation)

For example, when Massachusetts state police began to give more tickets for driving infractions from 2001 to 2003, there was a significant decrease in car accidents. (gives an example)

More traffic tickets would not only serve as a reminder to drivers to be more careful, but would also allow police to warn serious offenders before they cause accidents. (gives a reason or explanation)

Practice 1

Read each topic sentence. Then identify the sentence that supports it in one of the ways described on the previous page.

Example:

1 *Topic sentence: Reducing the amount of waste we send to landfills should be a real priority in our cities.*

  (a) *For one thing, we are running out of space for landfills anywhere near our cities.*

  b *Alternative energy sources are also important.*

  c *That is why we need to put less garbage in our landfills.*

2 Topic sentence: Payday loans are exploiting lower-income people in the United States.

  a Credit card interest has risen in the last few years.

  b Most people who take out payday loans fall into a cycle of debt that can last for months or years.

  c A lot of payday loan offices are in storefronts.

3 Topic sentence: The city of Pompeii came to a tragic end.

  a It was near what is now Naples, Italy.

  b It was destroyed when the volcano Vesuvius erupted.

  c It was at an important trading crossroads.

Practice 2

Read each topic sentence. Then circle the letter of the sentence that supports it in one of the ways described on the previous page.

1 Topic sentence: The cactus is a most unusual plant.

  a It has flowers but has no actual leaves.

  b The cactus grows in different parts of the world.

  c It is often seen in the deserts of the American west.

2 Topic sentence: Robert Frost's "The Death of a Hired Man" is an excellent example of a narrative poem.

  a Another narrative poem is "The Highwayman."

  b It is one of my favorite poems.

  c Like all narrative poems, it tells a story.

3 Topic sentence: The primary purpose for studying grammar is increased clarity in writing and speaking.

  a My English teacher takes off points for poor grammar and punctuation.

  b If the speaker or author uses articles incorrectly, it can confuse the audience.

  c And that is why grammar is so important.

CONCLUDING SENTENCES

Concluding Sentences

Concluding sentences summarize the important ideas in a paragraph and sometimes provide a final thought. They are usually the final sentence in a paragraph.

Concluding sentences can have three parts:

Conclusion Signals = *To sum up, In conclusion, Finally, To conclude, Thus*

Review of Ideas = a summary of points or re-statement of the topic sentence

Final Thought = why the information in the paragraph is important. This usually consists of an opinion, suggestion, or prediction.

Sample Paragraph:

There are four types of investments you can make if you want to save money. The first way is to keep your money in a savings account. Saving accounts generally have a very low interest rate, so there isn't a high return. Another way is to buy a certificate of deposit (CD), which accrues interest for a set period of time. The interest rate here is usually higher than it is for a savings account. Next, if you are planning for the long term, you can put your money in an individual retirement account (IRA). These accounts are tax deductible, and the interest rate is quite high compared to savings accounts and CDs. The final way to save money is to buy some stock in a company. If the value of the company's stock goes up, you can make a lot of money, but if the value goes down, you lose a lot of money. There can be a lot of risk associated with buying stock.

Possible Concluding Sentences:

1. To sum up, savings accounts, CDs, IRAs, and stocks are all great ways to invest in your financial future.

   The writer provides a review of contents.

2. Investment tools, such as savings accounts, CDs, IRAs and stocks all have unique advantages and disadvantages; thus, it is essential to think carefully about where to put your money.

   This is a review with a suggestion.

3. Investment tools are important to self-sufficiency. Anyone who doesn't invest is risking welfare or poverty.

   This is a review with an opinion.

4. The advantages and disadvantages of various investment tools may be confusing, but with some good advice, you should be able to find the one that is right for you.

   This is a review with a prediction.

Practice 1

Read the topic sentence. Then read each concluding sentence and circle the letter of its function.

Topic Sentence: Students in the United States should be required to wear school uniforms for a number of reasons.

1 In sum, research shows that school uniforms positively affect the classroom by reducing obvious differences in wealth and social status so that students can focus on school work.
   a review only
   b suggestion
   c prediction

2 To conclude, if we want to make egalitarian classrooms a goal, we should consider having students wear uniforms in U.S. public schools.
   a review only
   b suggestion
   c prediction
   d opinion

3 In conclusion, studies on the effects of school uniforms all lead to the same conclusion: they will make public schools safer and less hierarchical.
   a review only
   b suggestion
   c prediction
   d opinion

Topic Sentence: Though Buddhism is significantly different from Hindu thought, the two religions share a number of similarities because of their shared origins.

4 Finally, although many Westerners are drawn to Buddhism because of its perceived lack of dogma, Buddhism and Hinduism have many beliefs and spiritual practices in common.
   a review only
   b suggestion
   c prediction
   d opinion

5 In order to gain a better understanding of Buddhism, it helps to recall that the central principles of Hinduism were adopted by Buddhists.
   a review only
   b suggestion
   c prediction
   d opinion

6 To sum up, many schools of Buddhism adopted key elements of Hinduism, such as the emphasis on karma and the importance of meditation in reaching enlightenment.
   a review only   b suggestion   c prediction   d opinion

Topic Sentence: The return of wolves to Yellowstone Park in the western United States has greatly benefited grizzly bears.

7 And so, as wolves reduce the population of elk, grizzlies appear to be getting all the berries they need to flourish.

    a review only

    b suggestion

    c prediction

    d opinion

8 Clearly, based on the example of Yellowstone, the resurgence of the wolf population has had and will continue to have a beneficial effect.

    a review only

    b suggestion

    c prediction

    d opinion

9 Therefore, based on what happened in Yellowstone, scientists and policy makers should study more closely the interrelationships among animals in the wild.

    a review only

    b suggestion

    c prediction

    d opinion

Practice 2

Read the paragraph and circle the letter of the best concluding sentence.

There are a number of important reasons for employers to give fathers paid paternity leave. First, the initial months of a child's life are crucial to bonding and attachment. Traditionally, people have discounted the importance of father-child bonding, but researchers have found that children who have bonded with both parents are healthier and more secure. Employers would have happier employees if men were allowed to take a little time off to enjoy fatherhood and bond with their children. Second, employers should consider paternity leave to maintain equal work practices. It's gender discrimination to forbid new fathers from taking leave. Finally, in the United States many people no longer live in single-income homes. Since both the husband and wife usually work, new families often have a hard time adjusting to life with a new baby and keeping up with work. Providing leave to both parents would make the adjustment less of a burden.

1 Concluding Sentence:

    a To conclude, happy employees are more able to be focused and productive at work.

    b For all these reasons, paternity leave is a good policy for enlightened employers.

    c Thus, there are a number of reasons to give employees paid paternity leave.

When conducting academic research for a college class, it is important to follow a few simple guidelines. The first step when conducting research is to decide what the research question is. Students need to have an idea of what they want to know in order to find it. Once a student knows what he or she is looking for, it is a good idea to write down a number of keywords that will guide the research. After defining the search terms, a student can begin researching databases, the Internet, and library catalogs. Colleges usually require students to look for primary sources or original documents first. Secondary literature can be consulted at a later phase of the research process. Finally, before you rely on a source for your research, you should also evaluate whether it is accurate and relevant.

2 Concluding Sentence:

    a Following these guidelines as you complete a research project will save you time and improve the quality of your paper.

    b It's true that the research process can be difficult if you don't get help.

    c When you evaluate your sources, ask yourself, who the author is, where the publication appeared, and if the information you have gathered is credible.

Mimar Sinan was, without a doubt, the most important architect in Turkish history. Working at the same time as the great Michelangelo, he was the architect who brought the domed mosque to perfection. His open interior plan, using exterior supports, made the central dome look almost as though it was suspended in air. His splendid mosques became the pattern upon which other architects based their designs.

3 Concluding Sentence:

    a Mimar Sinan was the Turkish counterpart to Michelangelo.

    b Mimar Sinan was an artist as well as an architect.

    c No Turkish architect before or since has had such a widespread influence.

UNITY

Presentation

Unity

A paragraph is unified if there is only one main idea discussed throughout the paragraph. Every supporting sentence should clearly connect to the topic sentence. To achieve unity in writing, check that each sentence is relevant where it is. Delete any sentences that are off-topic or meaningless to the main idea of the paragraph. You can also move sentences to a more appropriate place.

Example Paragraph:

The three greatest composers of all time, at least in the Western tradition, are generally considered to be Bach, Beethoven, and Mozart. Bach was the creator of most of the musical inventions that are the foundation of Western music. His works are extremely complex and intellectual, yet highly expressive. The combination makes them well worth listening to again and again. Beethoven laid the basis for the entire Romantic movement in music. His music is beautifully structured and yet wild and emotional. He was deaf in the later years of his life. [Not relevant] A great prodigy, Mozart had a genius for melody, and he produced a remarkable collection of work. He wrote symphonies, operas, sonatas, chamber music, masses, and dozens of other musical forms. Bach wrote what was probably the greatest work of sacred music, the *Mass in B Minor.* [Relevant but not appropriate here, it should be moved to discussion of Bach.] Music lovers may argue endlessly about which of these men is greatest, but their three names continue to lead every list of great composers. Schubert and Debussy are also great composers. [Not relevant]

Practice 1

Circle the letter of the best description for each sentence in the paragraph.

Topic Sentence: In a tough job market, it is essential to prepare properly for a job interview.

1 The job market has been particularly difficult ever since the housing crisis.
  a Relevant   **b** Off-topic   **c** Wrong place

2 Preparing answers to questions you think will be asked is a good first step.
  a Relevant   **b** Off-topic   **c** Wrong place

3 An interviewee should be able to talk about his or her experience, education, strengths and weaknesses.
  a Relevant   **b** Off-topic   **c** Wrong place

4 One should not forget to address these questions in a thank you letter after the interview.
  a Relevant   **b** Off-topic   **c** Wrong place

5 The interviewee ought to do some research on the company and the position in order to appear knowledgeable.
  a Relevant   **b** Off-topic   **c** Wrong place

6 It's helpful to appear neat and clean in a professional outfit.
  a Relevant   **b** Off-topic   **c** Wrong place

7 Interviewers are often impressed with candidates who ask specific questions that demonstrate a good understanding of the job.
  a Relevant   **b** Off-topic   **c** Wrong place

8 Finally, a person should think carefully about appearance and dress.
  a Relevant   **b** Off-topic   **c** Wrong place

9 The most appropriate colors for interview clothes are blue, black, and grey because they are neutral and classic.
  a Relevant   **b** Off-topic   **c** Wrong place

10 A good second step is to get a good night's sleep and try to relax before the interview.
  a Relevant   **b** Off-topic   **c** Wrong place

Practice 2

Read the paragraph. Underline three sentences that are off-topic or in the wrong place.

Sibling rivalry is a problem which has several solutions. It is common for brothers and sisters to get upset and fight over toys, activities, and adult attention. Some parents punish children for fighting with time-outs, and others resort to spanking. One simple way to reduce sibling rivalry is to actively teach children to share with each other. If children see their brothers and sisters as allies and not as competitors, they are less likely to argue and fight with each other. Often, parents will buy two or three of the same toy for each child to reduce fighting. A second way to decrease rivalry is for each parent to spend individual time with each child. Individual time doing what each child wants can help the child feel accepted and loved for who he or she is. Experts have shown that children who feel more secure about their parents' love don't fight as often with their siblings. In fact, researchers suggest that children who have siblings develop their personalities by being different from their older and younger siblings. It is clear that parents can encourage better relationships between their children by teaching, sharing, and spending time individually with each child.

COHERENCE

Presentation

Coherence

In coherent writing, ideas follow one another logically, and readers understand how they are connected. Writers repeat keywords, use synonyms, and use pronouns within paragraphs to improve coherence and reduce repetitive phrasing.

How to Repeat Keywords and Key Phrases

Use the same words and phrases to talk about the key people, places, things, and concepts in writing.

Example:

Def Leppard, an English rock band, is coming out of retirement to do a final tour. They plan to tour ten cities in the next three months. Def Leppard hasn't played as a band in a few years.

Be careful not to overuse keywords and phrases. Use them to remind the reader what or who you are talking about, or use them when the meaning wouldn't be clear with a pronoun.

Example:

Academic dishonesty is a problem in college for many reasons. Researchers have discovered the top reasons for academic dishonesty are a lack of consequences for offending students and a lack of awareness of their actions by those students. Many colleges are creating strict rules to deal with academic dishonesty.

(The key phrase, "academic dishonesty," is overused. A pronoun or synonym might be more appropriate.)

How to Use Pronouns

Use pronouns to rename keywords and phrases, but make sure the reader is clear who or what you are referring to.

Example:

Academic dishonesty is a rising problem in college for many reasons. Researchers have discovered the top reasons for this are a lack of consequences for offending students and a lack of awareness of their actions by those students. Many colleges are creating strict rules to deal with it.

(This clearly refers to academic honesty, but it might confuse the reader. Does it refer to academic honesty, the lack of consequences, or the lack of awareness?)

Pay attention to pronoun agreement. Use the correct pronoun (gender, person, and number) to rename keywords. Only use pronouns when they clearly refer to a previously named person, place, thing, or concept in the paragraph.

Example:

The band is auditioning a new guitar player. They plan to take him or her on their next tour.

(*Band* is singular, not plural.)

Be careful to avoid gender bias.

Example:

We want someone who can type. We need to hire him or her.

(Use of both genders to avoid bias can be awkward.)

Alternatives:

We want people who can type. We need to hire them. (Use plural to avoid using both genders.)

We want someone who can type. We need to hire you. (Use 2nd person.)

How to Use Synonyms

Use a synonym or similar phrase to reiterate ideas without repeating them.

Example:

Def Leppard, an English rock band, is coming out of retirement to do a final tour. This famous band plans to tour ten cities in the next three months. They haven't played together in a few years.

Do not overuse synonyms. Use them to add variety to your writing; if used too much, they can confuse the reader.

Example:

Academic dishonesty is a rising problem in college for many reasons. Researchers have discovered the top reasons for cheating include lack of consequences and lack of awareness. Many colleges are creating strict rules to deal with plagiarism.

Practice 1

Underline the six mistakes in coherence in the following paragraph. Look for overuse of keywords, mistakes with pronoun agreement, mistakes with pronoun reference, gender bias, and confusing use of synonyms.

New immigrants could be encouraged to improve his English and become active members in American society in several ways. Often, language difficulties and unfamiliar customs can cause newcomers to the United States to move to a neighborhood where other people from their country live. This can provide a great deal of comfort for the newcomers; thus, he or she may not venture far outside. However, the problem is that they never fully integrate himself into American society. It is important to develop programs that encourage newcomers to learn the language and get familiar with them. They provide low-cost or free English classes for immigrants which may help immigrants with the language barrier. Currently, colleges offer classes on campus, but it might be more well-attended if they were offered in immigrant neighborhoods or at workplaces where immigrants are employed. To sum up, language classes can help immigrants feel more connected and less isolated.

Practice 2

Underline the noun, synonym, or pronoun that best completes each sentence in the paragraph. Use formal academic style.

Asperger's syndrome is a mild form of autism. Like (1) [autism, / its cousin / it], (2) [its / Asperger's / the syndrome] is a disorder in which (3) [you / he or she / a person] has difficulty with normal social behavior. Unlike (4) [someone / them / persons] with (5) [the problem / autism / it], (6) [people with Asperger's / those with Asperger's / a person with Asperger's] does not develop severe problems with language and thinking skills. However, (7) [they / he or she / him] may struggle with appropriate social behavior in a way that someone with autism does. A person with (8) [this mild disorder / a syndrome / it] often has trouble understanding the feelings of others. Someone with Asperger's syndrome doesn't interpret body language correctly, so (9) [they / he / he or she] misses important social cues. Also, someone with this disorder may be excessively dependent on routine in order to cope with daily life. Friends and family of a person with Asperger's might have trouble with (10) [their / his or her / your] inflexibility and insensitivity.

Essays
INTRODUCTIONS

> ### Presentation
> #### Introductions
>
> An essay's introductory paragraph usually starts with an opening "hook," a word, phrase, or sentence that serves to interest the reader in the topic. That can be a quote, a question, or a startling fact—almost anything that will get the reader's attention. It is good to follow that with your thesis statement, which is the controlling idea of your essay. You may then write sentences that hit the main supporting points for your thesis, especially if you are writing a long essay. In a shorter essay, this is usually not necessary. The final sentence should contain a transition so the reader moves on to the rest of the essay. The introductory paragraph should tell the reader what the essay is about and provide a basis (*what is the content of the essay, and what is my perspective on it?*) for reading the rest of the essay.
>
> **Essay Openings:**
>
> - Give *background* or historical information about the topic
> - Tell a *story* related to the topic
> - Make a *surprising statement* (fact or statistic) related to the topic
> - Provide a famous *quote* related to your topic
> - Ask a thought-provoking *question* about the topic
>
> **Sample Introductory Paragraph:**
>
> In the United States, students at private independent and religious schools have always worn uniforms, while students in public schools have not been required to do so. This trend is changing, however. More and more public schools across the nation, including the influential New York City school system, with its 550,000 elementary school children, *are requiring students to wear uniforms for a number of reasons.*

Practice 1

Read each of the following essay openings. Then identify what type of "hook" it is.

1 The hummingbird is the only bird that can fly backwards!
   a background
   b story
   c surprising statement
   d quote
   e question

2 What could be more exciting than a trip around the world?
   a background
   b story
   c surprising statement
   d quote
   e question

3 African Americans have fought in every American war since they first came to these shores in 1619.

a background

b story

c surprising statement

d quote

e question

4 "The buck stops here," was one of President Harry S. Truman's most famous statements.

a background

b story

c surprising statement

d quote

e question

5 Who invented the automatic dishwasher and why?

a background

b story

c surprising statement

d quote

e question

6 When I first met Margo, she told me that she was going to be famous one day, and I believed her.

a background

b story

c surprising statement

d quote

e question

7 The actor Helen Hayes said, "Age is not important unless you're a cheese."

a background

b story

c surprising statement

d quote

e question

8 Many countries tried to build a canal through Panama before the United States successfully completed one.

a background

b story

c surprising statement

d quote

e question

9 Believe it or not, the flamingo eats with its head upside-down.

  a background

  b story

  c surprising statement

  d quote

  e question

10 Could the main character of a full-length novel actually be a rabbit?

  a background

  b story

  c surprising statement

  d quote

  e question

Practice 2

Read each of the following essay openings. Then identify what type of "hook" it is.

1 How could an author win both the Pulitzer Prize and the Nobel Prize for Literature and not be considered a great writer?

  a background

  b story

  c surprising statement

  d quote

  e question

2 Clara Barton built on the work of the British nurse Florence Nightingale, who established a hospital for soldiers of the Crimean War.

  a background

  b story

  c surprising statement

  d quote

  e question

3 Amazingly, 80 percent of the human brain is water.

  a background

  b story

  c surprising statement

  d quote

  e question

4 Goethe, the great German writer, said, "Every day we should hear at least one little song, read one good poem, see one exquisite picture, and, if possible, speak a few sensible words."

  a background

  b story

  c surprising statement

  d quote

  e question

5 What was the most important scientific discovery of the second half of the 20th century?

   a background

   b story

   c surprising statement

   d quote

   e question

6 A whooper swan has been recorded flying at a height of 27,000 feet!

   a background

   b story

   c surprising statement

   d quote

   e question

7 To fully understand Texas, it is important to know that it was once a part of Mexico.

   a background

   b story

   c surprising statement

   d quote

   e question

8 When I walked into my new neighborhood, I saw children working in a community garden and, although I didn't know it then, that changed my life.

   a background

   b story

   c surprising statement

   d quote

   e question

9 "I always wanted to be somebody," said Althea Gibson, Olympic tennis player.

   a background

   b story

   c surprising statement

   d quote

   e question

10 Why is Jane Austen's *Pride and Prejudice* such an important book?

   a background

   b story

   c surprising statement

   d quote

   e question

THESIS STATEMENTS

Presentation

Thesis Statements

A thesis statement announces the main point in an essay. The sentence or sentences should limit the scope of the essay to a single assertion or opinion. A thesis statement tells us what the author will say about the given topic. The thesis statement is contained in the introductory paragraph.

The thesis statement:

- States the topic
- States the writer's perspective on the topic (This is also called the controlling idea.)
- Indicates how the essay will be structured (whether through argument, cause and effect, classification, comparison and contrast, definition, narration, problem/solution, or process analysis)

Thesis Statement Tips:

Make sure the thesis responds to the question in the assignment. This will keep the thesis on the topic.

Express an opinion about or a perspective on a given fact, in a thesis statement. Do not simply state a fact. For example, "Christopher Columbus was Italian," is a fact. "When Christopher Columbus discovered Hispaniola for the Europeans, he initiated genocide," on the other hand, is a thesis statement since it gives a perspective on the fact.

Craft a thesis that constrains the topic so that it is possible to write about it coherently. Avoid making statements that are too general or too broad.

On the other hand, be sure that a thesis isn't too specific that it cannot be supported or developed.

Sample Thesis Statements

Topic: Technology Overload

Too much technology—in the form of cell phones, tablets, etc.—can cause problems, but there may be simple, practical solutions.

The writer plans to discuss the problem and offer solutions. This thesis statement is appropriate.

It is becoming increasingly clear that staying constantly connected through technology can deprive us of many of life's joys and emotional necessities.

The writer plans to argue that too much technology can be harmful in several ways. The thesis statement is appropriate.

Today, more people have access to cell phones than to working toilets.

This is a factual statement. There is nothing to support, so it is not a thesis statement. It needs a perspective or an opinion.

> *Modern technology causes a lot of problems.*
>
> The statement is too general for the thesis of an essay.
>
> *It might help to have a technology-free space in your home.*
>
> This statement is too narrow for a thesis statement. It provides an example of how to deal with technology overload. A thesis statement needs to show what the author intends to say about the topic.

Practice 1

Circle the topic and the controlling idea for each thesis statement.

1 Adult students can face a number of challenges when they decide to return to school.
   a The topic of the thesis is: adults, challenges, returning to school, students.
   b The controlling idea is: adults, challenges, returning to school, students.

2 Though many people associate success with fame, wealth, or power, at its root, success is simply the result of completing a goal.
   a The topic of the thesis is: completing a goal; fame, wealth, and power; results; success.
   b The controlling idea is: completing a goal; fame, wealth, and power; results; success.

3 Barack Obama, like Franklin D. Roosevelt, leads a country with many economic and social challenges; however, their respective approaches to these challenges are quite different.
   a The topic of the thesis is: Barack Obama and Franklin D. Roosevelt face similar challenges, different approaches, similar economic and social challenges.
   b The controlling idea is: Barack Obama and Franklin D. Roosevelt face similar challenges, different approaches, similar economic and social challenges.

Practice 2

Read the assignment question and the thesis statement. Circle the letter for true if the thesis statement is appropriate and false if it is too broad, too narrow, or factual.

Describe the process of fermentation in the muscle cells in the body.

Thesis Statements:

1 Lactic acid fermentation is the process by which the muscles produce energy when oxygen is not present.
   a true
   b false

2 Fermentation, one of the processes by which muscle cells produce energy, occurs in a number of steps.
   a true
   b false

3 There are a few different processes that turn simple sugars into energy.
   a true
   b false

Describe the most common reasons for the outbreak of the Civil War and evaluate which is the most likely.

4 Differences over slavery caused the American Civil War.

   a true

   b false

5 Of the commonly cited reasons for the American Civil War—the economic differences between the North and the South, states' rights, and slavery—economic differences was probably the most significant reason for the outbreak of war between the North and South.

   a true

   b false

6 The main reason for the outbreak of the Civil War was differences in opinion over the economy.

   a true

   b false

Discuss the unemployment problem in the United States. Give at least one economic solution.

7 There are a number of different types of unemployment that have several economic causes.

   a true

   b false

8 High unemployment, poverty, and a lack of government resources are all economic problems in the United States today.

   a true

   b false

9 The two different ways to solve the unemployment crisis in the United States offered by many economists are increasing government spending and giving private businesses incentives to hire more employees.

   a true

   b false

CONCLUSIONS

> **Presentation**
>
> ## Conclusions
>
> A concluding paragraph is the final paragraph in the essay. It summarizes the main point and sub-points, and ends the essay with a final thought, opinion, suggestion, or prediction related to the thesis statement.
>
> Concluding paragraphs have three parts:
>
> **Conclusion Signals** = *To sum up, In conclusion, Finally, To conclude, Thus*
>
> **Review of Ideas** = a summary or re-statement of the topic sentences and the main ideas
>
> **Final Thought** = why the information in the essay is important (offer an opinion, suggestion, or prediction)

Essay Body Summary

Shopping online can be a rewarding experience when one follows some simple steps. (thesis) Before you begin shopping, it is important to familiarize yourself with issues of Internet safety in order to avoid identity theft. Once you are prepared to protect your information, you are ready to use consumer reviews to find the best product. The next step is to find the most reputable website offering that product with the lowest price. The final step is to purchase the item and make decisions about shipping.

Sample Concluding Paragraphs

To sum up, (*conclusion signal*) the steps to a successful online shopping experience involve taking time to research the choices available and protecting your financial information. (*thesis*) Many people find shopping online very convenient and cost-effective because it can offer a vast array of choices. (*review of ideas*) This variety is better for the consumer, since he or she gets the best type, quality, and price available. (*final thought—opinion*)

In conclusion, (*conclusion signal*) the Internet can provide an amazing shopping experience if you use safety guidelines to protect your financial information and read consumer reviews to find the best product and price. (*thesis and review of ideas*) If you are new to online shopping, you may wish to familiarize yourself with the most current Internet safety guidelines, which can be found on the Federal Trade Commission's website. (*final thought— suggestion*)

Finally, (*conclusion signal*) it is important to research safety guidelines carefully and protect your financial information when you shop online. (*thesis and review of ideas*) As more and more people become comfortable using the Internet, online sales will increase. It is possible that, in the future, most of our shopping will be done from the home. (*final thought— prediction*)

Practice 1

Read the essay and the three concluding paragraphs. Identify the structure of each concluding paragraph. Then circle the letter of the most appropriate concluding paragraph for the essay.

Qualities of a Good Marriage

Divorce is more common than not in the United States. A recent study found that almost 60 percent of marriages end in divorce. As a result, many psychologists have begun to study interactions between married couples in order to determine what qualities of the relationship seem to produce the best results for maintaining the marriage. According to some studies, long-lasting marriages seem to have three important qualities: good communication, unconditional acceptance, and humor.

First, researchers have found that communication is vital to a healthy relationship. Couples need to be honest about their needs and desires. If they are not honest, the decisions that they make together about work, family, housing, and money will lead to one partner feeling resentful.

Next, people in strong relationships often maintain an attitude of unconditional acceptance about their partner's faults. Studies have shown that feelings of disdain and contempt in a marriage increase the likelihood of divorce. Feelings of contempt are often directed towards the person, not the objectionable behavior. Couples that are more forgiving in general tend to argue and fight less.

In addition, because there will inevitably be conflict in relationships, humor is an important quality in a happy, long-lasting relationship. Research has shown that couples who laugh together have more positive feelings about their marriage.

Concluding Paragraphs:

1 To conclude, couples that work on communication, acceptance, and humor will likely have a successful marriage. These qualities can be learned and practiced. If your marriage is in trouble, it is a good idea to work on developing these relationship skills.

   a opinion

   b suggestion

   c prediction

2 Finally, healthy marriages are honest, forgiving, and fun. If a relationship is lacking these qualities, the marriage will probably face challenges. Once couples stop communicating and having fun together, they often develop contempt and resentment toward each other. If these feelings aren't resolved, separation and divorce may be inevitable.

   a opinion

   b suggestion

   c prediction

3 In conclusion, research clearly suggests that married couples can avoid divorce by cultivating a few simple attitudes and behaviors. Even though marriage research is still nascent, it is obvious that healthy marriages are not accidental. Honesty, forgiveness, and humor are the best ways to increase overall satisfaction with the relationship.

   a opinion

   b suggestion

   c prediction

4 Which of the three concluding paragraphs is the most appropriate for the essay?

   a 1

   b 2

   c 3

Practice 2

Read the essay and the three concluding paragraphs. Identify the structure of each concluding paragraph. Then circle the letter of the most appropriate concluding paragraph for the essay.

Reasons for Finishing a College Degree as an Adult

When Jim S. lost his job as a manager last year, he found that he couldn't find work to support his family. His caseworker at the unemployment office suggested that he go back to school to finish his accounting degree. At 45 years old, he never thought he would be returning to the classroom, but it turned out to be the best decision he had ever made. When he graduated last year, he immediately got a job earning twice the salary he earned as a manager.

Like Jim, many adults find it necessary to finish their degrees in order to get a promotion or change careers. In fact, there are a number of reasons to finish a degree as an adult. The number one reason is that people with a college education often make more money and enjoy more job security than people who aren't college-educated. People with only a high school education often earn the lowest wages. It is almost impossible to support a family with a very low wage, and without a secondary education, it is almost impossible to get promoted. In addition, entry-level work has little job security. Workers with limited formal education are easy to replace, so companies don't invest in them.

Other reasons to complete a college degree include the networking opportunities on a college campus and the vast field knowledge acquired through higher education. College can be an important place to meet people in the field you are interested in and talk to them about the kind of job you might want to do when you are finished. Teachers and other students often become valuable resources for information about the field and potential jobs.

Concluding Paragraphs:

1 Going back to school to finish a degree could contribute to your family's success in a number of ways. In previous generations, people could expect to work at one job their entire lives, so they often didn't need to get a college degree. However, that is not the case anymore. It may just be that formal education will be the norm in the future.

   a opinion

   b suggestion

   c prediction

2 To sum up, the reasons to return to college as an adult to finish a degree include increased job satisfaction and knowledge. Workers who make an effort to complete their formal education and increase their knowledge are more able to be flexible in a changing job market.

   a opinion

   b suggestion

   c prediction

3 Thus, completing a college degree can significantly increase your chances of having a successful career. If you are thinking about returning to school to complete a program, degree, or certificate, it is a good idea to speak with a college admissions counselor to discuss your options.

   a   opinion

   b   suggestion

   c   prediction

4   Which of the three concluding paragraphs is the most appropriate for the essay?

   a   1   **b**   2   **c**   3

ESSAY STRUCTURE

Presentation

Essay Structure

Essays, like paragraphs, have three main parts: an introductory paragraph, body paragraphs, and a concluding paragraph.

An introductory paragraph starts with a hook to get the reader interested in the topic. The sentences progress from general statements to more specific statements, and conclude with a thesis statement as the last sentence or sentences.

Essay Openings:

- Give background information or history about the topic
- Tell a story related to the topic
- Make a surprising statement (fact or statistic) related to the topic
- Provide a famous quote or saying that reflects your topic
- Ask a thought-provoking question about the topic

Thesis Statements:

- State the topic or general subject
- State the writer's idea about the topic. This is called the controlling idea.
- Say why the writer is writing (indicate the pattern of development)
- Possibly explain how the topic will be divided or show how the topic will develop

Body paragraphs divide the thesis statement into sub-topics that further support and provide evidence for the claim. Each body paragraph has a topic sentence, supporting sentences, and a concluding sentence.

- **The Topic Sentence** of each body paragraph states the sub-topic related to the thesis statement.
- **Supporting sentences** provide facts, examples, details, and explanations about the topic sentence.
- **Concluding sentences** review the ideas in one body paragraph and transition to the next body paragraph.

A concluding paragraph summarizes the main point and sub-points and finishes up the essay with a final thought, suggestion, or prediction related to the reason for writing.

Practice 1

Read the essay and identify the parts: hook, thesis, body paragraphs, sub-topics, and concluding paragraph. Then circle the letter of the correct answer to the question.

The Benefits of Native Plants

(1) What can a coneflower do that a pansy can't? (2) The answer to that question is just part of the powerful case to be made for putting native plants into our gardens, parks, and fields. (3) Often seen as weeds, native plants can help our soil, our water, and even the air we breathe. (4) But we have to plant them first.

(5) A native plant is one that belongs to a certain area. (6) That is to say, it has not been brought into the area from outside in recent centuries. (7) It has adapted to the soil and climate of that area over thousands of years. (8) The result is that it knows how to survive there. (9) It can thrive on the soil, whether it is clay or sand or rich loam. (10) It can flourish on the amount of rain that falls, whether it is one inch a year or a hundred. (11) It is at home.

(12) Native plants are part of the environment in which they live. (13) They provide food for native insects and other small critters. (14) (Some insects don't even recognize non-native plants as food.) (15) And the insects that live on native plants provide food for the birds that are native, which provide food for other wildlife, and so on.

(16) Native plants help protect their environment. (17) On a prairie, native plants put down deep roots to find water. (18) Their roots help keep the soil from eroding or blowing away. (19) In swamps, native plants help filter the water, keeping it clean for fish and other aquatic animals.

(20) As gardeners, citizens, and city planners, we can bring the benefits of native plants into our urban areas. (21) They will require far less care than non-natives, and they will enrich our lives with their beauty.

1 Which sentence is the introductory hook?
  a 1   **b** 2   **c** 3   **d** 4

2 What type of opening does the essay have?
  a background   **b** story   **c** question   **d** quote

3 Which sentence is the thesis statement?
  a 1   **b** 3   **c** 4   **d** 2

4 Which supporting sentence states the reason native plants can survive?
  a 7   **b** 6   **c** 8

5 Which of the topic sentences discusses the benefits of native plants for the environment?
  a 1   **b** 5   **c** 16   **d** 12   **e** 20

6 Which supporting sentence provides an explanation for why native plants keep the water clean?
  a 12   **b** 16   **c** 19

7 Which of the sentences provides a conclusion for the ideas expressed in the paragraph?
  a 6   **b** 9   **c** 11

8 How does the writer conclude the essay?

    a With a question.

    b With a final thought.

    c With a prediction

Practice 2

Read the essay. Write the number of the sentences in the correct order to complete the outline.

About Reading

Do you remember learning how to read? Many people don't. Unlike listening and speaking, reading is a skill that has to be learned, so chances are that someone taught you. Reading has many components. Thus, when a person learns to read, there are a number of skills he or she learns. The process of reading requires an automatic, conscious interaction involving decoding symbols on a page and using critical thinking skills.

A reader uses a variety of skills to decode letters into words, and words into sentences. He or she has to understand the relationship between the letters and their sounds in order to sound out and recognize words. For example, to say the word *cat*, a person must know the sounds for the letters *c, a,* and *t* and how to put the sounds together to form a word.

In addition to word recognition, one needs to understand the basic relationships between words in order to read and understand a given text. Knowledge of parts of speech, grammar, and meaning can help a person decode and understand individual sentences. It's also important for a reader to track meaning across sentences through the use of critical thinking skills. A critical reading experience has the reader questioning what they are reading. He or she should ask, for example, "What is this about? Why is it important? How does it connect to the previous ideas?"

A reader needs to be able to switch automatically between decoding words and understanding sentences. This is called automaticity. Furthermore, a good reader notices when he or she has failed to understand something and then takes action by re-reading or by using a tool, such as a dictionary, to understand the mistake. For instance, a person might read the sentence, "They went to cook in the chicken." He or she would realize this sentence is nonsensical by using critical thinking skills and by re-reading. Awareness of context is also a critical skill when reading.

Reading involves a number of skills that work together to help a reader understand text. People who have trouble reading often need help with the basic skills involved in the reading process. Understanding the discrete skills involved in the reading process is the best way to help readers who struggle.

1 Reading involves a number of skills that work together to help a reader understand a text.

2 A reader has to think critically about sentences to determine importance.

3 A reader needs to be able to switch automatically between decoding words and understanding sentences to deal with any misunderstandings.

4 The process of reading requires an automatic conscious interaction of decoding and critical thinking skills.

5 A reader first uses a variety of skills to decode letters into words and sentences that have meaning.

6 A reader should be aware of mistakes and repair them.

7 A reader needs to understand the relationship between letters and sounds.

8 One needs to understand the basic relationship between words in order to understand the meaning and importance of text.

I. Introduction

Thesis: _____

II. Body Paragraphs

A. _____

1. _____

2. A reader decodes to recognize words.

B. _____

1. A reader uses grammar to understand sentences.

2. _____

C. _____

1. The ability to switch between decoding and understanding should be automatic.

2. _____

III. Conclusion

In conclusion, _____

COHESION

Cohesion

When writing is cohesive, ideas move smoothly and logically from sentence to sentence in a paragraph and from paragraph to paragraph in an essay. We can improve the cohesion within the paragraph with transition signals to connect ideas. Transition signals help us understand the structure, or format, of an essay. There is a complete list of transition signals in the **Appendix**. We improve cohesion by connecting the concluding sentence of the previous paragraph to the topic sentence of the following one.

How to Use Transition Signals

1 Use transition signals to indicate how one idea connects to the next. For example, if you make a general statement and illustrate it with an example, the transition signal from general idea to signal might be *for example*. It is important to choose the correct transition signal to help your reader move easily through the text.

Example:

Recent research suggests that certain environmental factors often play a more important role in mental health than we think. For instance, a combination of two negative factors seems to lead to schizophrenia. They are viral infection during the first trimester of pregnancy followed by an unusual level of stress during puberty.

2 Be careful not to overuse transition signals. Too many will interrupt the flow of your sentences.

Example:

Recent research, in fact, suggests that certain environmental factors often play a more important role in mental health than we think, indeed. For instance, they have found a combination of two negative factors seem to lead to schizophrenia, such as a viral infection during the first trimester of pregnancy, followed by an unusual amount of stress during puberty.

3 Add a dependent clause to a sentence to indicate transitions:

Example:

Given the inclement weather, the family has stayed indoors for the last week.

4 Connect clauses in a sentence to indicate transitions:

Example:

Elena came to school despite the fact that she had a cold.

5 Use transition signals to show how sentences relate to one another:

Example:

Many historians believe that Abraham Lincoln wanted to issue a proclamation ending slavery at the start of the Civil War. However, he waited until the first Union victory for political reasons. (The transition signal shows that they are contrasting ideas.)

How to Connect Paragraphs in an Essay

1 Restate the main idea from the previous paragraph in the topic sentence

2 Use sentence connectors and adverbial phrases (*of course, in this way*) to connect ideas from one paragraph to another

3 Use articles (*the, another*) and pronouns (*this, that, it*) to refer to previous information

The following sentences would be part of a cohesive essay about the education systems in the U.S. and China:

Thesis: There are a number of similarities and differences between the educational systems of the United States and China.

End of the first body paragraph: Like in many other countries, the public school systems in China and the U.S. continue to require a rigorously scheduled curriculum.

Start of the second body paragraph: Though the U.S. and China agree on the subject matter and scheduling in education, the level of teacher intervention in the two countries can be quite different.

End of the second body paragraph: Chinese teachers, unlike American teachers expect all students to do well, so they intervene if a student is falling behind.

Start of the third body paragraph: Of course, Chinese teachers are more equipped to intervene because Chinese parents are more consistently involved in their children's education where American parental involvement varies widely.

End of the third paragraph: The differences in parental participation in the two countries can have a large effect on student outcomes.

Start of the fourth paragraph: In addition to the differing levels of involvement, these countries also use standardized testing quite differently.

Relationship	Coordinating and Paired Conjunctions	Subordinating Conjunctions	Conjunctive Adverbs	Prepositions and Phrases
Addition	and, nor both ... and not only ... but also neither ... nor		also, besides, furthermore, in addition, moreover, as well	an additional, a final, with, in addition to, as well as
Choice	or either ... or whether ... or		alternatively, on the other hand, otherwise	
Comparison	and both ... and not only ... but also	as as + adverb + as as if, as though *(the manner in which)*	similarly, likewise	the same as just like, like, similar to

Conclusion			finally, in conclusion, to conclude, for these reasons, last of all, in summary, in conclusion	it is clear that, you can see that, these examples show that
Condition		if, unless	instead, on the contrary, rather	
Contrast	but	while, whereas	on the other hand, in contrast	except for, instead of
Examples			for example, for instance	such as, an example of, like
Explanation			in other words, that is, in particular, indeed, in fact	
Location		where, wherever, everywhere, anywhere		above, across, against, next to, at, beside,
Logical Order			above all, first and foremost, first of all, more importantly, most important, more significantly, most of all	the first, an additional, a more important, the best/worst
Manner		as, as + adverb + as, as if, as though		
Opinion			in my opinion, in my view	according to, to believe/think/feel (that), for, against
Purpose		so that, in order that		
Reason	for	as, because, since	for this reason	due to, because of, as a result of, to cause

Result	so	so + adj/adv + that such + noun + that so much/many / little/few + noun + that	accordingly, as a result, consequently, hence, therefore, thus	the cause of, the reason for, provided that, to result in, to have an effect on
Time Order		before, after, when, while, since, as soon as	first, second, after that, next, subsequently, then, meanwhile, in the meantime, finally	the first, another, the last, the final, during, since, for, until, before, after
Contrary to Expectation	yet not ... but	although, even though, though	however, nevertheless, nonetheless, still	in spite of, despite, unlike

Practice 1

Underline the transition signals that make the essay more cohesive. Use the chart to help you.

The Effects of Social Media on Politics

Social media, such as Facebook and Twitter, is rapidly changing our society. With the click of a button, people share data with a large audience of friends, family, acquaintances, and even strangers. More and more, people are turning to the Internet to discuss whatever is on their minds. (1) [Besides / For this reason / Alternately], social media is having an increasing influence on modern politics in important ways.

(2) [First of all / Finally / In my opinion], free public access to Twitter, blogs, Facebook, and other social media sites has provided people with the ability to comment on political decisions and breaking news immediately. Virtually anyone can make his or her voice heard publicly about issues that affect him or her in real time. Often, people respond to posts immediately. (3) [Besides / Although / Therefore], there tends to be more debate about any given issue than there was previously. The conversation can provide people with varying viewpoints while they are forming their own opinions. (4) [However / For example / Finally], there is a tendency for people to "flame," or attack, others personally for their viewpoints, instead of giving a well-reasoned counterargument.

(5) [However / First of all / Secondly], politicians and people in power are increasingly likely to read what people are saying online about the issues of the day. Politicians can get a sense of how their constituents feel about important issues. When they read and aggregate these responses, they are better able to make political decisions that are in tune with what people want. (6) [In conclusion / Consequently / In contrast], social media can have an important democratic influence on government decision-making.

(7) [Finally / First and foremost / For this reason] people are no longer dependent on traditional media outlets to communicate with each other, organize, and protest. They can use the Internet and social media sites to sign petitions, engage in civil action, and coordinate protests. (8) [As a result / Since / As a result of], online social movements are difficult to suppress because everyone gets involved. (9) [After / In addition / Alternatively], social activism on the Internet is diffuse, so there is often no single leader to remove, and participation can be anonymous. Through social media, people can participate and get involved, particularly in countries that suppress people's right to protest and organize.

(10) [In conclusion / Besides / As well], social media allows a large sampling of people to participate in contemporary issues in a way that creates a more democratic global society than before. The Internet can be very empowering to people who feel strongly about politics.

Practice 2

Underline the transition signals and connecting phrases that improve cohesion in the essay. Pay attention to grammar, meaning, and the use of keywords, phrases, pronouns, and synonyms.

The Cornell Method

The transition from high school to college can be challenging for students. College is more demanding, and students are expected to master much more material than they did in high school. Professors also ask students to do more with what they are learning. (1) [Therefore / In conclusion / Alternatively], it is necessary for students to be organized so they can learn and memorize material quickly. One way to organize material is to take notes during class and while reading. There are a variety of strategies for note-taking, but many counselors recommend using the Cornell Method to take notes (2) [although / because / for example] it helps students organize and remember information.

(3) [The first step / Furthermore / In addition] of the Cornell Method is to set up one horizontal section for each of the main headings for the lecture or reading. Most professors provide an agenda of main points at the beginning of their lectures; those can be turned into main headings in a student's notes. Chapters in college textbooks are also organized into sections in this same way. In the Cornell Method, a student can write these main points as headings in the left columns of the page. Students should make sure to leave a significant amount of space between headings so that there is enough room for supporting ideas on the right.

(4) [In order to / After / Moreover] one has outlined the main ideas to the left, (5) [on the other hand / for this reason / the next step] is to divide the page into two vertical columns for supporting points and helpful examples. The left column should already contain the main headings for the lecture or reading, but the right columns will include all of the important supporting information about the heading. It's important to not try to write down every example and detail. Students should be more concerned with the sub-topics for each section. They only need to write enough detail so that they remember the topic of the lecture or reading. A simple explanation and example should be enough.

(6) [As a final step / First and foremost / As a result], the student reviews the main headings and supporting information, writing a couple of sentences that summarize the notes for the reading or lecture. This step separates the Cornell Method from other note-taking systems. (7) [Above all / Consequently / For instance], as students review their notes, they will probably remember the information well. (8) [Accordingly / In addition / In conclusion], they are more likely to notice mistakes or misunderstandings and ask questions. After the student has reviewed the information, he or she should write a short summary about the entire lecture or reading in one or two sentences. The summary sentences will help the student organize the information.

(9) [To conclude / First / For this reason], students can follow the steps of the Cornell note-taking method for greater success in their college classes. It is particularly helpful for students who have trouble summarizing because it forces students to organize information as they hear or read it.

Body Paragraphs
LOGICAL DIVISION OF IDEAS

Presentation

Logical Division of Ideas

One way to organize an essay is to divide the ideas into a logical structure. To do this, divide a topic or main idea into distinct parts based on a particular method. Then discuss each one in a separate body paragraph. Depending on the topic or main idea, a logical division might be by method, type, quality, reason, advantage, disadvantage, cause, effect, problem, or solution.

Thesis statements that divide ideas logically state the topic (main idea) and either the number of sub-divisions or the name of the sub-divisions. This statement is the controlling idea of the essay.

Body paragraphs divide the thesis statement into equal sub-topics that support and provide evidence for the claim made in the thesis. These sub-topics appear in logical order (most to least important, general to specific, familiar to unknown, or simple to complex) in the essay. Use transition signals to connect sentences within the paragraph and to connect the paragraphs to each other.

Example:

Thesis Statement:

>   *Government tax collection can be divided into four basic types.*

Topic Sentences for the Body Paragraphs:

1   The first type, proportional taxation, involves taxing everyone at the same rate.

2   Second, regressive taxation, reduces the tax for people with higher incomes.

3   Unlike the regressive tax system, the third method, progressive taxation, reduces taxes for people with lower incomes.

4   Last of all, in a lump sum tax system, the government collects the same amount of money from each person.

Transition Signals for a Logical Division of Ideas

Sentence Connectors: *first, first of all, second, third, next, last, finally, also, in addition, moreover, furthermore*

Coordination: *and, both…and, not only…but also*

Other Phrases: *One/ Another/ An additional/ The first cause, reason, factor, problem, advantage, result, etc.*

In addition to …

Relationship	Coordinating and Paired Conjunctions	Subordinating Conjunctions	Conjunctive Adverbs	Prepositions and Phrases
Addition	and, nor both … and not only … but also neither … nor		also, besides, furthermore, in addition, moreover, as well	an additional, a final, with, in addition to, as well as
Choice	or either … or whether … or		alternatively, on the other hand, otherwise	
Comparison	and both … and not only … but also	as as + adverb + as as if, as though *(the manner in which)*	similarly, likewise	the same as just like, like, similar to
Conclusion			finally, in conclusion, to conclude, for these reasons, last of all, in summary, in conclusion	it is clear that, you can see that, these examples show that
Condition		if, unless	instead, on the contrary, rather	
Contrast	but	while, whereas	on the other hand, in contrast	except for, instead of
Examples			for example, for instance	such as, an example of, like
Explanation			in other words, that is, in particular, indeed, in fact	
Location		where, wherever, everywhere, anywhere		above, across, against, next to, at, beside,

Logical Order			above all, first and foremost, first of all, more importantly, most important, more significantly, most of all	the first, an additional, a more important, the best/worst
Manner		as, as + adverb + as, as if, as though		
Opinion			in my opinion, in my view	according to, to believe/think/feel (that), for, against
Purpose		so that, in order that		
Reason	for	as, because, since	for this reason	due to, because of, as a result of, to cause
Result	so	so + adj/adv + that such + noun + that so much/many / little/few + noun + that	accordingly, as a result, consequently, hence, therefore, thus	the cause of, the reason for, provided that, to result in, to have an effect on
Time Order		before, after, when, while, since, as soon as	first, second, after that, next, subsequently, then, meanwhile, in the meantime, finally	the first, another, the last, the final, during, since, for, until, before, after
Contrary to Expectation	yet not . . . but	although, even though, though	however, nevertheless, nonetheless, still	in spite of, despite, unlike

Practice 1

Write the signals and phrases that indicate logical order in the essay.

furthermore	simple solutions	Either of these deterrents
several simple solutions	Some popular distractions	the main reason
another simple solution	the most popular solution	Long-term solutions like

Ways to Curb Nail Biting

Onychophagia, or nail-biting, is a disorder that usually begins in childhood. It is a habit that develops to relieve stress, and it is related to obsessive-compulsive disorders. The habit can be difficult for a person to stop. However, there are (1) _____ that have proven effective.

Substitution is (2) _____ for nail-biting. Psychologists believe that (3) _____ people develop the habit is to cope with high levels of stress. Nail-biting can give people a feeling of control in the midst of unmanageable life events. Thus, to stop nail-biting, people may need to find an equally calming and constructive physical activity. For example, some nail-biters go for walks or meditate during stressful times. Positive substitutes like walking and meditation have no harmful effects; (4) _____ , these activities can be quite effective in stopping nail-biting.

(5) _____ substitution can take time to develop, so at the outset psychologists recommend (6) _____ like distraction. Nail biters are advised to notice when they feel an urge to bite their nails, and find ways to interrupt the habit. (7) _____ are snapping a rubber band around the wrist, counting numbers, or reciting the alphabet. These distractions are not particularly productive, so they are not recommended for long-term use, but they do provide an outlet for the urge when someone is just beginning to stop.

Using a deterrent is (8) _____ psychologists might recommend. Some people paint a foul-tasting polish on their nails. Others go to the nail salon and get acrylic nails that they can't bite through. (9) _____ would make it difficult to continue nail-biting. These are definitely meant to be short-term solutions.

Practice 2

Underline the best signal or phrase that would indicate a logical division of ideas in the essay.

Advantages of Owning a Pet

If you are a single adult living alone in the United States, you are not alone. There are over 52 million unmarried Americans living alone, according to the last U.S. Census. A lot of these people only interact with others at work or when they meet friends. In fact, many report feelings of loneliness and isolation. In a world where more people are isolated and disconnected from the communities they live in, pet ownership can have a number of (1) [disadvantages / solutions / advantages], including companionship, improved self-worth, and increased social interaction.

(2) [One disadvantage / First / Both], pets can provide a person who lives alone with companionship. It can be lonely coming home to an empty house. A dog or cat can offer the comfort and physical affection that is lacking for someone who lives alone. Cats, for instance, are particularly responsive to attention and petting. Studies have shown that when people pet cats, their heart rate slows and they seem to be more relaxed.

(3) [Therefore / Not only / A second advantage] to pet ownership is that taking care of a pet can improve a person's feelings about him- or herself. When a person takes care of an animal, he or she engages in nurturing behaviors that can be beneficial. Psychologists believe that nurturing behaviors help people develop compassion. (4) [And / Either / Additionally], people develop a sense of pride and increased self-worth from taking responsibility for others.

(5) [Furthermore / Addition / A third solution], pets can give a single person living alone a reason to interact socially with others. For example, many dog owners take their pets to dog parks where they can meet and talk to other dog owners. (6) [Next / Moreover / In addition to], cat owners often make an effort to get to know neighbors (7) [for / in order to / because] have someone cat-sit if they go out of town. Having a pet can also be a great topic for small talk at work and other social events. People with pets often find they have an instant common interest for discussion when they first meet.

(8) [Thus / The final reason / In addition to], a single adult who lives alone might consider getting a pet because there is evidence to suggest that pet ownership might help with (9) [isolation, self-esteem, and loneliness / self-esteem, isolation, and loneliness / loneliness, self-esteem, and isolation]. Many pet owners have a parent-child relationship with their pet that can be very deep and cathartic.

CHRONOLOGICAL ORDER

Presentation

Chronological Order

An essay can be organized chronologically to describe the order of events in a process, procedure, plan, event, story, or biography. In this type of essay, a topic is divided into steps or events, and each one is discussed in a separate body paragraph.

Thesis statements that indicate chronological order provide an overview of the story or process (main idea). They lay out the order in which the steps, events, or phases happen. (the controlling idea)

Body paragraphs divide the thesis statement into individual events, stages, phases, or steps that support and provide evidence for the thesis. Use chronological transition signals to link sentences within the paragraph and link the paragraphs to each other in the correct order. See the example below.

Example:

Thesis:

In the essay "My Name" from *The House on Mango Street*, Sandra Cisernos describes how she feels about her name as she matures into an adult.

Topic Sentences for the Body Paragraphs:

The essay begins with Cisernos *defining her original first name, Esperanza, which in English means "hope."*

Next*, she explains that her parents named her after her grandmother, who was a fiercely independent woman with a very hard life and a sad story.*

Finally*, she concludes that she wants to change her name because she doesn't like the associations she has with the word.*

Transition Signals for Chronological Order

Sentence Connectors: *first, first of all, second, third, next, last, finally, also, in addition, moreover, furthermore*

Subordination: *after, as, as soon as, before, since, until, when, while*

Other Phrases: *The first/second step, day, etc.*

later that week, after, for x months, in 2013, several days ago, in the next minutes

Practice 1

Write the signals and phrases that indicate chronological order to complete the essay. Some of the answers have been marked already.

Soon after	As the story proceeds	Upon arriving
After the dinner ends	Finally	After Gretta finishes
When	Eventually	

Review of James Joyce's "The Dead"

"The Dead" is a short story published by the Irish writer James Joyce (1882–1941) in his 1914 collection, called *Dubliners*. The story is remarkable for its blend of what Joyce called "scrupulous meanness" and the quiet but transfiguring realization with which it ends. (1) _____ at the annual winter dance and dinner that his aunts hold, Gabriel Conroy, the protagonist, immediately strikes the reader as being as insecure as he is pretentious. (2) _____ he ridicules a maid about her marriage prospects, we see him grow flustered. _____ Then _____ , he pulls "his waistcoat down more tightly on his plump body" and crassly offers her money as a Christmas present. _____ Before the dinner begins _____ , he worries that his little speech will not be understood by those in attendance, whom he assumes are not as well-read as he is. As Gabriel will soon realize, he is, in his own words, a "nervous, well-meaning sentimentalist."

(3) _____ , it becomes overstuffed with details of food and drink being consumed, the dancing and the drifting conversations about travel and politics. (4) _____ , however, if we pay close attention, we realize this dinner party, which seems so full of life, is permeated with allusions to death and life's passing.

_____ After the dinner ends _____ , Gabriel and his wife, Gretta, board a cab for their hotel. It is snowing, and Gretta is unusually silent. Gabriel tries unsuccessfully to coax her into talking. (5) _____ , at the hotel, Gretta tells Gabriel that a song she'd heard earlier reminded her of her young love, Michael Furey. Theirs was a forbidden love, and Furey, delicate and ill, died after walking through the rain to see her. (6) _____ her story, she cries and falls asleep, leaving Gabriel to imagine the passion his wife once had for a delicate boy. He thinks of his own life, tame and passionless, and realizes that he does not know his own wife, that he has not lived, and that he is fading into middle age. (7) _____ this epiphany, as snow taps on the window, Gabriel's identity merges with all those who have passed out of life, as he imagines snow falling all over Ireland, "upon all the living and the dead."

Practice 2

Write the signals and phrases that indicate chronological order to complete the essay. Pay attention to grammar, meaning, and the use of keywords, phrases, pronouns, and synonyms. Some of the answers have been marked already.

First	the stages of the writing process	As you receive feedback
As soon as		The final stage
As you write	Before	

The Writing Process

Non-native speakers of English often find academic writing difficult because they lack vocabulary, and they struggle with grammar and sentence structure. It is important for these students to give themselves a lot of time when completing an assignment. Following (1) _____ can help non-native speakers of English have more success with academic writing.

(2) _____ you begin writing, it's a good idea to do some planning. Planning for an assignment involves two steps. (3) _____ , familiarize yourself with the assignment. You need to know what the assignment is and what the teacher expects. _____ Once _____ you know what to expect, you can either jot down some ideas in a list or free associate. It is particularly important for non-native speakers to spend extra time coming up with ideas because brainstorming helps them prepare for the vocabulary and grammar they will need when they write.

(4) _____ you have a list of ideas from brainstorming, you are ready to organize your ideas and write a draft. It is helpful to re-read your ideas in order to choose which ideas you will write about and which ideas you will discard. _____ Next _____ , you will need to organize the ideas using an outline or map. The outline or map will help you stay focused when you are writing. (5) _____ , follow the outline.

(6) _____ of the writing process after you have a draft is to get feedback and revise the draft multiple times. You should choose who you get feedback from carefully. Your teacher is the best source, followed by other students and tutors in the writing center at your college. In addition to these sources, you should also re-read the draft yourself and make notes about problems you see. (7) _____ , you should review the suggestions and use them to revise your draft. It is a mistake to revise only one time. The best essays are revised multiple times.

This writing process is particularly important for writers for whom English is not a native language. It takes them longer to complete an assignment, but the extra effort is worth it.

COMPARISON SIGNALS

Presentation

Comparison Signals

A comparison shows how one thing is similar to another. Use comparison signals in an essay to compare people, places, things, and concepts that are similar.

Thesis statements set up comparisons between or among at least two people, places, things, or ideas.

Body paragraphs divide the thesis statement into ideas that support and provide evidence for the comparative claim. The sub-topics appear in a logical order (most to least important, for example). Use comparison transition signals to link sentences within the paragraph and to link the paragraphs to each other.

Example:

Thesis Statement:

> *Though the technology has changed, modes of communication over the last 25 years still share* ***a number of similarities***.

Topic Sentences for the Body Paragraphs:

> *Current and older telephonic technology allows people to call each other from a distance.* ***Similarly****, telephones a few decades ago were* ***just as*** *capable as current telephones of recording a message.*

> ***Likewise,*** *sending written communications was as possible 25 years ago* ***as*** *it is today.*

Transition Signals for Comparison

Comparatives: *as…as*

Sentence Connectors: *similarly, likewise, also, too*

Coordinating Conjunctions: *and, nor*

Paired Conjunctions: *both…and, neither…nor, not only…but also*

Subordinating Conjunctions: *as, just as*

Prepositions: *similar to, equal to, like, the same as, just as, in common, as*

Practice 1

Write the signals and phrases that indicate comparison to complete the essay.

a number of parallels	Both	quite like	similar resolutions
and	Similarly	just as deceptive	share

10 Things I Hate About You: A Modern Adaptation of *The Taming of the Shrew*

Hollywood has a long tradition of remaking classic literature into made-for-teen movies. In fact, the plots of many of the romantic comedies set in high school come directly from Jane Austen's novels, Shakespeare's plays, or stories by Nathaniel Hawthorne. For instance, *10 Things I Hate about You,* the 1999 teen movie with Julia Stiles set in a modern American high school, shares (1) _____ to Shakespeare's play *The Taming of the Shrew*.

(2) _____ the play (3) _____ the movie are about two very different sisters. In the play, Katherina, the elder sister, is bad-tempered and is considered to be unmarriageable. Bianca, the younger sister, has several suitors who are vying to win her hand. (4) _____ , in the teen movie, the older sister, Kat, is unpopular because of her angry disposition, while the younger sister, Bianca, is popular for her kindness.

The play and the movie also (5) _____ plot devices. In *The Taming of the Shrew*, one of Bianca's suitors, Hortensio, has his friend, Petruchio, woo Katherina while he woos the sister Bianca, disguised as her music tutor. The high school boys in the movie are (6) _____ the men in the play. Cameron, who likes Bianca, enlists Patrick to woo Kat so that he can date Bianca. Cameron even pretends to tutor Bianca in French to get close to her.

Finally, the two stories have (7) _____ . In Shakespeare's play, Petruchio and Katherina fall in love after a series of arguments and misunderstandings. In the movie, Patrick and Kat fall in love despite a rocky courtship and many upsets. Furthermore, in both the movie and the play, Bianca falls for the sincere but not wealthy suitor, Cameron, and has to trick her father in order to be with him.

As you can see, the characters, plot, and resolution in *10 Things I Hate about You* are (8) _____ the characters, plot, and resolution in *The Taming of the Shrew*.

Practice 2

Write the signals and phrases that indicate comparison to complete the essay.

similar	the same	equally
Not only	both	but they also
common	as likely as	a number of similar geological features

Similarities between Earthquakes and Volcanoes

Volcanoes and earthquakes are geological events that share
(1) _____ origins, processes, and geography.

Volcanoes and earthquakes have similar origins. Geologists have discovered that the top layer of the Earth, called the crust, is made up of unstable plates of rock that move and shift. Underneath the crust is a mantle made up of hot, molten rock. Scientists who study plate tectonics, or the movement of the Earth's crust, have discovered that plate tectonics is responsible for (2) _____ volcanoes and earthquakes. Shifting plates can cause vibrations and tremors along fault lines or explosions of hot molten rock from the mantle.

(3) _____ do volcanoes and earthquakes share similar origins in the Earth's crust, (4) _____ are caused by the same processes. There are three types of plate shifting when the Earth's crust moves. Each can either cause an earthquake or a volcano, and, depending on the conditions, one may be (5) _____ the other. In a convergent boundary shift, two plates collide head-on, and one plate will often buckle underneath the other. Additionally, two plates can move side by side in a transform boundary shift. Convergent and transforming boundary shifts in the Earth's crust are (6) _____ likely to result in a volcano or an earthquake. By contrast, in a divergent boundary shift two plates drift apart and leave the mantle exposed. This shift, unlike the other two, most often results in volcanoes because the gap between the plates allows hot magma to explode out of the earth's crust.

In addition to having (7) _____ processes, the majority of volcanoes and earthquakes occur along (8) _____ fault lines. Fault lines form where two plates meet. One of the largest fault lines in the Western hemisphere is located at the edge of the Pacific Plate, which runs along the entire west coast of both North and South America. Some of the biggest earthquakes and volcanoes have been reported along this line.

To sum up, there are (9) _____ shared by earthquakes and volcanoes, though the results of an earthquake are different from those of a volcano. In an effort to better predict these devastating natural phenomena, geologists are learning more and more about them.

CONTRAST SIGNALS

Presentation

Contrast Signals

Use contrast signals in an essay to highlight differences among people, places, things, and concepts. There are two types of contrast signals: signals that indicate an unexpected result; and signals that indicate direct opposition.

The **thesis statement** introduces two to three similar people, places, things, or ideas (main idea) and then outlines how they are different. (the controlling idea)

Body paragraphs divide the thesis statement into a number of differences that support and provide evidence for the thesis. The sub-topics appear in a logical order (most to least important, for example). Use contrast transition signals to link sentences within the paragraph and to link the paragraphs to each other.

Example:

Thesis:

> In the last 25 years, technology has drastically changed how we communicate, and there are a **number of important differences between** the way we communicate now **and** the way we communicated then.

Topic Sentences for the Body Paragraphs:

> Twenty-five years ago, telephones were **larger** and **less** mobile than they are today.

> In the past, one could either speak or leave a message when calling; **by contrast,** telephones today can be used for **different types** of messaging, such as voice mail or texting.

> The postal system is **not as successful as** it was 25 years ago because of the many **faster** ways to send written communications.

Transition Signals for Contrast:

Comparatives: *more/less…than, the most/least…*

Sentence Connectors: *however, nevertheless, nonetheless, still* (unexpected result)
in contrast, on the other hand, on the contrary, in/by comparison (direct opposition)

Coordinating Conjunctions: *yet (*unexpected result*), but* (direct opposition)

Paired Conjunctions: *not…but* (direct opposition)*; not as…as*

Subordinating Conjunctions: *although, though, even though (*unexpected result*) while, whereas* (direct opposition)

Prepositions: *despite, in spite of* (unexpected result)

different from, dissimilar to, unlike, instead of (direct opposition)

Practice 1

Write the signals and phrases that indicate contrast to complete the essay.

a smaller group	Another important difference between	as opposed to	a better scientific reputation than
but now		Unlike conventional medicine	
more heavily	some of the differences between		In contrast

Differences between Naturopathic and Conventional Medicine

In Western society, practitioners of naturopathic medicine used to be a rarity, (1) _____ naturopathic medicine has become more scientifically accepted. In fact, health insurance companies now often cover naturopathic doctors as well as conventional doctors. When deciding whether to visit a naturopathic or conventional doctor, it is important to understand (2) _____ them.

First of all, conventional medicine has traditionally enjoyed (3) _____ naturopathic medicine. Part of the reason naturopathic medicine has had such difficulty becoming established as a respected scientific practice is because of its roots in folk remedies and ancient Eastern traditions. These are considered to be unscientific by some. (4) _____ , conventional medicine grew out of the trial and error of scientific inquiry. Medical practices had to be tested before they were accepted. Today, just like modern medicine, naturopathic medicine employs scientific inquiry. However, naturopathic studies, when compared to conventional medical studies, are often tested on (5) _____ of participants, and sometimes they rely (6) _____ on qualitative (7) _____ quantitative methods of research.

(8) _____ naturopathic and conventional medicine has to do with how a patient is treated. When a person goes to a conventional doctor, the doctor will focus on treating the problem. For example, if someone goes to a conventional doctor with back pain, he or she will usually leave with a prescription to reduce the pain. Conventional doctors often treat only the immediate problem. By contrast, in naturopathic medicine, one is expected to go to the doctor to prevent illness. (9) _____ , treatments in naturopathic medicine often involve lifestyle changes and holistic remedies for building the systems of the body. If a person comes in with back pain, a naturopathic doctor might prescribe exercise or massage or suggest vitamins to help the nervous system cope with stress.

Both conventional and naturopathic medical practices provide treatment for a variety of different illnesses, although the relationship with science and the approach to illness can be quite different.

Practice 2

Write the signals and phrases that indicate contrast to complete the essay.

| However | Despite | Nevertheless | though |
| different from | But | But in the last few years, | In contrast |

Cities Now Growing Faster Than Suburbs

Every decade since the invention of the automobile, suburban populations in the United States have grown at a faster rate than cities have. (1) _____ that trend has been moving in the opposite direction. Cities are now growing faster than suburbs, as more Americans are choosing city life over the roomier, quieter expanses of suburbia.

Before 2010, suburbs were growing at triple the rate of cities.
(2) _____ from 2010 to 2011, cities with a population of at least a million grew at a faster rate than suburbs. This reversal was largely an effect of the crumbling suburban housing market brought on by the recession of 2007–2009. Before the recession, many people were buying new homes and leaving the cities, and suburbs were booming. (3) _____ , the recession forced many of those potential suburbanites to put their moving plans on hold and remain where they were—in the cities—or even move back in with their parents. On top of that, today's suburbs, with their endless sprawl, long commutes, and fewer cultural attractions, are much
(4) _____ their village-like predecessors and have less and less appeal.

(5) _____ , cities are luring more residents, particularly young people, by cleaning up downtowns, offering more cultural attractions, and creating more job opportunities, as factories are leaving and high-tech companies are moving in. As a result, many major U.S. cities that were population losers in the 2000s saw a population growth in 2011. (6) _____ the overall growth, however, some cities still lost population in 2011. (7) _____ , they did so at a slower rate than in previous years.

Experts say that this population shift from suburbs to cities is evidence of the profound effects of the recession of the late 2000s, and (8) _____ it will not spell the end of migration to the suburbs, it has definitely slowed it down.

CAUSE AND EFFECT SIGNALS

Cause and Effect Signals

Use cause signals to indicate the causes, or reasons, for something happening. Use effect signals to indicate the effects, or results, for an event, occurrence, phenomenon, issue, or problem.

A **thesis statement** presents an event, occurrence, phenomenon, issue, or problem (main idea) and reviews the causes, effects, or both (the controlling idea).

Body paragraphs divide the thesis statement into causes and/or effects to provide evidence for the claim that is made. The sub-topics appear in a specific order (most to least significant, for example). Use cause and effect transition signals to link sentences within the paragraph and to link the paragraphs to each other.

Example:

Thesis Statement:

The reasons that *children become bullies are quite complex.*

Topic Sentences for the Body Paragraphs:

One reason *children bully is that there is too little discipline or supervision at home or in school.*

In addition, *bullies often mirror behavior that they learn at home;* ***therefore***, *many children who bully have also been bullied by their older siblings or parents.*

A third and final reason for bullying is that a bully acquires cachet among his or her peers by hurting someone else.

Types of Cause and Effect Signals:

Sentence Connectors: *as a result, as a consequence, therefore, thus, consequently, hence, for this reason*

Coordinating Conjunctions: *so, for*

Subordinating Conjunctions: *because, as, since*

Other Phrases: *to result in, to cause, to have an effect on, to affect, the cause of, the reason for, thereby*

Practice 1

Write the signals and phrases that indicate cause and effect to complete the essay.

because the symptoms	because of their PTSD	As a result	In order to avoid
	as a consequence	can be affected in	as their behavior
can affect anyone	caused by combat	the effects of	

PTSD and Returning Veterans

PTSD (Post-Traumatic Stress Disorder) is a condition that (1) _____ who has suffered a severe event. It's normal for a person who has suffered trauma to have initial feelings of fear and anxiety; however, people with PTSD continue to have symptoms related to the traumatic event long after it has ended. Many veterans returning from war suffer from PTSD. The difficulty that vets have in re-integrating into society when they return from battle is well-known; nevertheless, the psychological problems (2) _____ are just now being understood. PTSD in veterans can be particularly damaging (3) _____ often go unrecognized, and veterans often don't feel comfortable seeking treatment. It is important for family members and friends of veterans to look for (4) _____ PTSD in order to get them the help that they need. There are two types of PTSD symptoms to be aware of.

Some veterans re-live their trauma. (5) _____ , they often experience nightmares and other sleep disturbances when they return from combat. If a veteran is having nightmares and flashbacks a few months after returning, there may be nothing to worry about. One should be more concerned about PTSD if the nightmares are accompanied by flashbacks and hyper-sensitivity to current events. For example, the sound of gunfire from a TV show can be very startling and upsetting for someone with this disorder. Veterans with PTSD can't stop thinking about painful memories, and, (6) _____ , they often overreact to everyday situations with fear and anxiety.

Unlike those who continually re-experience trauma, other veterans often repress their feelings of panic and fear. Some veterans with PTSD may seem completely uninterested in daily life and depressed (7) _____. They may stop doing activities they previously loved. They may stop seeing friends. (8) _____ their feelings and memories, they may begin to use drugs or alcohol. Veterans with these symptoms can be difficult to diagnose (9) _____ may not immediately seem connected to PTSD.

Thus, veterans experiencing PTSD (10) _____ two very different ways. Scientists are not sure why some people get PTSD and others do not, but it's clear that someone suffering from PTSD will need to get help to cope with his or her disorder. If friends and family are aware of the potential problems veterans may experience, they may encourage those who suffer from PTSD to get help before their symptoms escalate.

Practice 2

Write the signals and phrases that indicate cause and effect to complete the essay.

effect	therefore	consequences	causes
results in	because	the cause	One reason

Causes of Climate Change

The majority of scientists in the field of climatology do not debate whether or not climate change is a reality. What is under debate, by a small minority, is whether or not the actions of humans are (1) _____ of climate change, also known as global warming.

We have known about the so-called greenhouse (2) _____ for more than a century. Carbon dioxide, which is produced by burning fossil fuels, absorbs infrared radiation (heat) and turns it into a kind of blanket, warming the Earth. This (3) _____ an elevation of temperatures.
Other (4) _____ of climate change include depletion of the ozone layer and loss of forests, which help convert carbon dioxide into oxygen.

(5) _____ that scientists worry about climate change is that its effects are severe. For example, both extremes of Earth's water cycle (drought and flooding) intensify. Also, as warmer temperatures melt ice sheets, sea levels rise, causing danger to coastal cities.

A tiny minority of scientists argue that we need not worry (6) _____ thousands of years of evidence from within Earth's ice sheets suggests that the Earth has warmed and cooled cyclically, with or without the presence of humans. While this is true, there is undeniable evidence that human behavior is contributing greatly to current changes, many of which could have disastrous (7) _____ on our way of life on Earth. We would (8) _____ do well to make some changes while we still can.

Describing a Process

Model Essay

How to Become a Citizen

Every year, at least one million immigrants come to live in the United States. There are many reasons people from around the world want to settle there. Some reasons people leave their home countries for the U.S. include study, work, and reuniting with their families. Many of these new immigrants hope for a long future in this new country, but the process to citizenship can be long and confusing. If you are interested in becoming a citizen, you should be aware of the requirements years before you apply. There are a number of procedures you should follow if you are interested in becoming a citizen.

At the beginning of the process, it is important to understand eligibility requirements. For example, you must be at least 18 years old. You must either have a green card or be married to a U.S. citizen in order to begin the process. At the time you apply, you will have to prove that the U.S. has been your main residence for a certain number of years. This means you will have to be physically present in the country for most of the waiting period.

Next, you will need to prove that you do not have a criminal record. The government will not give citizenship to people who don't obey the law. There is a requirement to be of "good moral character" to become a citizen. To be a citizen you must not have committed serious crimes. You also must pay taxes if you are working. Above all, you must not lie on any part of your application. In addition, if you are a man between the ages of 18 and 26 years, you may be required to sign up for the Selective Service. Once you have established your eligibility, you should prepare for the citizenship tests. There are two required tests you will take as a part of the citizenship process. The first one tests your English language skills. It's a good idea to enroll in low-cost or free ESL classes. You can find these classes at local colleges, in community centers, or at your neighborhood library. The second one tests your knowledge of U.S. history, the government, and citizen rights and responsibilities. There are many books, websites, and free civics classes available to help you prepare for this test.

To sum up, the process for becoming a U.S. citizen can take many years, so it is important to plan carefully. If you are aware of the requirements beforehand, you will be prepared to complete your application when the time comes.

Write an essay about one of the topics listed below or the topic your teacher assigns. You will have 50 minutes.

Describing a Process

An essay can describe a **process,** procedure, plan, or sequence of events. In this type of essay, a topic is divided into steps, and each one is discussed in a separate body paragraph. All essays have three main parts: an **introduction paragraph,** a number of **body paragraphs,** and a **concluding paragraph.**

An introduction paragraph starts with an **opening hook** to get the reader interested in the topic. The introductory paragraph explains the purpose of the writing and includes the *thesis statement.*

The thesis statement describes the process or event the essay will discuss. This is the main idea of the paragraph. It will also indicate the number of steps or events involved or provide the name of the stages or phases involved. This is the controlling idea.

Body paragraphs divide the thesis statement into a number of individual events, stages, phases, or steps that further support and provide evidence for the thesis statement. These are the sub-topics, and you should try to put the sub-topics into order (e.g., most to least important, general to specific, familiar to unknown, or simple to complex). Use chronological transition signals to link sentences within paragraphs and between paragraphs.

Transition Signals for Describing a Process:

Opening Expressions

the process of, the procedure for, a plan to, the five stages of, several phases of

Sentence Connectors

first, first of all, second, third, next, last, finally, also, in addition, moreover, furthermore

Subordination

after, as, as soon as, before, since, until, when, while

Other Phrases

The first/second step, day, etc.

later that week, after, for x months, in 2013, several days ago, in the next minutes

A concluding paragraph summarizes the main point and sub-points and concludes the essay with a final thought, suggestion, or prediction related to the reason for writing.

1 In a five- or six-paragraph essay, describe an everyday scientific or mechanical process you are familiar with, such as boiling water or starting a car.
2 In a five- or six-paragraph essay, describe how a caterpillar turns into a butterfly. You may describe another similar natural transformation you are familiar with, such as an animal growing from a baby into an adult.
3 In a five- or six-paragraph essay, describe the process of learning to speak or write in a new language.

Editing Checklist

- Are the grammar, sentence structure, mechanics, and punctuation correct?
- Is the vocabulary appropriate?
- Are the words spelled correctly?
- Is the essay well organized, well developed, and clear?

_____

_____

_____

_____

_____

_____

_____

_____

_____

_____

_____

_____

_____

_____

_____

_____

_____

_____

_____

_____

_____

Writing a Problem–Solution Essay

Model Essay

Protecting Your Privacy

The Internet has completely changed modern society. People now have access to information, services, and resources anytime. The Internet has made privacy almost impossible. Nonetheless, there are some very effective actions anyone can take to protect his or her privacy.

There are serious consequences to having your information online. Every time you go on the Internet, your personal information is saved on a data farm somewhere. Companies track your online information in order to sell you products. For example, Facebook looks at what you write and share with your friends and family. Then, it changes the ads on your page. Your private information is not just available to companies, it is also available to the average person. Anybody can search and find your address, phone number, and photos. Some people have been fired because of information they reveal on social networking sites. Many others have experienced harassment or even identity theft.

Lack of privacy online can be frightening, but there are a few solutions to this problem. First, people should regularly review what information about them is online. If you want to see what companies and other people can see about you, try googling yourself. It is a good idea to use your full name and even the cities you have lived in to see what there is about you. If you are uncomfortable with the information you find, you can ask the site's webmaster to remove it. Next, you can take security measures. Most of your private information online comes from your email and social networking accounts. However, it is easy to protect your privacy when you use these accounts. Facebook, Gmail, and Yahoo allow you to change your account settings to keep your information private and safe. For instance, on Facebook you can set up your account so that only your friends can see your information. Remember that the default setting allows everyone, including strangers, to see your information. You therefore have to take time to make your online presence secure.

The Internet can be an amazing tool. In contrast, unwanted advertising, identity theft, and harassment can make being online unsettling or even dangerous. There are two ways to protect your privacy online. Check your information regularly, and take action to ensure safety. If you are careful, you can enjoy the Internet without worrying about the safety of you or your family.

Write an essay about one of the topics listed below or the topic your teacher assigns. You will have 50 minutes.

Problem-Solution Essay

A **problem-solution essay** discusses a problem and ways to solve it. All essays have three main parts: an *introduction,* a *body* with a number of paragraphs, and a *conclusion.*

The introduction paragraph opens with a description of the problem. An introduction might describe the importance of the problem. The **thesis statement** might discuss causes of the problem and solutions.

Body paragraphs divide into a number of sub-topics that provide support for the thesis statement. Each body paragraph has a topic sentence and supporting sentences. **The topic sentence** identifies the solution and **supporting sentences** provide facts, examples, details, and explanations.

A concluding paragraph summarizes the possible solutions for the problem and provides a final thought. Some strategies include drawing a conclusion about the problem or making a prediction about the success of the solutions offered.

1 Write a five- or six-paragraph essay describing an urban problem and solutions for improving the situation.
2 Write a five- or six-paragraph essay describing some challenges faced by families today and solutions for making it easier to face those challenges.
3 Write a five- or six-paragraph essay describing a political conflict you've heard about in the news and possible solutions for resolving that conflict.

Editing Checklist

- Are the grammar, sentence structure, mechanics, and punctuation correct?
- Is the vocabulary appropriate? Are the words spelled correctly?
- Is the essay well organized, well developed, and clear?

_____

_____

_____

_____

_____

_____

_____

_____

WRITING ASSIGNMENTS

Writing an Argumentative Essay

Presentation

Model Essay

State-Subsidized College Education

In the current economy, many students graduating from high school face a very difficult choice. They wonder whether they should take a low-paying, entry-level job or enroll in college. If they do enroll in college, they may come out of school with better job prospects, but they often finish with huge debts. In uncertain times, many students have begun to wonder whether a college education is worth the time and money. However, job trends show that there are fewer and fewer well-paying jobs for high school graduates. Since a college degree has become necessary to finding a well-paying job, it is a wonder that the government has not considered ways to make college education more affordable than it is. Although many opponents to state-subsidized college education would disagree, there are several important reasons to make college education affordable for anyone who wants to attend.

Opponents of state-subsidized college education feel that a college education is optional and mostly unnecessary. In the 19th and early 20th centuries, schools prepared students to work on farms or at manufacturing jobs. People didn't need to continue past high school. A person was able to obtain a job that provided a stable, middle-class income after high school. However, the United States has changed dramatically in the last 50 years; college education is no longer regarded by many as unnecessary.

The first reason for providing an affordable college education is to prepare people for the changing job market. Farming and manufacturing jobs have all but disappeared in the current economy. Now, the majority of stable, middle-class jobs require a college education. In fact, current unemployment rates in a slow economy reflect this trend. According to the U.S. Department of Labor, the unemployment rate for college graduates is less than six percent, while the unemployment rate for high school graduates is more than 11 percent. While having a college education doesn't guarantee a job in a slow economy, it does make it easier to find one.

Secondly, a college education has become too expensive for students to pay by themselves. As colleges are becoming more and more expensive, the federal government has steadily been reducing the amount of financial aid it offers students. More and more students are saddled with huge amounts of debt before they get their first job. On average, college graduates can make $10,000 more than high school graduates, but they may end up spending that extra money paying off their student loan debt. Americans must ask themselves if they want the next generation to struggle to pay off education debts instead of investing in the economy, buying a house, and preparing for retirement.

Finally, it is the government's responsibility to provide an education that creates a well-trained workforce. In the United States, public education was created to prepare children for citizenship and the workplace. Opponents of publicly funded college education might argue that the United States government cannot afford such an expense. With a slow economy, high unemployment, and a large national debt, their fears about adding another burden to the national budget are well-founded. Nevertheless, the question is, "Can we afford not to invest in the future of the United States?" We know that well-paying jobs in the United States require a higher level of education. Thus, we need to provide a well-trained workforce capable of doing the jobs that are currently available. Otherwise, companies will either move their business overseas or import workers who have the right qualifications.

To sum up, the changing American economy has made a college or professional degree necessary. Therefore, the American government should make this education possible. Moreover, other countries have shown state-subsidized education is possible. By raising taxes, the government can ensure that students will graduate with limited student loan burdens.

Write an essay about one of the topics listed below or the topic your teacher assigns. You will have 50 minutes.

Argumentative Essay

An **argumentative essay** gives the writer's position about a controversial issue and supports the point of view with reasons and evidence. In writing that aims to persuade the reader of a particular view, an argument has credibility if it has data to support it. Also, the writer should address opposing viewpoints and arguments. All essays have three main parts: an ***introduction,*** a ***body*** with a number of paragraphs, and a ***conclusion.***

The introduction paragraph starts with an ***opening hook*** to get the reader interested the issue. The introductory paragraph also explains the purpose of the writing, why the issue is important, and includes the ***thesis statement,*** which provides the writer's point of view on the issue.

The thesis statement states the issue (main idea) and the writer's position or view (the controlling idea).

Body paragraphs divide the thesis statement into a number of reasons for the writer's claim, including rebuttals to any strong counterarguments. Rebuttals and reasons are supported with evidence, such as facts, examples, anecdotes, expert opinions, and statistics. Ideas can be organized in block or point-by-point pattern.

- In a Block Pattern, provide first a rebuttal to counterarguments. Then support your argument with data and reasons.
- In a Point-by-Point Pattern, organize the arguments by "points." In each paragraph, provide a rebuttal to counterarguments. Give the reasons and data for your argument. Use this pattern when your arguments are closely related to the counterarguments.

A concluding paragraph summarizes the main point and sub-points and finishes up the essay with a final thought, suggestion, or prediction related to the reason for writing.

Transition Signals for Persuasive Writing	
Presenting Arguments I think/feel/believe, in my opinion, to me, it is my belief that, it seems to me, from my point of view, I am certain that	
Presenting Counterarguments Opponents of ____ are certain that . . . , Some people feel/ believe that . . . , Many think/say that . . . , It may be true that . . .	
Presenting Rebuttal	**Presenting Reasons and Evidence**
Sentence Connectors However, Nevertheless, On the other hand Subordination Although, Even though, While, Whereas	**Sentence Connectors** first, first of all, second, third, next, last, finally, also, in addition, moreover, furthermore
Coordination But, yet, not only . . . but also, neither . . . nor	**Coordination** and, both . . . and, not only . . . but also
Other Phrases Despite the fact that, In spite of the fact that	**Other Phrases** One/ Another/ An additional/ The first *reason, factor,* etc. In addition to *noun phrase,*

1 Write a five- or six-paragraph essay arguing for or against capital punishment.

2 Write a five- or six-paragraph essay arguing for or against nuclear energy.

Editing Checklist

- Are the grammar, sentence structure, mechanics, and punctuation correct?
- Is the vocabulary appropriate? Are the words spelled correctly?
- Is the essay well organized, well developed, and clear?

_____

_____

_____

_____

_____

_____

_____

_____

_____

_____

_____

_____

_____

_____

_____

_____

_____

_____

_____

_____

_____

_____

Writing a Fictional Story

Presentation

Model Fictional Story

Nothing Ever Changes

The clock in the tower of the town hall said what it always said, three o'clock. The large hand was, as usual, on the twelve, and the small hand was, as always, on the three. Those hands had been in that same position for as long as Virgie could remember. Just like the town of Mallow, they never changed.

To Virgie Owen it seemed that there never had been and never would be anything exciting or interesting in Mallow. Not like Paris. Or London. Or even Des Moines. And, of course, she was stuck here. At the age of 16, she didn't have a lot of options. Her parents certainly weren't going to let her go willingly, and running away was such a bad idea. For one thing, she'd have to take the bus.

Just as Virgie said the word bus, the Greyhound turned the corner. There wasn't any actual station in Mallow. The town was too small for that. But you could buy a ticket in the drugstore and wait just inside the door. The bus stopped, sat at the curb for a couple of minutes, and then drove away, revealing a tall young woman in jeans and a dark green shirt, carrying a backpack and standing on the curb. She walked straight to Virgie, stuck out her hand in a forthright manner and said, "Hi. I'm Jane, and I need a job."

"Could you paint a barn?" asked Virgie. "A small barn?"

Jane smiled a wide, engaging smile. "I can paint anything on the planet," she said, "and paint it better than you can easily imagine."

So Virgie took Jane home with her and introduced her to Mr. Owen, Virgie's father. Mr. Owen hesitated. "There's no place to stay in town," he said. "No hotel. No boarding house."

"What about the barn?" said Jane. "I have a blanket in my backpack and I'm a barn sleeper from way back."

It took Jane only a few minutes to get Mr. Owen to come around. She ate dinner that evening with the family, slept that night in the barn, and looked over the available paint in the shed first thing in the morning. Mr. Owen said to use the red paint, but when Virgie came home after school, she saw every color in the rainbow. At the top of the barn, under the room, Jane had painted a blue sky, with white clouds tinged in pink. Below that purple mountains with white snowcaps loomed over a field of green. Jane was scattering yellow and white wildflowers through the field as Virgie approached.

"Wow," said Virgie, and Jane smiled her wide smile.

"Lovely, isn't it?" said Jane.

"But my father . . ." began Virgie.

> "He's seen it," said Jane. "And I don't have to paint it over just so long as I paint Owen's Hardware up there in the sky. Which I will do when the blue paint dries. There's something you need to know, Virgie. Nothing ever happens unless you do it yourself. And nothing ever changes except you. Now, tomorrow I have a job at the town hall. The mayor hired me to fix the clock. Would you like to assist me?"

Write a fictional text about one of the topics listed below or the topic your teacher assigns. You will have 50 minutes.

Writing a Fictional Story

A fictional story often describes an event. Fiction writers often show rather than tell. That is, they use dialogue and description to convey their meaning, rather than making direct statements about it. There are a number of elements common to many fictional stories:

- The **characters** (those who act or whom the action affects. The story is often from one or more characters' perspectives. It may also detail their feelings or thoughts.)

- The **setting** (where and when the story happened)

- The **plot** (recounts the most important moments of the story: the problem, the climax, the resolution)

- A logical **sequence of events** (stories generally have a beginning, middle, and end, in that order)

- A **point of view** (the person telling the story, whether it's a narrator or one of the characters)

When writing a fictional story choose a single event and organize your ideas. Consider the following structure:

- **An introduction** introduces the characters, the setting, and the plot (who, what, where, when, why, and how).

- **The body** describes the event or the plot. The paragraphs can be organized using various methods, such as chronological order, spatial order, etc. whichever organization best suits the story. Usually a problem is presented followed by a climax (the most exciting moment in the story) and ending with a resolution.

- **The conclusion** reflects on the resolution of the story. You might consider one of two strategies: you can explain what was learned; or you can report a change in behavior or thinking.

1 Write a short five- or six-paragraph fictional story about a person who makes a surprising discovery.

2 Write a short five- or six-paragraph fictional story from the point of view of an animal.

3 Write a short five- or six-paragraph fictional story from the point of view of a child.

Editing Checklist

- Are the grammar, sentence structure, mechanics, and punctuation correct?
- Is the vocabulary appropriate? Are the words spelled correctly?
- Is the story well organized, well developed, and clear?

_____

_____

_____

_____

_____

_____

_____

_____

_____

_____

_____

_____

_____

_____

_____

_____

_____

_____

_____

_____

Writing a Speech or Oral Presentation

> **Presentation**
>
> ## Model Outline for a Speech or Oral Presentation
>
> **I.** Introduction
>
>   **a.** Quote: "If you fail to plan, you plan to fail."
>
>   **b.** Many students end up paying more money for college because they don't know where, when, and how to get money to pay for college.
>
>   **c.** Today, I'm going to talk about the steps you will need to complete in order to apply for financial aid at this college.
>
> **II.** Body
>
>   **a.** Different types of financial aid
>
>   1. Federal money
>
>   2. State funds
>
>   3. Private scholarships
>
>   **b.** Collecting information
>
>   1. When to start
>
>   2. What you need to complete the Free Application for Federal Student Aid (FAFSA)
>
>   3. Finding out about scholarships
>
>   **c.** Making an appointment with the Financial Aid office
>
>   1. What to bring
>
>   2. What to ask
>
> **III.** Conclusion
>
>   **a.** To conclude, it is important to start early and look for funds from multiple sources.
>
>   **b.** Your financial aid specialist at the college is there to help you navigate the system. Make an appointment with one today.

Write an outline for a speech about one of the topics listed below or the topic your teacher assigns. You will have 50 minutes.

Speeches and Presentations

Short speeches and longer oral presentations with visual aids follow the same structure: an **introduction, a body with a number of main points,** and a **conclusion.**

The introduction starts with an *opening hook* to get the listener interested in the topic. Examples of a hook might be a funny or personal story, an important fact, or a famous saying. The introduction also includes any *background* information about the topic that might be unfamiliar to the audience. Finally, the speaker should clearly state the *topic and purpose* of the speech and provide an agenda of points to be made.

The body of a speech is divided into a number of *sub-topics* that further support and provide evidence for any claims. All points should be illustrated and explained with *supporting details* (facts, examples, statistics, expert opinions, anecdotes). Use *logical order transition signals* to organize your ideas. Use *visual aids and techniques for audience participation* (graphs, photos, research, activities, handouts, and discussion questions) to support your claims in a longer presentation.

The conclusion provides a *re-statement* of the main idea and sub-topics and finishes up the speech with a *final thought* related to the main idea of the speech. Examples of a final thought are a call to action, recommendation, or final observation.

It's a good idea to organize your thoughts in a formal outline before you give a speech:

I Introduction
   a Hook
   b Background information
   c Topic, Purpose, and Main Points

II Body
   a Point 1
      1 Supporting details
      2 Visual aids
      3 Techniques for audience participation
   b Point 2
   c Point 3
   d Point 4

III Conclusion
   a Summary of Main Points
   b Final Comment

1 Prepare an outline for a 15-minute speech or presentation to tell the story of how you chose to study English.

2 Prepare an outline for a 15-minute speech or presentation to give advice to parents about bringing up their children.

Editing Checklist

- Are the grammar, sentence structure, mechanics, and punctuation correct?
- Is the vocabulary appropriate? Are the words spelled correctly?
- Is the outline well organized, well developed, and clear?

_____

_____

_____

_____

_____

WRITING ASSIGNMENTS

Writing a Résumé and Cover Letter

JOB ANNOUNCEMENT

The Northshore YMCA is looking for a temporary summer entry-level *administrative assistant* whose values align with our organization's values: respect, responsibility, honesty, and caring. Job responsibilities include answering phones, assisting YMCA clients, and writing business correspondence, reports, brochures, and other texts. Requirements include the following:

- State-approved first aid certification and CPR certification
- Two years or more of related experience

Speaking knowledge of Spanish and experience with diverse populations preferred.

COVER LETTER

Mr. Anthony Delpina
1200 Broadway Avenue
Seattle, WA 98122

April 14, 2013

Northshore YMCA
118 NE 15th St.
Seattle, WA 98122

RE: Position as an Administrative Assistant

I am writing in reference to the position as administrative assistant at the Northshore YMCA. I believe I have the qualities you are looking for and will make a positive addition to your team.

I am interested in working for the YMCA because your mission to help others and respond to the needs of individuals and families in the community closely aligns with my own values. While I do not have a lot of work experience in office administration, I recently received a certificate in office assistance at Central College. I am highly trained in all basic computer applications, and I have strong writing and editing skills. For the last two years, I have been volunteering in the office at my church for 15 hours a week. As a volunteer, I answer questions, assist church participants, write business letters and other correspondence, and file important documents. In addition to my strong education background and volunteer experience, I am able to work with a variety of people. I speak fluent Spanish and Tagalog, so I would be particularly helpful to your Hispanic and Filipino clients.

I have attached a copy of my résumé with this cover letter. I look forward to answering any questions you may have in a personal interview. Please feel free to contact me at a.delpina@gmail.com or call me at (206) 322-2345. Thank you in advance for your consideration.

Best regards,

Anthony Delpina

ENC: Résumé

FUNCTIONAL Résumé

Mr. Anthony Delpina
1200 Broadway Avenue
Seattle, WA 98122
(206) 322-2345
a.deplpina@gmail.com

OBJECTIVE: To obtain a position as an office assistant

AREAS OF ACCOMPLISHMENT:
Customer Service
- Able to interpret client concerns to help them find what they want
- Able to answer telephones and handle messages in a professional manner
- Able to work with diverse populations
- Able to communicate effectively in Spanish and Tagalog, as well as English

Office Skills
- Copying, sorting, and filing office documents using different record-keeping systems
- Accurate typing (40 wpm) and data entry (80 kpm)
- Excellent writing and editing skills

EDUCATION:
CPR and First Aid Certification (Expected Completion: May 2013)
Central Community College, Seattle, WA
Certificate, Office Assistant 2009–2012
ESL Classes 2007–2009

EXPERIENCE:
Office Volunteer, St. Paul's Church, Seattle, WA 2010–2012
Sales Clerk, Harper's Department Store, Bellevue, WA 2008–2010
Driver, Grocery Delivery, Tukwila, WA 2004–2008

Write a résumé and a cover letter about one of the topics listed below or the topic your teacher assigns. You will have 50 minutes.

You will need a **résumé** and a **cover letter** every time you apply for a job. Résumés list the most important experience, education, and skills for the job for which you are applying. You should update your résumé regularly. Cover letters explain why you are the most qualified person for the job. The purpose of the résumé and cover letter is to get an employer interested in interviewing you for the position. It is important to research the company and study the job description before writing your résumé and cover letter in order to tailor them to the job.

Information to Collect for Résumés and Cover Letters:

1. Volunteer and work experience for the last ten years

Job or volunteer title (name of the position)

The company name, city, and state or country

Responsibilities and duties

Start and end dates

2. Education starting with high school

School name, city, state or country

Diploma, degree, certificate, license, etc.

Field of study

Start and end dates

3. Special skills

Languages

Office skills (typing, filing, writing, computers)

Academic or professional awards

4. Professional references

Guidelines for Résumés:

Organize the sections to put your strongest qualifications first. Chronological résumés put work experience first. Functional résumés put education or skills first.

List most recent work history and education first.

Use short phrases beginning with action words (usually past tense verbs) to describe responsibilities and job duties.

Only include high school education if you haven't completed college or job training.

Guidelines for Cover Letters:

Use standard business letter rules and organization.

Only discuss the most important qualifications relevant to the job for which you are applying.

Prepare a résumé and cover letter to apply for your dream job. Focus on your abilities, talents, and experience.

Editing Checklist

- Are the grammar, sentence structure, mechanics, and punctuation correct?
- Is the vocabulary appropriate? Are the words spelled correctly?
- Are the resume and cover letter well organized, well developed, and clear?

_____

_____

_____

_____

_____

_____

_____

_____

_____

_____

_____

_____

_____

_____

_____

_____

_____

_____

_____

Writing a Business Memo

Presentation

MEMORANDUM

DATE: May 23, 2013
TO: Parents, Teachers, and Staff of Bright Horizons Elementary School
FROM: Andrew Hines, Director, Bright Horizons School
RE: New Safety Precautions for School Zone

The Bright Horizons community was saddened when one of our children was hit by a car outside of our school last week. Fortunately, the child in question was not seriously hurt; however, the incident has raised some concerns about some of our policies.

NEW POLICIES

The parent-teacher board has taken some precautions to increase the safety of our children when they are at school.

Drop-Offs and Pick-Ups

We have asked the city to install a one-way street sign on 8th Avenue to limit the amount of traffic coming and going on the street outside the school. Parents should be aware of the following new rules:

- You can travel only east on 8th Avenue now. Do not attempt to drive west on this street.
- Drive slowly. Stay under the 15 mph speed limit.
- Drop off and pick up your children in front of the school doors only. Do not drop off or pick up at the end of the block.
- If there is a line to drop off or pick up, wait your turn.
- Please respect other parents. Limit the amount of time you are parked to under 5 minutes.

New Personnel

In addition, we have hired two safety guards to wait at the school doors and assist children in getting to their cars safely. Let's welcome Amanda Greeves and James Clements, our new safety guards. They will be wearing yellow safety vests, and they will be at the doors from 7:00 to 9:00 a.m. for drop-offs and from 2:00 to 4:00 p.m. for pick-ups. If they ask you to do anything, please follow their instructions.

We hope these new precautions will prevent another accident. Please take some time to familiarize yourself with the new policies and let us know if you have any questions. My phone number is (206) 722-1110 and my email address is ahines@brighthorizons.edu.

Write a memo about one of the topics listed below or the topic your teacher assigns. You will have 50 minutes.

A Memorandum

A **memorandum** (memo) is a business correspondence written for people within a company or department to announce a change, recommend actions, or explain a process. Memos aren't as formal as business letters because they are internal, but we still avoid informal language, jokes, stories, personal information, slang, and abbreviations. Pay close attention to mechanics, organization, and format.

1 Title your memo first. It is enough to just say Memorandum in capital letters. It is common to use company letterhead with the title of the document.
2 Date your memo.
3 Include the list of people or departments the memo is addressed to.
4 Include the sender's information (full name, job title, and/or department).
5 Include the subject of the memo. The subject should be a 5–7 word phrase describing the purpose and topic of the memo.
6 Start with 1–2 sentences about the topic and purpose of the memo. Are you writing to announce a change, make a recommendation, or give an explanation?

Major Heading

Organize the topic into sections with major and minor headings.

Minor Heading

• Use lists to organize instructions, recommendations, or suggestions.
• Use bullets, numbers, or letters to separate points.

Close the memo with what you want to happen (a call to action). Give contact information (email and/or phone number). It's not necessary to give a closing.

1 Write a short business memo to inform employees about a visit to the office by colleagues from overseas.
2 Write a short business memo to inform employees about a renovation of their offices that will start later this year.

Editing Checklist

• Are the grammar, sentence structure, mechanics, and punctuation correct?
• Is the vocabulary appropriate? Are the words spelled correctly?
• Is the memo well organized, well developed, and clear?

_____

_____

_____

_____

Writing a Business Letter

Tammy Nguyen
341 NW Main Street
Seattle, WA 98103

February 14, 2013

Andrew Hines, Director
Bright Horizons Child Care
100 8th Avenue
Seattle, WA 98103

Dear Mr. Hines:

I am a student at Central College, and I am writing to you for information about jobs and opportunities in early childhood education.

I am in my first quarter of the early childhood education program at Central College though I don't plan to graduate until June 2014. I enrolled in this program when I lost my job in a local factory, so I am re-training for a new profession. I love working with children, and I am excited to be doing such important work, but I have a lot of questions. I met you recently when you gave a presentation about the early childhood education field in my Issues and Trends class at Central College. During your presentation, you mentioned that you would be willing to meet with any student to talk more about the early childhood education field and our job prospects after we graduate.

I was hoping you would be willing to meet with me for a short time to discuss my questions. I look forward to any insight and advice you would be willing to share. I plan to call you next week to discuss a date and time for an informational interview with you, but feel free to contact me at (206)-633-4637 or email me at tnyguyen@central.edu.

Sincerely,

Tammy Nguyen, ECE Student

Write a business letter about one of the topics listed below or the topic your teacher assigns. You will have 50 minutes.

Business Letter

A business letter is a formal letter written to ask a question, make a request, make a complaint, or apply for a job. Avoid informal language, jokes, stories, slang, and abbreviations. Pay close attention to mechanics, organization, and format.

Format:

HEADING:

1 Start with your full name and address. This information goes in the upper left corner.

2 Leave one space under the address; include the date below that.

3 Leave one space under the date. Then write the recipient's full name, company name, and address.

4 Leave one space. Then start the letter with a greeting. Use a title and the last name in the greeting for formal letters. For example, Dear Mr. Jones:

FIRST PARAGRAPH: Write one or two sentences about the purpose of the letter. Are you writing to make a request, express a concern about an issue, ask a question, or apply for a job?

SECOND PARAGRAPH: Explain more about the reason for writing. What information does the person need to complete your request, address the issue, answer your query, or give you an interview for a job?

THIRD PARAGRAPH: State what you want to happen as a result of the letter. Do you want the person to give you information, take an action, answer a question or give you an interview? Make sure you make your plans clear, give contact information, and thank the person for his or her time.

CLOSING:

1 Close the letter with a formal closing. For example: Sincerely, Best wishes, In closing, Thank you, Yours truly, etc.

2 Include spaces for your written signature in blue or black ink.

3 Type your full name.

1 Write a business letter from a company to its customers announcing a new product or service.

2 Write a business letter from a customer to a company asking for information about a new product.

Editing Checklist

- Are the grammar, sentence structure, mechanics, and punctuation correct?
- Is the vocabulary appropriate? Are the words spelled correctly?
- Is the business letter well organized, well developed, and clear?

_____

_____

_____

_____

_____

_____

_____

_____

_____

_____

_____

_____

_____

_____

_____

_____

_____

_____

_____

Writing a Summary

Model Summary

A Summary of "Get a Knife, Get a Dog, but Get Rid of Guns"

According to American political commentator Molly Ivins, gun use should be restricted in the United States because of the inherent danger guns pose to the security of the United States. In her essay "Get a Knife, Get a Dog, but Get Rid of Guns," she argues that the Second Amendment to the United States Constitution does not propose that every citizen should have the right to own a gun. In fact, as she points out, the Second Amendment ensures that the American people have only a "well-regulated militia," not that little boys carry guns or that religious cults possess an arsenal. Indeed, she feels that the Second Amendment has been grossly misinterpreted by people who oppose gun control. She compares gun ownership laws to the laws and regulations that exist for automobile owners. Ivins mentions that cars can also be dangerous, but constraints on total freedom, such as speed limits and stop signs, exist to prevent accidents. We should have similar regulations for gun ownership and licensing, she argues.

Furthermore, she highlights the decreasing need for guns in a society that is becoming more modern and urban. For Ivins, gun laws should require some kind of training and testing in order to guarantee that the gun owner is aware of the responsibilities of gun ownership. Finally, she discusses the strong language against regulation by groups such as the NRA (National Rifle Association). She alludes to its campaign to prevent existing laws from changing, and suggests that this small but vocal group is at least part of the reason many Americans die every year from gunshot wounds.

Ivins, Molly. "Get a Knife, Get a Dog, but Get Rid of Guns," *Nothin' but Good Times Ahead.* Vintage Books: New York, 1993. Print.

Write a summary about one of the topics listed below or the topic your teacher assigns. You will have 50 minutes.

1 Write a short summary of a news story you heard recently.

2 Write a short summary of a TV show you saw recently.

Writing a Summary

A **summary** briefly recounts the most important main points about a source text (book, article, lecture, workshop, website).

Summaries:

- include the main points, but not the supporting details
- describe the author's ideas using the student's own words
- don't include the student's opinion or interpretation
- are shorter than the original text
- include citations to avoid plagiarism

When writing a summary, organize your ideas in the following way:

- **A topic sentence** provides basic information about the source text: author, title, and type of text. It gives an overview of the topic.

- **Supporting sentences** state the main ideas of the source text: topic, purpose, supporting points. Relate these in your own words. It's OK to use important names and keywords. Avoid including supporting details, facts, and examples. Do not include your opinion or other ideas not discussed in the source.

- **A concluding sentence** re-states the overall main ideas found in the source text.

Editing Checklist

- Are the grammar, sentence structure, mechanics, and punctuation correct?
- Is the vocabulary appropriate? Are the words spelled correctly?
- Is the summary well organized, well developed, and clear?

_____

_____

_____

_____

_____

_____

_____

_____

_____

_____

_____

_____

_____

_____

Paraphrasing

Original Paragraph

MSW statistics from the Environmental Protection Agency

U. S. municipal solid waste is material discarded in United States towns and cities. Paper and paperboard account for 28 percent of municipal solid waste generated in 2011. Food waste accounted for 14.5 percent. Yard trimmings accounted for 13.5 percent. Plastics accounted for 12.7 percent. Metals accounted for 8.8 percent. Rubber, leather, and textiles (cloth) accounted for 8.2 percent, and wood for 6.4 percent. Glass made up 4.6 percent of all municipal solid waste generated, and other materials made up 3.3 percent. Of materials recycled, paper and paperboard were 52.8 percent and yard trimmings 22.2 percent (compost). Metals were 6.6 percent and glass 3.7 percent. Plastics made up only 3.1 percent, wood 2.7 percent, and food waste 1.6 percent. Other materials accounted for 5.3 percent of all recovered municipal solid waste.

Paraphrase

Information from the U. S. Environmental Protection Agency provides a picture of how Americans dispose of trash and garbage. The largest category of trash is paper and paperboard, which made up more than a quarter of solid waste in American towns and cities in 2011. That same year, paper and paperboard made up more than half of all recycled materials. Food waste was the next largest category of waste, making up almost 15 percent of MSW. But food waste accounted for only 1.6 percent of recycling. About 13.5 percent of all MSA was yard trimmings, and they accounted for almost a quarter of recycled material because they were composted. About 12.7 percent of all waste in 2011 was made of plastic. Plastics, on the other hand, made up only a little more than 3 percent of recycled materials. About 8.8 percent of waste was made of metal and about 8.2 percent of rubber, leather, or cloth. Metals were 6.6 percent of recycled materials, and rubber, leather, and cloth were not recycled enough to show up as a separated item on the recycling list. Wood, which was 6.4 percent, showed up on the recycling list at 2.7 percent, just below plastics and just above food waste.

Write a paraphrase about one of the topics listed below or the topic your teacher assigns. You will have 50 minutes.

Paraphrasing

A paraphrase recounts all of the main points and important supporting details about a source text, whether it is a book, article, lecture, workshop, or website.

Paraphrases:

When writing a paraphrase about a source, organize your ideas including:

- an introduction that cites the source information (author, title, and type of source) and gives an overview of the topic.
- a body that states the main ideas of the source (topic, purpose, supporting points) in your own words. It's OK to use important names and keywords. The body also includes supporting details, facts, and examples with an explanation. Do not include your opinion or other ideas not discussed in the source.
- a conclusion that re-states the overall main idea or ideas found in the source.

1 In no more than a few sentences, paraphrase a famous speech.

2 In no more than a few sentences, paraphrase a story you heard or read about in the news.

Editing Checklist

- Are the grammar, sentence structure, mechanics, and punctuation correct?
- Is the vocabulary appropriate? Are the words spelled correctly?
- Is the paraphrase well organized, well developed, and clear?

_____

_____

_____

_____

_____

_____

_____

_____

_____

_____

_____

_____

Writing a Journal

Model Journal Entry

Thursday evening.

Last night, I was watching the latest episode of *Glee*. I really like that show. The performers do their own music and dance routines, and they usually choose the most popular new songs, so it's a good way for me to figure out what is popular, which is not always easy for me. I just don't have that "thing" that tells some people what's new. I mean, *Glee* shows the latest fashions and trends, and I learn a lot when I watch the show.

Anyway, Tina, one of the main characters, said something about one of the outfits she was wearing. She said it was a new style of clothes called "steampunk." She was wearing these metal, futuristic goggles that reminded me of the goggles that pilots of small planes or motorcyclists wear. She also had a very feminine lacy dress on with a military fitted jacket.

I think I've seen this style before, but I didn't know it had a name. It sort of reminds me of the clothes in the movies *Sherlock Holmes* and *9*. You know, it's sort of old fashioned, sweet, and romantic, and I'm like that sometimes. But it's got these parts of it that are futuristic and industrial. And I'm like that, too. Steampunk seems like a combination of two very different times in history. And I can relate to that.

Write a journal entry about one of the topics listed below or the topic your teacher assigns. You will have 50 minutes.

Writing a Journal

People write journals not only for private use, but also for an audience online (blog) or in a classroom setting. There are a number of reasons for keeping a journal:

* To increase confidence and speed in writing without fear about a grade
* For self-exploration and creative expression
* To experiment with new ideas, vocabulary, and grammar structures

Types of Journals:

Diary – Write on a regular basis about your life, thoughts, and feelings for private or public consumption.

Free-writing – Write about any topic without correction or a grade. This kind of writing may be assigned by a teacher in class to practice fluency.

Guided Response Journals – Write about a specific topic assigned by the teacher.

Dialogue Journals – Write about a topic that is later reviewed and commented on by a classmate or the teacher.

Blogs – Write your personal opinion about different topics, and make your writing available online to the public.

Sample Topics:

- Write about an educational goal or career plan.
- Write about a challenge in your life and brainstorm some solutions.
- Write about your most or least favorite celebrity, landmark, style, or trend.
- Write about a current or historical event.
- Write about a time you felt happy, embarrassed, ashamed, or uncertain.
- Write about similarities and differences between people, places, and things.

1 Write a short journal entry about your progress in English.
2 Write a short journal entry about your plans for the year.

Editing Checklist

- Are the grammar, sentence structure, mechanics, and punctuation correct?
- Is the vocabulary appropriate? Are the words spelled correctly?
- Is the journal entry well organized, well developed, and clear?

_____

_____

_____

_____

_____

_____

_____

_____

_____

_____

_____

_____

_____

_____

_____

_____

_____

Analyzing a Literature or Media Piece

Presentation

Model Literary Analysis

"*Sonnet 30*" by William Shakespeare

When to the sessions of sweet silent thought

I summon up remembrance of things past,

I sigh the lack of many a thing I sought,

And with old woes new wail my dear time's waste:

Then can I drown an eye, unused to flow,

For precious friends hid in death's dateless night,

And weep afresh love's long since cancelled woe,

And moan the expense of many a vanished sight:

Then can I grieve at grievances foregone,

And heavily from woe to woe tell o'er

The sad account of fore-bemoanèd moan,

Which I new pay as if not paid before.

But if the while I think on thee, dear friend,

All losses are restored and sorrows end.

William Shakespeare's "*Sonnet 30*" is one of the most beautiful—and beautifully crafted—poems ever written. As a sonnet, it is well-made. As an example of effective and musical language, it is near perfection. And as an exploration of memory and its sorrows, it is insightful and moving.

The form of the poem is that of an English, or Shakespearean, sonnet. Like all sonnets, it has 14 lines, divided into an octet (eight lines) and a sestet (six lines). The octet is made of two four-line stanzas, rhyming alternate lines. The sestet is a four-line stanza, also rhyming alternate lines, and a rhymed couplet.

From the first line of the poem, Shakespeare's extraordinary mastery of his craft is apparent. Alliteration is seldom used as skillfully as in the repeated "s" sounds of "When to the sessions of sweet silent thought, I summon up . . ." And, smooth as those sounds are, the line does not flow too quickly. The poet uses the final "t" sounds of "sweet silent thought" to slow our tongues as he slows our thoughts.

As the poem continues, we encounter more alliteration, as well as other techniques that contribute to the music. There are the "w" sounds in "And with old woes new wail my dear time's waste . . ." and "death's dateless night." There is the repetition in "grieve at grievances foregone" and "Which I new pay as if not paid before."

Impressive as the craft of the sonnet is, its insight into memory is most important. The poet speaks of sighing for what he tried to get and didn't. He cries again for sadnesses of the past and time wasted. He mourns the loss of friends gone long ago and feels again the grief he thought had passed. Memory makes him experience all of these memories anew. But memory also gives him relief for his sadness because he thinks of his friend.

Write an analysis about one of the topics listed below or the topic your teacher assigns. You will have 50 minutes.

Literary Analysis

A **literary analysis** gives an overall impression about a theme in a story, performance, or movie. It's common to present a viewpoint on what the author says in his or her narrative. A literary analysis has three main parts: an **introduction,** a **body** with a number of paragraphs, and a **conclusion.**

An **introduction paragraph** starts with an **opening hook** to get the reader interested in the topic. The introductory paragraph explains the purpose of the writing and includes the **thesis statement.**

The thesis statement provides the name of the text you will analyze and identifies themes of the text and your perspective on them.

Body paragraphs divide the thesis statement into a number of sub-topics that further support and provide evidence for the thesis statement. Each sub-topic should be supported with evidence from different parts of the text (beginning, middle, and end) that support the thesis statement.

A **concluding paragraph** summarizes the body paragraphs and provides a final thought on the subject.

1 Write a five- or six-paragraph analysis of a movie with which you are familiar. Describe the plot and the characters, the characters' motivations, and the main theme. Evaluate how successfully you think the movie achieves its goal.

2 Write a five- or six-paragraph analysis of a TV show with which you are familiar. Describe the format of the show, the people who appear in it, and the main purpose of the show. Evaluate how successfully you think the show achieves its goal.

Editing Checklist

- Are the grammar, sentence structure, mechanics, and punctuation correct?
- Is the vocabulary appropriate? Are the words spelled correctly?
- Is the analysis well organized, well developed, and clear?

_____

_____

_____

_____

_____

Writing a Classification Essay

Write an essay about one of the topics listed below or the topic your teacher assigns. You will have 50 minutes.

Classification Essay

A classification essay divides a complicated topic or subject into different parts. In this type of essay, a topic or main idea is divided into distinct parts, and each one is discussed in a separate body paragraph. Depending on the topic or main idea, a logical division might divide a topic into methods, types, kinds, qualities, reasons, advantages, disadvantages, causes, effects, problems, or solutions. All classification essays have three main parts: an **introduction,** a **body** with a number of paragraphs, and a **conclusion.**

An **introduction paragraph** starts with an **opening hook** to get the reader interested in the process or event. The introductory paragraph explains the purpose of the writing and includes the *thesis statement.*

Thesis statements for a classification essay indicate logical division of ideas and state the topic (main idea). They also state either the number of sub-divisions or the name of the sub-divisions (the controlling idea).

Body paragraphs divide the thesis statement into a number of sub-topics that further support and provide evidence for the claim in the thesis statement. Put the sub-topics into some logical order (most to least important, general to specific, familiar to unknown, or simple to complex). Use logical division transition signals to link sentences within the paragraph and between paragraphs.

Sentence Connectors

first, first of all, second, third, next, last, finally, also, in addition, moreover, furthermore

Coordination

and, both…and, not only…but also

Other Phrases

One/ Another/ An additional/ The first cause, reason, factor, problem, advantage, result, etc.

In addition to…

A concluding paragraph summarizes the parts of the subject and provides a final thought about the subject.

1 Classify the different food groups and discuss the benefits of each to a healthy diet.
2 Classify different types of vacations that would appeal to people of different interests and income levels.

Editing Checklist

- Are the grammar, sentence structure, mechanics, and punctuation correct?
- Is the vocabulary appropriate? Are the words spelled correctly?
- Is the essay well organized, well developed, and clear?

Writing a Description Essay

Model Essay

In the Rain Forest

The people of Washington state call it the "Mist-ical Peninsula," a play on words based on the beautiful mists and fogs that a traveler might encounter any day of the year on the Olympic Peninsula. And it is an appropriate name because of the almost mystical beauty of one of the world's three temperate rain forest regions. But there is more to this remarkable place than 500-year-old trees and ground-clouds. That's what I discovered when I spent a little time in a cabin near Lake Quinault.

Let me begin with the rain. About 150 inches of rain fall every year in the Lake Quinault area. As a comparison, Seattle gets about 38 inches. Phoenix gets 8. As you might guess, that means that everything grows fast and big. Douglas firs soar 300 feet into the sky, with moss dripping from their branches. Ferns grow waist-high. And the mushrooms! In the fall, mushrooms fill the forest like wildflowers, with colors that are almost as bright.

Right in the middle of this is Lake Quinault itself, about 3 miles wide and 5 miles long. It's fed by melting glaciers, making it so cold that you almost need a wet suit to swim in it. Clear and deep, it's surrounded by small mountains and tall trees and is owned by the Quinault tribe. The tribe stocks it with salmon and allows no motorboats to disturb its peace. On a rainy day, I have stood, perfectly dry, on the shore of the lake and watched rain move toward me from the opposite shore.

Around Quinault and reaching up towards Canada are the Olympic Mountains. Not very tall, they are nonetheless beautiful, with an extraordinary number of snowfields and glaciers. As the glaciers melt in the summer, they create waterfalls all over the mountains. And if you hike the paths, you will step into subalpine meadows filled with lupine, daisies, asters, and paintbrush.

The people who live in this wonderland are homesteaders and the children of homesteaders. They're loggers and the children of loggers. They love the trees that surround them and don't think there's anything wrong with cutting a bunch of them down. They have a pretty little library nestled in the woods between the school and the volunteer fire station, and they go there on a chilly afternoon to sit in front of the woodfire and read a magazine. Most of all they believe they live in the most beautiful place in the world, and they don't know why anyone would ever want to live anywhere else.

And after you've been in Quinault for awhile, you'll feel exactly the same way.

Write a description about one of the topics listed below or the topic your teacher assigns. You will have 50 minutes.

Description Essay

A description essay reports an overall impression about a person, place, thing, or concept. A description includes:

the **key characteristics** of the subject

use of sensory details

the **emotional connection** to the subject

the **history** of the subject

When writing a descriptive essay, choose a single person, place, thing, or concrete idea to describe and organize your ideas into three main parts: an **introduction,** a **body** with a number of paragraphs, and a **conclusion.**

An **introduction paragraph** starts with an **opening hook** to get the reader interested in the topic. The introductory paragraph explains the purpose of the writing and includes the **thesis statement** or **controlling idea.**

The **thesis statement / controlling idea** indicates the person, place, thing, or concept you will describe (main idea) and provides an overall impression of the person, place, thing, or concept that you are describing.

Body paragraphs divide the description into a number of sub-topics that further inform and support the overall claim. It is a good idea to put the sub-topics into logical order (most to least important, general to specific, familiar to unknown, or simple to complex). Use logical division transition signals to link sentences within the paragraph and between paragraphs.

Sentence Connectors

To/on the left/right, in front of, next to, behind, first, first of all, second, third, next, last, finally, also, in addition, moreover, furthermore

Coordination

and, both…and, not only…but also

A **concluding paragraph** summarizes the subject and provides a final thought about the subject.

1 In a five- or six-paragraph essay, choose a product or invention and describe how it works.
2 Describe the town or city where you live.
3 Describe a family member. Include physical characteristics and personality.

Editing Checklist

- Are the grammar, sentence structure, mechanics, and punctuation correct?
- Is the vocabulary appropriate? Are the words spelled correctly?
- Is the description well organized, well developed, and clear?

_____

_____

_____

_____

_____

_____

_____

_____

_____

_____

_____

_____

_____

_____

_____

_____

_____

_____

_____

_____

Comparing and Contrasting

Presentation

Model Essay

Block Organization

Yoga Practices in India and the United States

Yoga is an ancient tradition that began in India over 5,000 years ago and has recently become popular in the United States. While there are some similarities between the yoga practices in India and the U.S., there are also a number of differences.

Yoga practices in both places include two types of activities. First, there is a series of poses called *asanas*. These are physical positions that people hold for one to three minutes at a time. The second type of exercise involves a special kind of breathing called *pranayama*. These breathing exercises help people focus and calm down. In both countries, teachers lead students through a series of *asanas* in yoga classes. A yoga practice in both countries will usually begin or end with *pranayama*.

Traditionally, people in India and the U.S. have practiced yoga for quite different reasons. Yoga began in India thousands of years ago as a spiritual practice. However, in the United States, it has become popular as a type of exercise.

In India, yoga is a part of the Hindu spiritual tradition. Traditional practitioners believe that yoga prepares the body and the mind for spiritual practice. The practice helps people calm down so that they can sit for long periods of time during meditation. In contrast, people in the U.S. see yoga as exercise. Many Americans feel that yoga treats a number of health issues, such as depression and heart disease. Unlike in India, yoga practices in the United States are often fast and athletic. This raises the heart rate and tones muscles. Breathing exercises relax and reduce stress.

In conclusion, it's clear that yoga is a prevalent practice in India and the United States for different reasons. Yoga is becoming increasingly popular in the United States because it has many benefits. Both Indians and Americans find that practicing yoga can be useful to them for a variety of reasons.

Point-by-Point Organization

Yoga Practices in India and the United States

Yoga is an ancient tradition that began in India over 5,000 years ago and has recently become popular in the United States. There are a number of similarities and differences in yoga practices in India and the United States.

In both countries, people practice yoga for mental and physical health; however, Indians and Americans have different cultural understandings about the physical benefits of yoga. In both countries, teachers lead students through asanas or a series of poses. These are physical positions which people hold for one to three minutes at a time. Each pose is designed to alternately stretch and contract different groups of muscles. Indians believe that the action of stretching and contracting helps to detoxify the body and purify it. In India, people do yoga to prepare the body for meditation and other spiritual rituals.

In contrast, Americans have a more pragmatic understanding about the health benefits of yoga. Unlike in India, yoga practices are often fast and athletic. This kind of practice raises the heart rate and tones muscles. Medical researchers have proven that yoga poses increase blood circulation.

In addition, yoga in both India and the United States typically focuses on breathing, though the understanding of the purpose of this practice may differ. A session in both countries will usually begin or end with a special type of breathing called *pranayama*. These breathing exercises help people focus and calm down. In India, the time devoted to *pranayama* in a daily practice might be 50 percent or more. Indians use *pranayama* to quiet the mind before meditation, so it is often considered more important than the *asanas*.

On the other hand, in the United States, *pranayama* is usually confined to five or ten minutes at the beginning and end of yoga. Americans tend to see the pragmatic value of *pranayama*, since it oxygenates the body. In fact, many American psychologists value *pranayama* techniques because it reduces anxiety and relieves depression. However, pranayama is not generally a yogic preparation for spiritual practice in the United States, as it is in India.

People in India and the U.S. practice yoga for quite different reasons. Yoga began in India thousands of years ago as one part of an entire spiritual system. Yoga is a part of the Hindu spiritual tradition, which also involves service, meditation, a vegetarian diet, and *ayurvedic* practices that prevent disease. However, in the United States, people tend not to focus on the spiritual aspects of yoga. It is, rather, regarded as one of many forms of exercise that deliver health benefits.

While it's clear that yoga is popular in both India and the U.S., the reasons for its popularity and the methods of practicing yoga differ between the two countries.

Write an essay about one of the topics listed below or the topic your teacher assigns. You will have 50 minutes.

Comparing and Contrasting

We often **compare and contrast** two or more options in an essay to come to a decision or explain a preference. When comparing and contrasting two or more options in writing, discuss similarities and differences between the two subjects. All essays have three main parts: an **introduction paragraph,** a number of **body paragraphs,** and a **concluding paragraph.**

An **introduction paragraph** starts with an **opening hook** to get the reader interested in the topic. The introductory paragraph explains the purpose of the writing and includes the ***thesis statement.***

The thesis statement indicates two or three people, places, things, or concepts (main idea) and compares and/or contrasts them to show their similarities and/or differences (the controlling idea).

Body paragraphs divide the thesis statement into a number of similarities and/or differences that further support and provide evidence for the claim. It is a good idea to put the sub-topics into some order (e.g., most to least important). Ideas can be organized in block or point-by-point pattern.

- In a **block pattern**, compare all of the similarities and then, contrast all of the differences, or discuss all of the points of comparison about each option separately.

- In a **point-by-point pattern**, organize by categories or "points of comparison." Discuss the similarities and differences for the options for each category.

- A **concluding paragraph** summarizes the main point and sub-points and finishes up the essay with a final thought, suggestion, or prediction related to the reason for writing.

Comparison Signals	Contrast Signals
Comparatives *as . . . as*	**Comparatives** *more/less . . . than,* *the most/least . . .*
Sentence Connectors *similarly, likewise, also, too, in addition, additionally*	**Sentence Connectors** *however, nevertheless, nonetheless, still (contrast)* *in contrast, on the other hand, on the contrary, in/by comparison (contrast)*
Coordinating Conjunctions *and, nor*	**Coordinating Conjunctions** *yet (contrary to expectation), but (contrary to expectation)*
Paired Conjunctions *both . . . and, neither . . . nor, not only . . . but also*	**Paired Conjunctions** *not . . . but (opposing alternatives)*
Subordinating Conjunctions *as, just as*	**Subordinating Conjunctions** *although, though, even though (unexpected result)* *while, whereas (opposing alternatives)*
Prepositions *similar to, equal to, like, the same as, just as, in* common, *as*	**Prepositions** *despite, in spite of (unexpected result)* *different from, dissimilar to, unlike, instead of (opposing alternatives)*

1 In a five- or six-paragraph essay, compare and contrast the development stages of a human baby and a baby chimpanzee.

2 In a five- or six-paragraph essay, compare and contrast two political systems, such as the different forms of democracy, or a dictatorship and a democracy.

3 In a five- or six-paragraph essay, compare and contrast the diets and foods of two different countries or cultures.

Editing Checklist

- Are the grammar, sentence structure, mechanics, and punctuation correct?
- Is the vocabulary appropriate? Are the words spelled correctly?
- Is the description well organized, well developed, and clear?

Describing Causes and Effects

Model Essay

Block Organization

Hurricane Katrina

New Orleans, Louisiana, is a fascinating city located on the Gulf Coast of the United States. It is a home of jazz and blues, and many writers and artists have found inspiration on its streets. The city has a rich history with traditions and customs influenced by French, Spanish, and African cultures, among others.

In 2005, New Orleans was changed forever, when Hurricane Katrina, one of the most lethal and costly storms in American history, slammed into this beloved city. Delayed evacuation, broken levees (embankments to prevent rivers from overflowing), and a lack of public aid contributed to devastation of New Orleans and its environs.

Residents of the towns and cities along the Gulf Coast are used to tropical storms during August and September. It is very rare that these storms require serious preparation or even evacuation, so people tend to stay at home and wait the storms out. In the case of Hurricane Katrina, the official order for mandatory evacuation came too late. Many people simply did not have the time or means to leave.

Moreover, New Orleans is below sea level. A web of canals and levees are meant to prevent the city from flooding during a storm. During Katrina, the levees broke and the city was flooded with water. Many believe that the levees failed because the U.S. Army Corp of Engineers (USACE) failed to maintain them properly. In fact, the USACE was sued and found liable in 2008.

After the storm hit and the levees broke, the emergency response from the government was slow and ineffective. Lack of cooperation between the governor of Louisiana, the mayor of New Orleans, the Federal Emergency Management Association, and the Coast Guard caused many people to go without food, water, and shelter for days after the storm. Of the over 50,000 people who remained, many tried to find shelter in the city's Superdome and Convention Center, but neither place had ever been prepared for such a purpose, and evacuation took weeks.

No government is able to stop storms from inflicting damage, but in the case of Hurricane Katrina mismanagement exacerbated the damage and destruction. In fact, New Orleans is still struggling to recover from the long-term effects of the disaster.

Hurricane Katrina devastated the infrastructure of New Orleans and surrounding areas. Over 1,800 people died in the initial days after the storm, and over one million people were relocated to other areas of the United States. Many of these people never returned to their original homes. Families were separated, and the rich cultural traditions of the city were changed forever. The migration of all these people represents the greatest U.S. migration since the Great Depression.

The storm also created irreversible environmental damage to the Southern coastal areas. The massive amount of flooding caused over 215 square miles of beaches, swamps, marshes, and islands to be completely covered in water. The storm also caused a number of oil refineries to malfunction, and there were over 40 oil spills. A total of seven million gallons of oil spilled.

Finally, economically, the hurricane cost local and federal governments over $100 billion dollars. The flood waters caused a huge amount of damage to structures in and around New Orleans. Rebuilding has cost a lot of money. Moreover, many people were unable to go back to work in the months after the storm. New Orleans's economic base (tourism, oil production, and fishing) disappeared in the weeks after the storm.

A number of factors during and after Hurricane Katrina permanently changed New Orleans and its surrounding areas in several important ways. Even today, parts of New Orleans are being rebuilt. The storm is still a defining moment in the lives of New Orleanians. Many have left and will never return, and the ones who stayed have horror stories about the days, weeks, and months after the storm. The storm also caused great controversy in some quarters. Many people felt the local, state, and federal governments did not respond quickly because the people in disaster zones were predominantly poor and African American. While various government agencies have promised this scale of damage will not occur again, no one can be certain it will not.

Chain Organization

Hurricane Katrina

New Orleans, Louisiana, is a fascinating city located on the Gulf Coast of the United States. It is a home of jazz and blues, and many writers and artists have found inspiration on its streets. The city has a rich history with traditions and customs influenced by a heritage that is a mix of, among others influences, the French, the Spanish, and the African. No one can visit this beautiful city and not fall in love with its food, people, and ambience.

In 2005, New Orleans was changed forever, when Hurricane Katrina, one of the most lethal and costly storms in American history, slammed into this beloved city. In late August, it smashed the Southern United States and destroyed some coastal areas of Florida, Mississippi, and Louisiana. Nowhere was the destruction worse than in New Orleans. Delayed evacuation, broken levees (embankments to prevent rivers from overflowing), and a lack of public aid contributed to devastation of New Orleans and its environs.

The first reason for the devastation was delayed evacuation. Residents of the towns and cities along the Gulf Coast are used to tropical storms during August and September. It is very rare that these storms require serious preparation or even evacuation, so people tend to stay at home and wait the storms out. In the case of Hurricane Katrina, the official order for mandatory evacuation came too late. Many people simply did not have the time or means to leave.

As a result, Hurricane Katrina devastated the infrastructure of New Orleans and surrounding areas. Over 1,800 of the people who didn't evacuate died in the initial days after the storm, and over one million people had to relocate to other areas of the United States. Many of these people never returned to their original homes. Families were separated, and the rich cultural traditions of the city were changed forever. The migration of all these people represents the greatest U.S. migration since the Great Depression.

A second reason for the devastation involves the failure of the levee system. New Orleans is below sea level. A web of canals and levees are meant to prevent the city from flooding during a storm. During Katrina, the levees broke, and the city was flooded with water. Many believe that levees failed because the U.S. Army Corp of Engineers (USACE) failed to maintain them properly. In fact, the USACE was sued and found liable in 2008.

Failing levees and flooding had serious consequences for New Orleans and surrounding areas. The storm created irreversible environmental damage to the Southern coastal areas. The massive amount of flooding caused over 215 square miles of beaches, swamps, marshes, and islands to be completely covered in water. The storm also caused a number of oil refineries to malfunction, and there were over 40 oil spills. A total of seven million gallons of oil spilled. In New Orleans, after the storm, fires from a malfunctioning chemical plant destroyed homes and property.

The final reason for the severe damage was the slow response by government agencies. After the storm hit and the levees broke, the emergency response from the government was slow and ineffective. Lack of cooperation between the governor of Louisiana, the mayor of New Orleans, the Federal Emergency Management Association (FEMA), and the Coast Guard caused many people to go without food, water and shelter for days after the storm. Of the over 50,000 people who remained, many tried to find shelter in the city's Superdome and Convention Center, but neither place had ever been prepared for such a purpose, and evacuation took weeks.

Since the government was slow to respond, the damages caused by the storm became very expensive. Economically, the hurricane cost local and federal governments over $100 billion. Water from the flooding took months to be pumped out of the city. Afterwards, there was a huge amount of damage to structures in and around New Orleans. Re-building cost a lot of money. Moreover, many people were unable to go back to work in the months after the storm. New Orleans's economic base (tourism, oil production, and fishing) disappeared in the weeks after the storm.

No government is able to stop storms from inflicting damage, but in the case of Hurricane Katrina, mismanagement exacerbated the damage and destruction. Even today, there are still areas in New Orleans being rebuilt and reconstructed. The storm is still a defining moment in the lives of New Orleanians. Many of them have left and will never return, and the ones who stayed have horror stories about the days, weeks, and months after the storm.

The storm also caused great controversy in some quarters. Many people felt the local, state, and federal governments did not respond quickly because the people in disaster zones were predominantly poor and African American. While various government agencies have promised this scale of damage will not occur again, no one can be certain it will not.

Write an essay about one of the topics listed below or the topic your teacher assigns. You will have 50 minutes.

Describing Causes and Effects

An essay can indicate the causes and/or the effects of an event, occurrence, phenomenon, issue, or problem. In a cause-effect essay, a topic or main idea is divided into reasons and results, and each one is discussed in a separate body paragraph. All essays have three main parts: an **introduction paragraph,** a number of **body paragraphs,** and a **concluding paragraph.**

An **introduction paragraph** starts with an **opening hook** to get the reader interested in the topic. The introductory paragraph explains the purpose of the writing and includes the ***thesis statement.***

The thesis statement indicates the event, occurrence, phenomenon, issue, or problem (main idea) and reviews the causes, effects, or both (the controlling idea).

Body paragraphs divide the thesis statement into causes and/or effects to provide evidence for the claim. It is a good idea to put the sub-topics into some order (most to least significant). Ideas can be organized in block or chain pattern.

- **A block pattern** organizes causes and effects into section blocks with short transition paragraphs between main ideas.
- **A chain pattern** alternates causes and effects (use when the reasons and results are closely linked).

Transition signals for describing causes and effects:

Sentence Connectors

as a result, as a consequence, therefore, thus, consequently, hence, for this reason

Coordinating Conjunctions

so, for

Subordinating Conjunctions

because, as, since

Other Phrases

to result in, to cause, to have an effect on, to affect, the cause of, the reason for, thereby

A concluding paragraph summarizes the main point and sub-points and finishes the essay with a final thought, suggestion, or prediction related to the reason for writing.

1 Write a five- or six-paragraph essay describing the causes of animal extinction and the effects extinction could have on our lives.
2 Write a five- or six-paragraph essay describing the causes of pollution and the effects it has on the environment.

Editing Checklist

- Are the grammar, sentence structure, mechanics, and punctuation correct?
- Is the vocabulary appropriate? Are the words spelled correctly?
- Is the description well organized, well developed, and clear?

APPENDICES

Appendix 1: Verb Forms

Base Form	Simple Past	Past Participle	Base Form	Simple Past	Past Participle
arise	arose	arisen	leave	left	left
be	was/were	been	lend	lent	lent
bear	bore	born	let	let	let
become	became	become	lie (to be at rest)	lay	lain
begin	began	begun	lose	lost	lost
bend	bent	bent	make	made	made
bet	bet	bet	mean	meant	meant
bid	bid	bid	meet	met	met
bite	bit	bitten	mistake	mistook	mistaken
bleed	bled	bled	overtake	overtook	overtaken
blow	blew	blown	pay	paid	paid
break	broke	broken	prove	proved	proved/proven
bring	brought	brought	put	put	put
broadcast	broadcast	broadcast	quit	quit	quit
build	built	built	read	read	read
burn	burned/burnt	burned/burnt	ride	rode	ridden
buy	bought	bought	ring	rang	rung
catch	caught	caught	run	ran	run
choose	chose	chosen	say	said	said
cling	clung	clung	see	saw	seen
come	came	come	seek	sought	sought
cost	cost	cost	sell	sold	sold
cut	cut	cut	send	sent	sent
deal	dealt	dealt	shake	shook	shaken
do	did	done	shine	shone/shined	shone/shined
draw	drew	drawn	shoot	shot	shot
dream	dreamed/dreamt	dreamed/dreamt	shrink	shrank	shrunk
drink	drank	drunk	shut	shut	shut
drive	drove	driven	sing	sang	sung
eat	ate	eaten	sit	sat	sat
fall	fell	fallen	sleep	slept	slept
feed	fed	fed	sneak	sneaked/snuck	sneaked/snuck
feel	felt	felt	speak	spoke	spoken
fight	fought	fought	spell	spelled/spelt	spelled/spelt
find	found	found	spend	spent	spent
flee	fled	fled	spill	spilled	spilled
fling	flung	flung	spoil	spoiled/spoilt	spoiled/spoilt
fly	flew	flown	spread	spread	spread
forbid	forbade	forbidden	spring	sprang	sprung
forecast	forecast	forecast	stand	stood	stood
forego	forewent	forgone	steal	stole	stolen
foretell	foretold	foretold	strike	struck	struck
forget	forgot	forgotten	sweep	swept	swept
forgive	forgave	forgiven	swim	swam	swum
forsake	forsook	forsaken	take	took	taken
get	got	gotten	teach	taught	taught
give	gave	given	tear	tore	torn
go	went	gone	tell	told	told
grow	grew	grown	think	thought	thought
hang (to put up)	hung	hung	throw	threw	thrown
hang (to kill by hanging)	hanged	hanged	undergo	underwent	undergone
			understand	understood	understood
have	had	had	undertake	undertook	undertaken
hear	heard	heard	wake up	woke up	woken up
hide	hid	hidden	wear	wore	worn
hold	held	held	weep	wept	wept
hurt	hurt	hurt	win	won	won
keep	kept	kept	wind	wound	wound
know	knew	known	withdraw	withdrew	withdrawn
lay	laid	laid	write	wrote	written
learn	learned/learnt	learned/learnt			

Appendix 2: Spelling Rules

Spelling of Plural Nouns Rules	Examples	
Add -s to form the plural of most count nouns.	pencil > pencils	
	cat > cats	
Add -es to form the plural of nouns that end in a consonant + o.	tomato > tomatoes	
Add -es to form the plural of nouns that end in ch, sh, x, or ss.	kiss > kisses	
	box > boxes	
	witch > witches	
	wish > wishes	
To form the plural of words that end in consonant + y, change the y to i and add -es.	party > parties	
To form the plural of words that end in vowel + y, add -s.	boy > boys	
Some plural nouns have an irregular plural form.	child > children	
	foot > feet	
	man > men	
	person > people	
	tooth > teeth	
	woman > women	
Some nouns have the same form for singular and plural.	pants > pants	
	clothes > clothes	
	deer > deer	
	fish > fish	
	sheep > sheep	
Some nouns have only a singular or plural form.	economics (is)	
	news (is)	
	the United Arab Emirates (is)	
	clothes (are)	
	glasses (are)	
	scissors (are)	
Nouns with Greek or Latin roots take irregular plural endings that must be learned.	appendix > appendices	
	cactus > cacti	

Spelling of Plural Nouns		
Rules	**Examples**	
	datum > data	
	medium > media	
	thesis > theses	
Add -*s* to the first noun in a compound noun.	father-in-law > father**s**-in-law	
	attorney general > attorney**s** general	
Add -*'s* to form plurals for letters.	p and q	p's and q's
Spelling of Third-person Simple Present Verbs		
Rules	**Examples**	
Add -*s* to form the third-person singular of most verbs.	to cook > cook**s**	
Add -*es* to verbs ending in *s, z, x, sh,* and *ch.*	kiss > kiss**es**	
	buzz > buzz**es**	
	fix > fix**es**	
	push > push**es**	
	watch > watch**es**	
If a verb ends in consonant + *y*, change the *y* to *i* and add -*es.*	try > tr**ies**	
If a verb ends in vowel + *y*, do not change the ending.	pay > pay**s**	
The verbs *have, do,* and *be* take irregular third-person singular forms.	be > is	
	do > does	
	have > has	
Spelling of Present Participles		
Rules	**Examples**	
Add -*ing* to the base form of most verbs.	walk > walk**ing**	
If a verb ends in *e*, drop the *e* and add -*ing.*	come > com**ing**	
If a one-syllable verb ends in consonant + vowel + consonant (CVC), double the last consonant and add -*ing.*	sit > si**tting**	
Do not double the last consonant if a word ends in *w, x,* or *y.*	flow > flow**ing**	
	fix > fix**ing**	
	play > play**ing**	
In words of more than one syllable that end in consonant + vowel + consonant (CVC), double the last consonant if the syllable is stressed.	permit > permi**tting**	

Spelling of Regular Past Participles Rules	Examples	
If a verb ends in a consonant, add -ed.	jump > jump**ed**	
If a verb ends in e, add -d.	like > like**d**	
If a verb ends in consonant + y, change the y to i and add -ed.	carry > carr**ied**	
If the verb ends in vowel + y, do not change the y to i. Just add -ed.	play > play**ed**	
If a one-syllable verb ends in consonant + vowel + consonant (CVC), double the last consonant and add -ed.	jog > jo**gged**	
Do not double the last consonant if a word ends in w, x, or y.	fix > fix**ed**	
In words of more than one syllable that end in consonant + vowel + consonant (CVC), double the last consonant if the syllable is stressed.	permit > permi**tted**	
British and American Spelling Differences		
Common American Spelling	fulfill, fulfillment, traveled, traveling, center, color, connection, defense, encyclopedia, burned, judgment, realize, realization	
Common British Spelling	fulfil, fulfilment, travelled, travelling, centre, colour, connexion, defence, encyclopaedia, burnt, judgement, realise, realisation	

Appendix 3: Noncount Nouns

Types of Noncount Nouns	Examples
names for a whole group	furniture, jewelry, mail, meat, equipment, luggage, software
fluids	water, juice, blood, gasoline, oil, wine, milk
solids	butter, cheese, ice, paper, poultry, beef, pork
gases	air, carbon dioxide, fog, smoke, fire, steam, exhaust
particles or small pieces	rice, corn, cereal, wheat, sugar, salt, flour
material	gold, wood, steel, brick, wool, chalk, dirt
abstract ideas	beauty, love, war, peace, advice, grammar, information
languages	Amharic, Arabic, Chinese, English, French, Korean, Spanish
fields of study	biology, literature, math, history, psychology, geography, physics
recreation/ activities	baseball, swimming, tennis, walking, singing, football, work
natural phenomena	weather, rain, fire, snow, thunder, lightning, heat

Appendix 4: Modals

Rules	Modals	Examples
Use *can*, *could*, and *be able to* to talk about ability.	*can* = ability in the present and the future	John **can** swim. Betsy **can't** (cannot) cook.
		Can Andrew sing at the wedding tomorrow?
	could = general ability in the past	When I was a child, I **could** speak Korean.
		I **couldn't** drive a car.
	be able to = completed task in the past; ability in all tenses	They **were able to** get the tickets after all.
		Have you **been able to** reach her?
Use *have to* and *must* to talk about necessity.	*have to* = what is required in statements and questions; what is not required	Why does she **have to** get her driver's license?
		She **has to** commute 20 miles to work.
		They **don't have to** study for that test.
	must = law or necessity in statements; it signifies what is not allowed	International students **must** apply for a visa.
		You **must not** smoke in public.
Use *can't*, *could*, *may*, *might*, and *must* to talk about possibility.	*can't* = no possibility	Jill **can't** be in the house. She called from the school.
	Could/could not = no possibility or or a small possibility	It's not likely, but the boys **could** finish cleaning their room on time. They **couldn't** possibly finish on time.
	Might/might not = no or a slight possibility	There **might not** be any way to reach them.
	May/may not = fair possibility or a good possibility	My friends **may** come if they have time. They **may not** be ready for the news.

	must = no or very strong possibility	The line is really long for the movie. It **must** be excellent. The line for the restaurant is short. It **must not** be very good.
Use *should, ought to,* and *had better* to give advice or make suggestions.	*should* = suggestion or advice; intentions, duty, or obligation in questions	Katie **should** break up with her boyfriend. He's not very nice.
		What **should** Kevin do after school?
		He **shouldn't** play video games. He does that all the time.
	ought to = suggestion or advice in a formal manner; not frequently used in negative statements	The medical group **ought to** evaluate their procedures.
	had better/had better not = strong suggestion for or against doing something in statements, not questions	You **had better** clean your room, or you can't go out to play!
		She **had better not** leave the house by herself. It's too dangerous.
Use *used to* and *would* to talk about past habits and routines.	*used to / would* = past habits and routines that we no longer have; frequently used in negative and affirmative statements and questions.	My sister **used to play** the piano when we were kids. My brother and I **didn't use to play** the piano. When I was in college, I **would stay up** all night studying. My roommate **wouldn't stay up** late. She worked in the morning. **Would you stay up** all night to work in college?

Appendix 5: Prepositional Phrases with Adjectives

Preposition	Example	Other Adjectives with this Preposition
about	I **am concerned about** my daughter. She's skipping classes.	crazy, curious, excited, glad, happy, nervous, worried
at	Angela is **angry at** her boyfriend. He forgot their anniversary.	amazed, awful, brilliant, good, slow
for	The manager is **responsible for** the work schedule.	grateful, known, prepared, remembered, ready
from	We got an alarm, so the house would be **safe from** burglars.	absent, different, divorced, made
of	Her father was **proud of** her accomplishments.	ashamed, aware, capable, certain, convinced, fond, guilty, incapable, scared
to	They are **accustomed to** Susan's lateness. She never comes on time.	committed, connected, dedicated, limited, opposed, similar, used
with	We will leave when my son is **finished with** his homework.	acquainted, associated, content, disappointed, familiar, fed up, pleased, satisfied

Appendix 6: Prepositional Phrases with Verbs

Preposition	Example	Other Verbs with this Preposition
about	She always **complains about** her in-laws.	dream, forget, learn, think, wonder
for	The prosecutor **is arguing for** the death penalty because the crime was so terrible.	apply, ask, blame, fight, forgive, search, wish
of	They have decided **to accuse** her **of** taking the money.	approve, consist, disapprove, remind, take advantage, take care
to	Helen **apologized to** Gary for her actions.	belong, compare, contribute, listen, object, respond, speak
with	The researchers **didn't agree with** the results of the previous study.	cooperate, disagree, interfere, meet, unite

Appendix 7: Phrasal Verbs

Phrasal Verbs	Examples	Synonyms
ask for	I asked for a raise.	request
believe in	We believe in her.	trust
break down	The car might break down.	fail
break up	My boyfriend and I broke up.	separate
bring on	Global warming has brought on climate change.	cause
bring up	Her friends were afraid to bring up her drinking problem.	mention
call back	Has the manager called him back?	return a telephone call
call off	They need to call off the party.	cancel
carry out	The team carried out the plan.	perform; execute
come across	She came across that book at the library.	find
come back	She refused to come back home.	return
come up with	We will need to come up with a better solution.	produce
deal with	How will we deal with the stress?	handle
depend on	My father has been depending on me since he got sick.	need
do without	I can't do without coffee. I need it.	forego
end up	If she doesn't start studying, she will end up failing.	result in
fall down	She fell down the stairs and broke her leg.	tumble
figure out	They can't figure out why the dog won't eat.	understand
find out	Have you found out the name of the restaurant?	learn
follow up	I called the company yesterday, but the problem isn't fixed. We should follow up tomorrow.	revisit
get back	I'm going to return the pants I bought and get my money back.	retrieve
get out of	Susan is never around when it is time to finish work. She always gets out of it.	avoid
give up	When she realized how badly she had played soccer, she decided to give it up.	quit
go back	After their son lost his job, he went back home to live with his parents for a while.	return
go into	Don't go into the building! There is a fire.	enter
go out	We went out with friends yesterday.	socialize
go through	The couple is going through a difficult time. They are thinking about a divorce.	experience

keep up	Good job! Keep up the good work.	continue
know about	Did you know about the scholarship?	be aware of
look at	Let's take some time to look at the problem again.	study
make up	The student needs to make up the test.	redo
meet with	Every summer, I meet with my friends and go on vacation.	reunite
move on	His ex-girlfriend has moved on. She is dating his friend now.	leave; get over something or someone
pick up	Can you pick the kids up from school today?	retrieve/collect
point out	The accountant has pointed out a number of inconsistencies in the report.	call attention to
put away	Every day, the children put away their toys before dinner.	tidy up
put on	The woman is going to put on her best dress for the party.	wear
put out	The firefighters arrived after the fire was put out.	extinguish
rely on	The neighbors rely on the elderly man to watch the neighborhood during the day.	depend on
run away	When I was a child, I would run away when I got mad at my mother.	escape
run out	Could you buy some toilet paper on your way home? We've run out.	finish
set up	Fran will come and help us set up for the party.	get organized
take care of	Jill will take care of the cat and water the plants while they are gone.	look after; watch
take out	It stinks in here. Did you take out the trash?	remove
try out	I have never eaten sushi, but I'll try it out.	test
turn off	When they left, they turned the lights off.	put off
turn on	They came into the house and turned on the lights.	put on
use up	We won't buy more paper for the printer until it is completely used up.	gone
work on	The man has been waking up late for work every day, but he is working on the problem.	attempting to improve
write down	The secretary will write down the main points made in the meeting.	record

Appendix 8: Prepositional Phrases

Meanings	Prepositions	Examples
Addition	in addition to with as well as	We have to shop for new shoes **in addition to** the other errands on Sunday. I'd like a hotdog **with** cheese. I like Spain **as well as** Germany.
Comparison	just like the same as similar to	Jeff cooks **just like** his mother. He has **the same** hair **as** his father. Mars is **similar to** Earth in some ways.
Exclusions/ Alternatives	except for instead of	Everybody came to the party **except for** Ellen. Sarah was there **instead of** Joyce.
Examples	such as like an example of	James plans to stay at home and take care of **such** tasks **as** cleaning his room and washing the floor. He eats fruits **like** apples and oranges. I can't think of **an example of** tax evasion more egregious than this.
Location/ Place	above across against beside next to in at on	The cat is sleeping **above** the radiator. The Smiths live **across** the street. The book is positioned **against** the door. The knives are **beside** the sink. She **next to** a garbage dump. Her wallet is **in** her purse. The class is **at** the school. Grab the pens **on** the desk.
Opinion	according to against for	**According to** my student Tan, he passed his test. The one team was **against** playing at the new field. The other team was **for** playing at the new field.
Reason	as a result of because of due to	**As a result of** the new carpet, the room smells. You have to take off your shoes **because of** the new carpet. The room smells **due to** the new carpet.
Result	the cause of the reason for	Actually, **the cause of** her depression should be obvious. Nobody knows what the **reason for** her depression is.
Time Order	after before during for since until	**After** school, the little girl walks home. **Before** school, she eats breakfast. **During** her school day, she learns. **For** a long time, she did not enjoy art class. **Since** the new teacher's arrival, however, she enjoys it. She is not satisfied **until** her meeting with her mathematics teacher.

	when	**When** that happens, she feels energetic.
	while	**While** learning math, she dreams about working for NASA.
	in	
	at	**In** July 2013, she is going to space camp. It is **in** the summer.
	on	
		It will start **at** 9:00 AM every day.
		On Mondays and Tuesdays, there will be field trips.
Unexpected Contrast	despite in spite of unlike	**Despite** feeling a little tired, Gary met his friends for dinner.

Appendix 9: Coordinating and Paired Conjunctions

Meaning	Examples
Addition *and, nor* *both … and* *not only … but* *also* *neither … nor*	Gary has lived in Spain, **and** Joanne has lived in Spain. **Both** Joanne **and** Gary have lived in Spain. **Not only** Gary **but also** Joanne has lived in Spain. Gary hasn't lived in France, **nor** <u>has he lived</u> in China. **Neither** <u>has Gary lived</u> in France, **nor** <u>has he lived</u> in China. (*Nor* has a negative meaning. Don't use a negative verb phrase in the second clause. This results in a double negative. Use a <u>question word order</u>.)
Choice *or* *either … or* *whether … or*	After the movie, we can go for a walk, **or** we can drive to my friend's party. We can **either** go for a walk **or** drive to the party. It's important to determine **whether** the experiment worked **or** failed. (two choices only)
Contrary to expectation *but*	It was a summer morning, **but** a cold shiver ran through my body.
Reason *For*	I couldn't buy lunch, **for** I had left my wallet at home. (The first sentence is the result of the second)
Result *So*	John didn't have any eggs for breakfast, **so** he went to the store. (The first sentence is the reason for the second)
Contrary to expectation *yet*	I didn't study at all, **yet** I passed the test.

Appendix 10: Subordinating Conjunctions

Meaning	Examples
Condition *If* *Unless*	**If** it rains, I will go home. I'll stay at the picnic **unless** it rains. (*unless means "except under the circumstances that"*)
Opposites *Whereas* *While*	**While** I am a good singer, my sister is not. My sister is not a good singer, **whereas** I am. *Use a comma in both positions with these subordinating conjunctions
Location *Where* *Wherever* *Everywhere* *Anywhere*	They prefer to study in the library **where** there are a lot of books. **Wherever** my daughter goes, she finds something to be curious about. **Everywhere** the singers performed, people gave them a standing ovation. Many people can access their bank records with an app **anywhere** they go.
Manner *as* *as + adverb + as* *as if* *as though*	Think **as** I think, and do **as** I do. (*in the same manner that*) The bridge was designed **as economically as** the architects could manage. People who deliver public speeches often behave **as though/as if** they aren't nervous.
Purpose *So that* *In order that*	I had to go home early **so that** I could work in the morning.
Reason *As* *Because* *Since*	She's going to the party **because** she wants to dance. **As** she wants to dance, she's going to the party. **Since** she wants to dance, she's going to the party.
Time *After* *As soon as* *Since* *Until* *When* *Whenever* *While*	The students met at the library **after** they finished their test. **As soon as** I finish reading this book, I'll call her back. They haven't seen each other **since** Susan had that party. We waited at the coffee shop **until** it was 5:30 pm. **When** we ran out of gas, we were almost home. I like to get a coffee **whenever** I go to Starbucks. **While** the children were walking, it began to snow.
Result *so + adj/adv + that* *such + noun + that* *so much/many /little/ few + noun + that*	The students were **so anxious that** the teacher sang them a song. The team wrote **such a great proposal that** they were awarded extra funds. She earned **so much** money **that** she retired early.
Unexpected Result *Even though Although* *Though*	**Even though** he was still a boy, he won the national chess championship. **Although** I like the sun, the desert was too bright and hot for me. **Though** I see it every day, I find the tree in front of my house enchanting.

Appendix 11: Conjunctive Adverbs

Meaning	Examples
Addition *also, besides, furthermore, in addition, moreover*	Maria's sister is a sales representative for a medical company; **furthermore**, she travels a lot.
Choice *alternatively, on the one hand, . . . on the other hand, otherwise*	I can't decide which movie to rent tonight. **On the one hand**, my friends really loved the documentary *Bowling for Columbine*; **on the other hand**, I might prefer a comedy like *Something about Mary*.
Comparison *similarly, likewise*	New Orleans and Paris are similar cities. They have similar architecture. **Likewise**, New Orleans and Paris share similar cuisine.
Conclusion *finally, in conclusion, to conclude, for these reasons, last of all, in summary, in conclusion*	**To conclude**, mammals have three specialized middle-ear bones and, at some point in their lives, hair.
Condition *instead, on the contrary, rather*	My grandparents refuse to turn on the heat; **instead**, they make a fire and sleep in front of it.
Opposition *in contrast, on the other hand*	My mother is a fabulous cook, **whereas** I can't boil water.
Examples *for example, for instance*	There are many perks to her job. She gets to drive a company car, **for example**.
Explanation *in other words, that is*	He hated his job and his colleagues, yet he worked at the same place for decades. **In other words**, he did it for the money.
Logical Order *above all, first and foremost, first of all, more importantly, most important, more significantly, most of all*	**First of all**, you will need seeds. **Most important**, you plant them in shaded soil. **Above all**, protect your new plants from deer.
Reason *for this reason*	He was feeling sick. **For this reason**, he visited a physician.
Result *as a result, consequently, therefore, thus*	My sister left food under her bed for a week. **As a result**, we now have ants in our house.
Time Order *first, second, after that, next, subsequently, then, meanwhile, in the meantime, finally*	**First**, she is going to finish her degree. **After that**, she will travel. **Then**, she will get a job.
Contrast *however, nevertheless, nonetheless, still*	The young girl spilled juice all over the table last night; **however**, she didn't clean it up. **Nevertheless**, her mother did not get angry.

Appendix 12: Transition Signals

Relationship	Coordinating and Paired Conjunctions	Subordinating Conjunctions	Conjunctive Adverbs	Prepositions and Phrases
Addition	and, nor both . . . and not only . . . but also neither . . . nor		also, besides, furthermore, in addition, moreover, as well	an additional, a final, with, in addition to, as well as
Choice	or either . . . or whether . . . or		alternatively, on the other hand, otherwise	
Comparison	and both . . . and not only . . . but also	as as + adverb + as as if, as though (the manner in which)	similarly, likewise	the same as just like, like, similar to
Conclusion			finally, in conclusion, to conclude, for these reasons, last of all, in summary, in conclusion	it is clear that, you can see that, these examples show that
Condition		if, unless	instead, on the contrary, rather	
Contrast	but	while, whereas	on the other hand, in contrast	except for, instead of
Examples			for example, for instance	such as, an example of, like
Explanation			in other words, that is, in particular, indeed, in fact	
Location		where, wherever, everywhere, anywhere		above, across, against, next to, at, beside,
Logical Order			above all, first and foremost, first of all, more importantly, most important, more significantly, most of all	the first, an additional, a more important, the best/worst

Manner		as, as + adverb + as, as if, as though		
Opinion			in my opinion, in my view	according to, to believe/think/ feel (that), for, against
Purpose		so that, in order that		
Reason	for	as, because, since	for this reason	due to, because of, as a result of, to cause
Result	so	so + adj/adv + that such + noun + that so much/many / little/few + noun + that	accordingly, as a result, consequently, hence, therefore, thus	the cause of, the reason for, provided that, to result in, to have an effect on
Time Order		before, after, when, while, since, as soon as	first, second, after that, next, subsequently, then, meanwhile, in the meantime, finally	the first, another, the last, the final, during, since, for, until, before, after
Contrary to Expectation	yet not . . . but	although, even though, though	however, nevertheless, nonetheless, still	in spite of, despite, unlike

Post-Test 1

In the timed Post-Test 1, you will demonstrate how well you understand sentence structure, grammar, punctuation, mechanics, and organization. You have 50 minutes to complete the test.

Grammar

Circle the letter of the correct answer.

1 Ana and her husband don't like their roommate Dan. They
  a will ask him
  b don't ask him
  c would ask him

to leave if they
  a don't need
  b need
  c didn't need

him to pay the rent.

2 I hope
  a to living
  b to be living
  c live

in my own apartment by this time next year.

3 I loved the color blue. In fact, when I was a child, I
  a was used to
  b would
  c didn't

wear a blue T-shirt every day.

4 **a** Should
  b Would
  c Could

your roommate still
  a be sleeping?
  b sleep?
  c have been?

I thought his final exam started 15 minutes ago.

5 The boys had two hours to get ready. They

    a must iron

    b could have ironed

    c could have been ironing

their clothes, but they obviously didn't. Look how wrinkled their shirts are!

6 The crops in the field died last week. They

    a had poisoned

    b have been poisoning

    c had been poisoned

by the toxins in the water.

7 When Jonas got home, he noticed his house

    a has been burglarized.

    b had been burglarized.

    c has been burglarizing.

8 How long

    a have you been studying

    b you have studied

    c you were studying

English at the community college?

9 Jodi met a really nice guy at the party last night. She

    a hopes

    b wishes

    c hope

he will call her.

10 The Destons love their new neighborhood. There are

    a a few

    b few

nice parks and

    a a little

    b little

traffic.

Circle the letter of the best reported speech for the original quote below.

11 "Don't move and put your hands up," says the police officer as the man starts to run.

The police officer told the man who

    a started to run not to move and to put his hands up.

    b starts to run don't move and put his hands up.

    c started to run to move and put his hands up.

12 The education department is receiving a $2 million grant,

    a some of it will be used to train

    b some of which will be used to train

    c that will be used to train

some of the faculty in new technologies.

13 New York has

    a so congested traffic

    b such congested traffic that

    c traffic congestion so that

many people choose to walk or take the subway.

14 The boy's mother

    a get him read

    b makes him read

    c helping him to read

for an hour every night before bed.

15 Angel started playing the piano in 1995. By the time she is 25 years old, she

    a will have been playing

    b will be playing

    c will have play

for 15 years.

16 The researchers are worried

    a that the power outage will adversely affect

    b the power outage will be affecting

    c which the power outage adversely affecting

the results of the experiment.

Circle the letter of the correct participial phrase to reduce the underlined clause.

17 Ana almost stopped running <u>after she was severely burned</u> in her kitchen.

Ana almost stopped running

    a after severely burned

    b severely burning

    c after being severely burned

in her kitchen.

18 One of the early jazz pianists, Art Tatum,

    a taught himself

    b teach him

    c to teach him

to play at a very young age.

19 He was determined the novel

    a be

    b is

    c were

true to his own life.

Punctuation and Mechanics

Circle the letter of the correct answer.

1 Which sentence is correct?

    a Since Irma Rombauer wrote *The Joy of Cooking: America's All-Purpose Cookbook*, it has become America's most published cookbook.

    b Since Irma Rombauer wrote *The Joy of Cooking America's All-Purpose Cookbook*, it has become America's most published cookbook.

    c Since Irma Rombauer wrote <u>*The Joy of Cooking, America's All-Purpose Cookbook*</u>, it has become America's most published cookbook.

2 Which sentence is correct?

    a My family does not live near me, so I sometimes feel isolated and lonely.

    b My family does not live near me so I sometimes feel isolated, and lonely.

    c My family does not live near me so I sometimes, feel isolated and lonely.

3 Which sentence is correct?

    a In *The Wizard of Oz*, Dorothy and her friends discover that the allpowerful wizard is just a man behind a curtain.

    b In *The Wizard of Oz*, Dorothy and her friends discover that the all-powerful wizard is just a man behind a curtain.

    c In *The Wizard of Oz*, Dorothy and her friends discover that the all powerful wizard is just a man behind a curtain.

4 Which sentence is correct?

    a The opponents of gun control (hunters, members of the National Rifle Association, and gun collectors) often argue that people kill, not guns.

    b The opponents of gun control; hunters, members of the National Rifle Association, and gun collectors often argue that people kill, not guns.

    c The opponents of gun control hunters, members of the National Rifle Association, and gun collectors often argue that people kill, not guns.

5 Which sentence is correct?

    a "Research suggests that language is not situated in just one part of the brain the scientist told the audience."

    b Research suggests that language is not situated in just one part of the brain the scientist told the audience.

    c "Research suggests that language is not situated in just one part of the brain," the scientist told the audience.

6 Which sentence is correct?

   a The faculty is in negotiations for its new contract, consequently, it has been meeting regularly with the union.

   b The faculty is in negotiations for its new contract; consequently, it has been meeting regularly with the union.

   c The faculty is in negotiations for its new contract: consequently, it has been meeting regularly with the union.

Sentence Structure

Circle the letter of the correct answer.

1 Everyone

   a who doesn't

   b who don't

   c who not

get health care from his or her employer can buy it under the new health care regulations.

2 The fire caused a lot of damage to

   a we

   b us

   c our

   d ours

home.

3 The Grand Canyon

   a a national park on the Colorado River

   b , a national park on the Colorado River,

   c which is a national park on the Colorado River

is a main tourist attraction in Arizona.

4 Would you mind

   a doing

   b making

   c taking

   d having

a favor for me?

5 Kaitlin is a runner

   a although

   b since

   c , whereas

her partner is a couch potato.

6 Not only

    a there are no more need-based scholarships,

    b are there no more need-based scholarships,

    c no more need-based scholarships

but also federal financial aid has been reduced.

7 The children

    a both need colored markers,

    b need both colored markers

    c need both colored markers,

and a journal for the project.

8 Taken together, are the underlined words a phrase, dependent clause, or independent clause? It's clear <u>that Fran isn't feeling well</u>.

    a Not a clause

    b Adverb clause

    c Adjective clause

    d Dependent clause

    e Independent clause

9 The company is giving the manager an award for her

    a imagination, persistence, and hard-working

    b imagination, persistent, and hard work.

    c imagination, persistence, and hard work

10 Darren often grows tired when reading his students' essays because he does so after work;

    a moreover,

    b unless

    c since

they are badly written and have many grammatical errors.

11 He is

    a devotion

    b devoted

    c devotee

to his work.

Paragraph and Essay Organization

Circle the letter of the correct answer.

Teacher Evaluation and Standardized Test Scores

Many Americans are concerned with failing public schools. Children often go to the next grade without the skills they need. American students' scores in reading, math, and science have been declining over the years. Though there are a number of social and economic reasons for the decline of American public schools, there is great awareness of the problem. <u>(a) Therefore, schools have responded by requiring annual standardized testing for every student</u>. These tests can be very helpful in determining whether a child is learning or not. However, schools in various cities now want to use test scores to determine whether a teacher is doing a good job.

1

   a There are a number of ways to measure teacher performance that would be more effective.

   b In my opinion, this could negatively affect curriculum, instruction, and student development.

   c Standardized testing is not a good measure of what students are able to do.

2

   a The first way it

   b Student test scores

   c First of all, an increased focus on standardized testing

would change a given school's curriculum in harmful ways. Standardized tests evaluate basic skills: reading, writing, math, and science in a timed setting using multiple-choice questions. They don't test history, music, arts, or physical education. Schools will feel pressured to drop these important subjects because

3

   a they

   b the fields

   c these important subjects

are not tested. Teachers of these subjects will be judged on the entire school's average, not on individual class performance. (b) Children need to study subjects such as geography and history in order to understand their world and become better citizens.

4

   a Furthermore, the arts

   b The arts, however,

   c For example, the arts

are important to creativity and self-expression, just as physical education is necessary to learn how to stay healthy.

5

   a Teachers nextly

   b Secondly, teachers

   c Teachers

will be less likely to use research-based classroom techniques because these would take time away from test preparation. Research suggests that students learn better when working with each other, but collaborative activities take a lot more time to prepare and execute than lecturing does. While collaboration teaches students important social skills necessary for success in the workplace, it doesn't prepare a student to do well on a multiple-choice, timed test. If teachers are evaluated on test scores alone, they will change their teaching methods to deliver good results on tests. (c) Research suggests that students as young as nine can give effective and helpful feedback about teacher performance; in addition, regular observations and teacher mentoring have also shown positive results. If scores are held to be paramount, it will become

6 a just as important to teach test preparation as
   b more important to teach test preparation than
   c important teaching test preparation

to teach social skills and teamwork.

Finally, students won't develop essential problem-solving and critical-thinking skills. Standardized tests evaluate what one knows, not the process through which one learns. There is only one correct answer

7 a , therefore,
   b , so
   c , for

a standardized test does not measure how well a student analyzes and solves problems. Critical reasoning skills are necessary for college preparation and job training. (d) Proponents of teacher evaluation through test scores have suggested that students who do well on standardized tests would also do well at critical thinking, but tests require very different skills than critical thinking demands. They require the student to remember

8

   a while
   b although
   c , whereas

critical thinking requires analytical skills.

In conclusion, while standardized testing is an important way to evaluate a student's progress, it is an ineffective assessment tool for teacher evaluation, since it neither improves the curriculum nor the teaching. While teacher evaluation is important, school districts should consider carefully the type of feedback they give teachers because it will affect how teachers deliver their lessons in the future.

9 The introduction of this essay begins with
   a a factual statement.
   b a question.
   c a quote.
   d a story.

10 Which of the supporting sentences in the essay (labeled a–d above) is off-topic or in the wrong place?
   a
   b
   c
   d

11 The conclusion ends with
   a a prediction.
   b a suggestion.
   c an opinion.

Post-Test 2

In the timed Post-Test 2, you will demonstrate how well you can write about a topic. Pay attention to sentence structure, grammar, punctuation, mechanics, organization, and vocabulary. You have 50 minutes to complete the test.

Write a five- or six-paragraph essay describing the causes and effects of the use of tobacco. Why do people smoke, and what effects does it have on others?

_____

_____

_____

_____

_____

_____

_____

_____

_____

_____

_____

_____

_____

_____

_____

_____

_____

_____

_____

_____

ANSWER KEY

PRE-TEST
Pre-Test 1

GRAMMAR pp. 1–3

1. b, b, 2. a, 3. c, 4. c, 5. b, 6. c, 7. b, 8. a, 9. b, 10. b, 11. c, 12. b, 13. b, 14. b, 15. a, 16. a, 17. c, 18. b, 19. a

PUNCTUATION AND MECHANICS pp. 3–4

1. b, 2. c, 3. c, 4. a, 5. c, 6. a

SENTENCE STRUCTURE pp. 4–6

1. a, 2. c, 3. b, 4. b, 5. a, 6. b, 7. a, 8. b, 9. c, 10. c, 11. a, 12. b, 13. c, 14. c

PARAGRAPH AND ESSAY ORGANIZATION pp. 6–8

1. c, 2. a, 3. b, 4. c, 5. a, 6. c, 7. b, 8. a, 9. b, 10. b, 11. b

Pre-Test 2 p.9

Answers will vary.

PUNCTUATION AND MECHANICS

Commas

Practice 1 pp. 11–12

1. a, 2. b, 3. b, 4. c, 5. a, 6. a, 7. c, 8. a, 9. c, 10. b, 11. c

Practice 2 pp. 12–13

1. c, 2. a, 3. a, 4. b, 5. b, 6. c, 7. a, 8. a, 9. c, 10. a

Parentheses

Practice 1 pp. 14–15

1. He was having a temper tantrum.

2. fifteen hundred dollars
3. ca. 150 million years ago
4. 5 feet 4 inches
5. Central Intelligence Agency
6. 1
7. after being silent for several minutes

Practice 2 p. 15

1. a, 2. b, 3. b, 4. a, 5. a, 6. a, 7. b, 8. a

Semicolons

Practice 1 pp. 16–17

1. a, 2. c, 3. b, 4. b, 5. c, 6. a, 7. b, 8. a, 9. a, 10. c

Practice 2 pp. 17–18

1. a, 2. b, 3. a, 4. a, 5. a, 6. a, 7. c, 8. a, 9. c, 10. a

Colons

Practice 1 pp. 20–21

1. a, 2. b, 3. a, 4. a, 5. c, 6. a, 7. b, 8. a, 9. c, 10. c

Practice 2 p. 21

1. ,
2. :
3. : ,
4. :
5. :
6. ; : : :
7. ,

Hyphens

Practice 1 p. 22

1. left-handed
2. sister-in-law
3. self-esteem
4. ex-wife
5. un-American
6. X-rays

7. twenty-one

8. two-door, four-wheel

9. two-thirds

10. Indian-American

11. five-minute

Practice 2 p. 23

1. good-tempered

2. part-time

3. twenty-four, duty-free

4. two-thirds, seventy-five

5. ex-boyfriend

6. happy-go-lucky

7. able-bodied

8. e-mail

Underlining and Italics

Practice 1 pp. 24–25

1. Moby Dick

2. The Nutcracker

3. coccinella septempunctata

4. r, l

5. and

6. Qigong

7. Gettysburg Address

8. The Mona Lisa

9. How to Win Friends and Influence People

Practice 2 pp. 25–26

1. b	3. b	5. a	7. a
2. c	4. c	6. c	

Abbreviations

Practice 1 p. 28

1. D.r.

2. US

3. Johns Hopkins Univ., French lit.

4. CA.

5. M.s., cosmetics corp.

Practice 2 pp. 28–29

1. b, 2. b, 3. a, 4. b, 5. c, 6. b, 7. c

Numbers

Practice 1 p. 30

The Soviet Luna III was the 3rd probe to be sent to the moon. It was launched in nineteen fiifty-nine by Russia. The probe was about 130 centimeters by 1,20 cm. It first approached the south pole of the moon at about 6,200 kilometers before traveling to the far side, which had never been seen at that time. The probe began to capture the first photographic images of the dark side of the moon at six-thirty A.M. on October 7, 1959, from a distance of 63,500 kilometers. 9 pictures were taken in all; the images detailed about 70% of the surface of the far side of the moon. Before the probe was lost, it transmitted some of the pictures to Earth. The 7 pictures recovered were the 1st pictures of the far side of the moon ever seen. It is believed that the probe burned up in the Earth's atmosphere in March 1960.

Practice 2 pp. 31–32

1. a, 2. a, 3. a, 4. b, 5. c, 6. c, 7. a, 8. c, 9. a, 10. b

Capitalization

Practice 1 p. 34

1. Olga is from Poland, but she speaks German and English fluently.

2. I had over 300 messages in my e-mail account by the time I returned home from vacation in Prague.

3. After William completes a master's degree in political science, he plans to move to Washington, D.C. and work for the Democratic Party.

4. Fanny Price is the famous heroine of the novel *Mansfield Park*.

5. The Declaration of Independence was signed on July 4, 1776.

6. Benjamin Franklin reportedly said, "We must all hang together, or most assuredly we shall all hang separately."

Practice 2 p. 35

<u>September</u> 23, 2015

<u>Camilla</u> <u>Frantz</u>

1234 <u>Devon</u> <u>Rd</u>.

<u>Denver</u>, <u>CO</u> 81102

<u>Dear</u> <u>Dr</u>. <u>Frantz</u>:

<u>I</u> am writing to apply for a position as a research intern at your lab.

<u>I</u> am a fourth year student at the <u>University</u> of <u>Colorado</u>. <u>I</u> expect to graduate in <u>June</u> 2016 with a bachelor's degree in organic chemistry. <u>I</u> plan to apply to the <u>CU</u> <u>Medical</u> <u>School</u> and eventually become a doctor. <u>I</u> am interested in this position because <u>I</u> am excited about the work you are doing at the cancer center, and <u>I</u> believe <u>I</u> could be a real asset to the lab.

<u>I</u> have attached a copy of my résumé with this cover letter. <u>Please</u> feel free to contact me at judith.eglos@uc.edu or call me at (333) 555-2345. <u>Thanks</u> in advance for your consideration.

<u>Sincerely</u>,

<u>Judith</u> <u>Eglos</u>

Quotation Marks

Practice 1 pp. 36–37

1. b, 2. a, 3. b, 4. a, 5. b, 6. b, 7. a, 8. b, 9. a, 10. b

Practice 2 pp. 37–38

1. b, 2. a, 3. a, 4. a, 5. b, 6. a, 7. b, 8. a, 9. b, 10. a

GRAMMAR

Complex Sentences

ADJECTIVE CLAUSES

Practice 1 p. 42

1. non-restrictive, yes
2. restrictive, no
3. restrictive, no
4. non-restrictive, yes
5. restrictive, no
6. non-restrictive, yes
7. non-restrictive, yes
8. restrictive, no
9. non-restrictive, yes
10. non-restrictive, yes

Practice 2 pp. 42–43

1. , who was upset with her daughter,
2. that were recently discovered in Denmark/ which were recently discovered in Denmark
3. where many famous jazz musicians began their careers
4. which the director wrote down / that the director wrote down
5. , who all suspected Agnes
   , all of whom suspected Agnes
6. , which compare the topic to a more common idea
7. that began in 1857
   which began in 1857
8. whom Hiram was referred to
   to whom Hiram was referred
   that Hiram was referred to
   Hiram was referred to
9. that Gary confided in
   whom Gary confided in
   in whom Gary confided
   Gary confided in
10. we eat
    that we eat
    which we eat
11. , which was thick with dust and grime,

ADVERB CLAUSES

Practice 1 pp. 44–45

1. a, 2. c, 3. b, 4. a, 5. a, 6. b, 7. a, 8. c, 9. a, 10. b, 11. c

Practice 2 pp. 45–46

1. She plans to accept the marriage proposal if her father approves.

2. To prevent identity theft, experts advise researching websites you want to do business with so that you can be sure the website is legitimate.

3. The lecturer brings her family with her everywhere she travels around the country to speak.

4. Since fossil fuels are not renewable, researchers have been developing alternative renewable energy sources.

5. Adrian is working longer hours so that he can save money to pay off his credit card.

6. Whenever pistol shrimp snap their claws, the resulting sound paralyzes their prey.

7. Space travel became possible only after the first rockets were developed by German scientists in the 1940s.

8. Jacob went back to school so that he could apply for a better-paying job.

9. She is careful with the antique vase, so that it can be preserved for future generations.

10. Although it has been passed down for generations in her family, the china still looks new.

11. While capital punishment still remains legal in some U.S. states, Canada has banned the practice altogether.

PARTICIPIAL PHRASES

Practice 1 pp. 47–48

1. a, 2. b, 3. b, 4. a, 5. c, 6. b, 7. a

Practice 2 pp. 48–49

1. a, 2. b, 3. a, 4. b, 5. a, 6. b, 7. b, 8. a, 9. b, 10. a

Causatives

Practice 1 pp. 51–52

1. a, 2. b, 3. a, 4. a, 5. b, 6. a, 7. b, 8. a, 9. a, 10. b

Practice 2 p. 52

1. a, 2. a, 3. b, 4. b, 5. a, 6. b, 7. b, 8. a, 9. b, 10. b, 11. a

Conditionals

REAL AND UNREAL CONDITIONAL SENTENCES

Practice 1 pp. 54–55

1. a, 2. a, 3. b, 4. a, 5. a, 6. b, 7. a, 8. b, 9. a, 10. b

Practice 2 p. 55

1. a, 2. b, 3. b, 4. a, 5. b

Hope vs. Wish

Practice 1 pp. 57–58

1. a, 2. c, 3. b, 4. c, 5. c, 6. b, 7. c, 8. a, 9. b, 10. c, 11. b

Practice 2 p. 58

1. hope	4. wish	7. hopes	10. wish
2. hope	5. hope	8. hope	11. hope
3. wish	6. wish	9. wish	

The Future

FUTURE PERFECT VS. FUTURE PERFECT PROGRESSIVE

Practice 1 pp. 60–61

1. b, 2. a, 3. a, 4. b, 5. a

6a. a	6c. a	6e. b
6b. a	6d. a	6f. a

Practice 2 p. 61

1. will have fallen asleep

2. will have researched

3. will have changed

4. will have been delivering / will be delivering

5. won't have become / will not have become

6. will have lost

7. will have been earning / will be earning

8. will be demanding / will have demanded

9. will have been producing / will have produced

FUTURE PROGRESSIVE

Practice 1 p. 63

1. a, 2. b, 3. a, 4. b, 5. b, 6. a, 7. b, 8. a, 9. b, 10. a, 11. b

Practice 2 p. 64

1. will be running
2. will be working / will work
3. will be running out / 'll be running out / will run out / 'll run out
4. will still be cooking
5. will be sleeping
6. will be walking / 'll be walking / will walk / 'll walk
7. will be sitting
8. will still be rehearsing / will still rehearse
9. will be dancing / will dance
10. will be fixing / will fix

Present Perfect vs. Present Perfect Progressive

Practice 1 pp. 66–67

1. a, 2. b, 3. a, 4. b, 5. a, 6. a, 7. a, 8. b, 9. b, 10. a

Practice 2 pp. 67–68

1. a, 2. a, 3. b, 4. b, 5. a, 6. b, 7. a, 8. a, 9. b, 10. a

The Past

SIMPLE PAST VS. PAST PERFECT

Practice 1 p. 70

1. ate, had missed
2. had just washed, began
3. saw, had read
4. started, had had, had worked

Practice 2 p. 70

Jackie had lived in the United States for almost six months when her father came for a visit. She had not received / hadn't received / 'd not received many letters from home, so she was eager to hear news about her family. Her father told her that her mother had not been / hadn't been well for several weeks during the summer, but she had recovered / 'd recovered completely by the time he left for the United States. She asked him why her mother had been so ill, and he said that she had had / 'd had the flu.

PAST PROGRESSIVE

Practice 1 p. 72

1. b, 2. a, 3. b, 4. a, 5. b, 6. a, 7. b, 8. b, 9. b, 10. a

Practice 2 p. 73

1. was writing
2. was fighting
3. was looking
4. was already sitting
5. was playing
6. was auditioning
7. was howling
8. was waiting
9. was playing
10. was worrying

Reflexive Pronouns

Practice 1 pp. 75–76

1. b, 2. a, 3. c, 4. c, 5. b, 6. a, 7. c, 8. a, 9. c, 10. b, 11. c

Practice 2 p. 76

When I was a child, both my parents worked outside the house, so my four siblings and I sometimes stayed home by ourselves. Our parents always encouraged us to be independent. It was not a problem for us to be alone because my older brother took care of us himself. We all knew we could depend on him to drop us off and pick us up from school. He was very strict, so we usually behaved ourselves around him. He didn't know how to cook, though, so my oldest sister had to prepare the meals by herself. As a result, from a young age, I learned to solve problems by myself. Today I am a father, too, and I also encourage my children to do as many things as possible for themselves.

Noun Clauses

Practice 1 p. 78

Our English teacher announced <u>that we would have a vocabulary test on Friday</u>.

Ms. Angela White is one of the most respected teachers in our school for several reasons. First, she takes the time to find out <u>who her students are</u>. She wants to know <u>what her students are interested in</u>, and she tries *to* connect her lessons to what her students want to learn. Second, her students say <u>that she is very fair</u>. She makes sure <u>that every person in her class gets an equal chance to participate</u>, and she never plays favorites. Next, Ms. White always gives clear instructions so that students understand exactly <u>what they are supposed to do</u>. In addition, she is sensitive to them. If they make mistakes, she knows <u>how to correct them</u> so that students do not feel ashamed. One last thing <u>that makes Ms. White such a good teacher</u> is her nice voice. Her students always mention <u>how much they enjoy listening to her</u>.

Practice 2 p. 78

1. that I should become a businessman
   what I wanted to do
2. what the homework is for Monday / what the homework for Monday is
3. A: how I can get there
   B: where that is
   A: that I won't find it / I won't find it
   B: whether you have GPS on your phone / if you have GPS on your phone
   B: how it works
4. who directed the movie *Titanic*
5. that we be at the auditorium no later than 7 P.M. / that we are at the auditorium no later than 7 P.M.
6. what time it is

The Subjunctive

Practice 1 p. 80

1. make
2. is, not turn in, doesn't learn / won't learn
3. be
4. follow, don't happen / won't happen
5. study, discuss, understands
6. meet

Practice 2 p. 81

1. that you make an appointment with the visa counselor
2. that you see your dentist twice a year
3. that you pay your phone bill on time / for you to pay your phone bill on time
4. that everyone not smoke cigarettes
5. that we call the fire department if we smell gas / to call the fire department if we smell gas
6. that American workers pay their income taxes by April 15 / for American workers to pay their income taxes by April 15
7. that I not procrastinate on my college applications
8. that a person see a doctor / to see a doctor
9. that you get your brakes checked / you to get your brakes checked
10. that I not wait to buy my textbooks / not to wait to buy my textbooks
11. that a few workers be laid off / laying a few workers off

Gerunds and Infinitives

Practice 1 p. 82

1. to study
2. to have
3. to carry
4. cheating, doing, copying, to get away with, to give, studying
5. to babysit
6. meeting

Practice 2 pp. 82–83

1. studying
2. to be picked up, to be held / held
3. cleaning
4. to go, to go out
5. studying, being, making
6. to learn
7. to offer
8. to tune

Direct and Indirect Speech

Practice 1 pp. 84–85

1. she didn't feel well
2. he had to finish the project that night
3. if the researchers were presenting there at the conference
4. not to turn the table over
   had been screwed in
5. yawning can be very contagious
6. how he could find a study group for that class
7. is a higher likelihood that a marriage will last if the couple has
8. to collect their things and go
9. workers had been taking too many breaks
10. drivers shouldn't talk on the phone
11. he would pick up the children from soccer practice

Practice 2 p. 85

1. she had met a cool guy the night before
2. where she had met him
3. they had been standing in line
4. whether he had been attractive
5. he had been nice-looking
6. whether they had exchanged
7. he had given her his number and asked her
8. the next day
9. if she was going to go out
10. wished she could, but she couldn't
11. she had decided

Modals

ABILITY AND POSSIBILITY

Practice 1 p. 86

1. Can you play
2. can't come / isn't able to com / may not come / might not come
3. may not join / might not join / can't join / couldn't join / isn't able to join
4. must not be / can't be / couldn't be
5. might be / must be / could be / may be
6. can't think / couldn't think
7. can't see / 'm not able to see
8. must still be / may still be / might still be / could still be
9. Could I sit / May I sit
10. could weaken / might weaken / may weaken
11. couldn't wear / weren't able to wear

Practice 2 p. 87

Switzerland is a very small country, but it has four official languages: German (70%), French (20%), Italian (4%), and Romansch (1%). Every school child must learn / can learn / may learn / is able to learn at least one second language in school. Furthermore, many children can pick up / are able to pick up a third or fourth language. Swiss people value multilingualism. As English is becoming increasingly popular in Switzerland, more Swiss people may choose / might choose to study English instead of one of the official languages. Thousands of tourists visit Switzerland each year, and most of them can't speak / aren't able to speak any of the countries official languages. Almost all of them can speak / are able to speak English, however. Some Swiss people are worried about the growing use of English in their country. They ask: "What effect might English have / may English have / can English have on the relationships between the different linguistic groups in the country?" These people are afraid that English may take / might take / could take over as the principal method of communication in the country and that this <u>could cause</u> the minor languages to die out. They say that the Swiss people <u>can't allow / mustn't allow</u> this to happen because multilingualism is an essential feature of Swiss history, culture, and identity.

NECESSITY AND ADVISABILITY

Practice 1 pp. 87–88

1. Should she have

2. must receive / have to receive

3. don't have to be

   do not have to be

4. doesn't have to study

   does not have to study

5. must not change / mustn't change / don't have to change / do not have to charge

6. ought to help / should help / must help / has to help / had better help / 'd better help

7. will have to cancel / should cancel / ought to cancel / had better cancel / 'd better cancel

8. have got to stop / have to stop / must stop / should stop / ought to stop / had better stop

9. had better not text / 'd better not text / must not text / mustn't text

10. Do you have to declare / Did you have to declare / Must you declare

11. should not get married / ought not get married / shouldn't get married / mustn't get married / must not get married

Practice 2 pp. 88–89

Have you thought about what would happen to your estate if you became disabled or died? Many people don't, but they <u>should consider / ought to consider / 'd better consider / had better consider</u> it carefully.

If you want to save your family from a headache and extra taxes, you <u>had better protect / have to protect / have got to protect / 'd better protect / ought to protect / should protect</u> your estate with a legal plan of some sort.

Here are three good reasons to have a plan: After you die, the courts <u>must follow / have to follow</u> state law if there is no legal plan. Your family <u>will have to complete</u> a legal process called probate to receive your property and possessions. During the probate process, the court can take about five percent of the estate. So, what <u>do you have to do / should you do</u>? There are three ways to protect your family in the event that you are disabled or die.

Most importantly, you <u>should set up / ought to set up / 'd better set up / had better set up</u> a trust for assets like bank accounts, houses, and cars. If there is a trust, your family <u>won't have to go / will not have to go / doesn't have to go / does not have to go</u> to court. You can use a kit to set up a trust. All you <u>have got to do / have to do</u> is choose a person called a trustee to be in charge of your trust after you die.

Additionally, you <u>ought to designate / should designate / 'd better designate / had better designate</u> or choose a beneficiary for your retirement and IRA accounts. You <u>must not include / mustn't include</u> these accounts in your trust. It's not allowed.

PAST HABITUAL ACTIVITY

Practice 1 pp. 89–90

1. wouldn't help

2. used to get

3. would get

4. would work

5. you use to go

6. become used to

1. wouldn't have

2. used to staying up

3. didn't use to have

4. Would you listen

5. Are you used to

Practice 2 p. 90

When I was seven years old, I <u>wouldn't go / 'd not go</u> near the water because I <u>used to be</u>

afraid. My mother <u>would bring / used to bring</u> my brothers to the pool for swimming lessons every Saturday. In the beginning, she <u>didn't used to require / wouldn't require</u> me to come. But after a while, she <u>would make / 'd make</u> me come because she wanted me to learn. My brothers <u>used to get / would get</u> in the water right away. They loved swimming. By that time, they had been swimming for over a year. However, I <u>used to start / 'd start / would start</u> crying when we got there. Eventually, though, I <u>got used to</u> the water. The teacher was very patient. She <u>would hold / used to hold / 'd hold</u> my hand and walk me down the stairs into the shallow end of the pool. Because of her, I'm not afraid anymore.

PERFECT FORMS

Practice 1 pp. 90–91

1. might have been out
2. should have bought / ought to have bought
3. should not have eaten / shouldn't have eaten
4. should have stayed / ought to have stayed
5. may not have finished / might not have finished
6. would not have gone / could not have gone
7. might have been / must have been
8. would not have made
9. should have paid
10. must have overslept
11. might have had / may have had

Practice 2 p. 91

WIFE: I had the worst day today. This morning the car would not start, so I had to find a different way to get to work.

HUSBAND: What did you do?

WIFE: Well, I <u>would have taken</u> the bus, but the bus station was too far to walk. I guess I <u>could have called / might have called</u> a taxi, but I was worried about money. Taxis are very expensive, and I know we

don't have much money right now. In the end, I called in sick again.

HUSBAND: Oh no, what <u>could have happened</u>?

WIFE: It <u>can't have been / couldn't have been</u> the gas. I just filled the tank. It <u>must have been</u> the battery. That's the only other thing I can think of.

HUSBAND: I thought you replaced it when you went to the mechanic last week. You <u>should have gotten / ought to have gotten</u> the battery replaced when you had the chance.

WIFE: I know, but I <u>couldn't have replaced</u> it last week. I hadn't been paid yet.

HUSBAND: You <u>shouldn't have waited</u>. I know you don't want to bother me, but <u>couldn't you have asked</u> me for the money? I <u>would rather have helped</u> than risk your missing any more work.

WIFE: I had no idea you <u>would have given</u> me the money. You are right. I <u>should have told / ought to have told</u> you what was happening.

PROGRESSIVE FORMS

Practice 1 p. 92

1. could be running
2. could have been flying / could be flying
3. would have been celebrating / would be celebrating / could be celebrating
4. has to be working / must be working
5. should I be doing / could I be doing
   could be calling / might be calling / ought to be calling / should be calling
6. shouldn't have been sleeping / should not have been sleeping
   have got to be leaving / have to be leaving / must be leaving

7. could he be doing / may he be doing / might he be doing

can't be watching

must be playing

Practice 2 p. 93

1. must be playing / might be playing / may be playing

can't possibly be studying

2. would have rather been skiing / would rather be skiing

3. might be working / could be working / might have been working / could have been working / would be working / would have been working / 'd be working / 'd have been working

4. could have been preventing / could be preventing / might be preventing / might have been preventing

might have been visiting / could have been visiting

might not have been feeling / would not have been feeling / wouldn't have been feeling / could not have been feeling / couldn't have been feeling

5. had better be starting up / should be starting up / ought to be starting up

6. may have been riding / might have been riding / could have been riding

couldn't have been riding / can't have been riding

The Passive Voice

Practice 1 pp. 94–95

1. is adjourned

2. was being tailored / was tailored

3. the refrigerator had been fixed

4. may be asked to revise

5. will be promoted / is going to be promoted / 's going to be promoted / 'll be promoted

6. was hired to plan and manage

7. is felt that

8. have been being read to / have been read to

9. being served

10. is going to be written

11. having been yelled at

Practice 2 p. 95

1. a, 2. b, 3. a, 4. a, 5. b, 6. b, 7. b, 8. a, 9. a, 10. b

Quantifiers

Practice 1 p. 96

1. several

2. The number of

3. hardly any, Most of the

4. Each of

5. several, a large amount of

6. a lot of, plenty of, much, many

Practice 2 p. 96

1. not much

2. a little, few

3. One of

4. a number of, many

5. many, and every one of

6. plenty of

7. some, not enough

Articles

Practice 1 p. 97

1. The	5. a	9. the
2. the	6. an	10. the
3. the	7. Ø	11. a
4. Ø	8. Ø	

Practice 2 p. 97

1. A, a, Ø	2. The	3. a
4. the, Ø, Ø, The, an, Ø		

SENTENCE STRUCTURE

Agreement

PRONOUNS

Practice 1 p. 99

1. a, 2. b, 3. c, 4. c, 5. b, 6. a, 7. a, 8. a, 9. c, 10. a

Practice 2 pp. 99–100

Bill Gates was born on October 28, 1955, in Seattle, Washington. His interest in software began at an early age. By 13, Gates had already begun programming computers, and by 20, he had co-founded Microsoft with his childhood friend, Paul Allen. Together, they began developing software for personal computers.

On January 1, 1994, Gates married Melinda French, and the couple had two children. Later, they founded the Bill & Melinda Gates Foundation. A person of great financial means (Forbes magazine has ranked him as the richest person in the world 15 times), Gates has made philanthropy an important part of his life. He and Melinda have endowed their foundation with more than $21 billion to support initiatives in global health and learning. Gates believes that " . . . if you show people the problems and you show them the solutions, they will be moved to act." And he uses his vast fortune to bring solutions to people most in need.

Gates also believes that personal computers have revolutionized how people communicate and interact worldwide. To him, " . . . personal computers have become the most empowering tool we've ever created. They're tools of communication, they're tools of creativity, and they can be shaped by their users" — that is, by people like you and me.

Although one of the wealthiest and most influential people in the world, Gates is, in many ways, just like the rest of us—he worries about his children and their future, and he complains about spam mail!! As he says, "Like almost everyone who uses email, I receive a ton of spam every day. Much of it offers to help me get out of debt or get rich quick. It would be funny if it weren't so irritating.

POSSESSIVE ADJECTIVES AND PRONOUNS

Practice 1 p. 101

1. our	6. their
2. My	7. Your
3. her	8. theirs
4. our	9. our
5. its	10. mine

Practice 2 p. 101

1. her	5. Whose	9. your
2. her	6. my	10. hers
3. his	7. yours	11. our
4. his	8. mine	

INDEFINITE PRONOUNS

Practice 1 pp. 102–103

1. c, 2. b, 3. a, 4. a, 5. b, 6. c, 7. c, 8. b, 9. a

Practice 2 p. 103

In the United States, anyone who wants to be a teacher must have a college education. No one is given a class to teach unless he or she also completes at least one year of supervised teaching. Many colleges offer five-year programs that give students more time in the classroom. Each new teacher is also required to pass tests to get a teaching certificate from his or her state. Several states require more than one test, while others have a video evaluation. Everything new teachers have to go through is worth it, though. Each time a child learns something new, one forgets about everything else. For most teachers, nothing else is better than that.

Collocations

Practice 1 p. 105

1. b, 2. a, 3. b, 4. a, 5. b, 6. a, 7. b, 8. a, 9. b

Practice 2 p. 106

1. a, 2. c, 3. c, 4. a, 5. b, 6. b, 7. a, 8. b, 9. a, 10. c

Correlative Conjunctions

Practice 1 p. 108

1. a, 2. a, 3. a, 4. a, 5. b, 6. a, 7. b, 8. b, 9. b

Practice 2 pp. 108–109

1. either
2. both
3. or
4. nor
5. but also
6. whether / if
7. Both
8. but
9. Not only

Parallel Structure

Practice 1 p. 111

1. she hopes to make
2. snow
3. they also use social media
4. blocking them from accessing any inappropriate sites
5. go to the pool
6. they also hope to live longer
7. save the money to pay for it
8. she also wanted an iPad

Practice 2 pp. 111–112

1. stop, drop, cover yourself
2. opened the shed, grabbed his tools, he headed towards the vegetable patch
3. he was doing a good job with his projects, [that] he wasn't working very well with his coworkers
4. an associate's degree, three years of experience, two letters of reference
5. to keep quiet, to turn off their phones
6. Jun's determination to win, [his **or** Jun's] willingness to work long hours

Word Forms

Practice 1 p. 114

Column 1: classify, demonstrate, effect, threaten

Column 2: demonstrability, inclusiveness, measurement, modification

Column 3: classifiable, exceptional

Column 4: creatively, threateningly

Practice 2 pp. 114–115

1. placement
2. critically
3. criticizes
4. distinguished
5. distinguished
6. establish
7. establishment
8. innovative
9. innovations
10. recognizably
11. recognition

Appositives

Practice 1 pp. 116–117

1. b, 2. c, 3. b, 4. b, 5. b, 6. b, 7. d

Practice 2 p. 118

Rosa Parks <u>the mother of the Civil Rights Movement who began the Montgomery Bus Boycott</u> was born Rosa Louise McCauley on February 4, 1913, in Tuskegee <u>a city in the state of Alabama.</u>

She left Tuskegee when her parents got divorced. She moved to a farm in Pine Level, where her grandparents lived. They had been slaves and opposed Jim Crow laws, laws segregating whites and blacks in the South. Rosa's early experiences with segregation affected her deeply. For example, she went to a segregated school for African Americans. Her school had no money for important resources <u>books, pens, paper, school buses,</u> whereas the white school had supplies and school buses for its children.

Rosa wasn't able to finish school because her grandmother got sick. When she was 18 years old, she married a barber Raymond Parks from Montgomery, another city in Alabama. Raymond Parks was a member of the NAACP, the National Association for the Advancement of Colored People a society dedicated to improving African American lives. He encouraged Rosa to finish school and get involved in the organization. Soon, she became the secretary to E.D. Nixon, the president of the NAACP.

Rosa's involvement in the Civil Rights Movement began on December 1, 1955. She was working as a seamstress a job sewing clothing and rode the bus to and from work. At that time, the law stated that African Americans and whites had to sit separately on buses, so blacks sat in the back of the bus, and whites sat in the front. If the bus got too crowded, blacks were asked to stand. Rosa was tired that day, so when she was asked to stand, she refused. She was arrested and taken to jail.

The people in the NAACP decided to protest her arrest and the law. They started the Montgomery Bus Boycott a city-wide boycott of the bus system. No African Americans in the city took the bus for almost one year. They walked, biked, carpooled, and took taxis. On December 20, 1956, Montgomery changed the law and stopped segregation on public buses. This initial success led to the Civil Rights Movement, a decade-long campaign against segregation in the South.

Simple Sentences

Practice 1 pp. 119–121

1. a, 2. a, 3. a, 4. b, 5. c, 6. a, 7. c, 8. c, 9. d, 10. a, 11. c, 12. a, 13. a, 14. b, 15. a

Practice 2 pp. 121–122

1. b, 2. a, 3. b, 4. a, 5. a, 6. b, 7. a, 8. a, 9. b

Compound Sentences

Practice 1 pp. 124–125

1. c, 2. b, 3. c, 4. a, 5. a, c, 6. b, 7. a, 8. a, 9. c, 10. a, 11. a

Practice 2 pp. 126–127

1. , for
2. , for
3. ;
4. ; otherwise,
5. ; therefore,
6. ; for example,
7. , or
8. , yet
9. not only … , but also
10. Either … , or
11. ; however,

Independent and Dependent Clauses

Practice 1 pp. 128–129

1. b, 2. b, 3. a, 4. b, 5. c, 6. a, 7. b, 8. a, 9. b, 10. a, 11. b

Practice 2 p. 130

Do you know the difference between an alligator and a crocodile? Many people confuse these reptiles because they look so similar and have comparable behaviors. Nevertheless, alligators and crocodiles are different in several ways.

One difference can be seen in the animal's nose, or snout. An alligator has a wide, round snout, whereas the snout of a crocodile is longer and more pointed.

A second difference is where the two animals can be found. Alligators are found only in two places in the world: the United States and China. In contrast, crocodiles are found in 91 countries, which is about 51 percent of all the countries in the world. However, they can only live in warm, wet climates. Therefore, there are no crocodiles in Canada, northern Europe, or Russia.

The wild alligator population in the United States is estimated to number more than 1 million animals; on the other hand, the Chinese alligator, which is smaller than its American cousin, is nearly extinct. American alligators outnumber American crocodiles by about 1,000 to 1. Since only about 500 wild crocodiles remain on the whole continent, crocodiles are considered a species that is endangered and needs protection by law. There are many myths about alligators and crocodiles. For example, many people believe that they can live for hundreds of years, but this is only a myth. In fact, though captive alligators and crocodiles may live 60 to 80 years, wild alligators and crocodiles usually only live to be 30 or 40 years old.

Complex Sentences

Practice 1 p. 132

1. a, 2. b, 3. a, 4. a, 5. b, 6. b, 7. a, 8. b, 9. a

Practice 2 pp. 133–134

1. a, 2. b, 3. a, 4. b, 5. a, 6. a, 7. a, 8. b, 9. a, 10. a

Compound-Complex Sentences

Practice 1 pp. 135–136

1. b, 2. a, 3. b, 4. a, 5. a, 6. b, 7. a, 8. b, 9. a

Practice 2 pp. 136–137

1. b, 2. d, 3. c, 4. a, 5. b, 6. d, 7. d, 8. a, 9. d, 10. c

Fragments

Practice 1 pp. 138–140

1. a, 2. d, 3. c, 4. b, 5. a, 6. d, 7. e, 8. c, 9. d, 10. e, 11. a

Practice 2 p. 140

Corn that is a native plant to the Western Hemisphere. The Indians of North and South America growing corn for thousands of years before Columbus arrived in the New World in 1492. Indeed, fossils of ancient corn cobs can be found in museums today. When Columbus and his ships landed in the West Indies. He traded with the natives there. Taking corn back with him to Spain. From there, corn was introduced to other Western European countries. And eventually to the rest of the world. When the first European settlers came to the New World, the Indians given them corn to eat. Thereby saving them from near-certain starvation. During their first harsh winter in America, the Indians called this life-saving food "ma-hiz." Which the settlers pronounced as "maize." Later, the Indians taught the settlers how to plant corn and use it in the preparation of various foods. Corn was very valuable in those days. That was used as a form of money and traded for meat and furs. Today, the United States grows about 80 percent of the world's corn. And the world's largest exporter.

Run-On Sentences and Comma Splices

Practice 1 pp. 142–143

1. c, 2. a, 3. b, 4. c, 5. c, 6. a, 7. b, 8. b

Practice 2 pp. 143–144

1. Unless there is a place where I can get a hot shower, I
2. good because they were missing their guitarist
3. is so terrible that people
4. in the United States; furthermore, it has OR in the United States. Furthermore, it has
5. As soon as I completed the online survey, I
6. While the woman was in the shower, the package
7. an auction in order to get donations
8. because of the snow, but avid skiers can't wait OR because of the snow, while avid skiers can't wait

9. this weekend, for we are going to

10. Whenever the students want to study late, they go

11. emergency procedures after the building

Choppy Sentences

Practice 1 pp. 145–147

1. a, 2. b, 3. a, 4. a, 5. b, 6. a, 7. b, 8. a, 9. a, 10. b

Practice 2 pp. 147–148

1. a, 2. b, 3. b, 4. a, 5. a, 6. b, 7. a

Stringy Sentences

Practice 1 pp. 150–151

1. b, 2. a, 3. b, 4. b, 5. a, 6. b, 7. a, 8. b

Practice 2 pp. 151–152

1a. However, he

1b. because it

1c. Unfortunately, he

2a. because they

2b. ; in addition, they

3a. However, the

3b. ; it is

3c. Furthermore, the

4a. in order to

4b. Nevertheless,

4c. , so

PARAGRAPH AND ESSAY ORGANIZATION

Paragraphs

TOPIC SENTENCES

Practice 1 pp. 154–155

1. b, 2. a, 3. b, 4. b, 5. b, 6. a, 7. b, 8. a, 9. a, 10. b, 11. b, 12. b

Practice 2 pp. 155–156

1. c, 2. a, 3. b

SUPPORTING SENTENCES

Practice 1 p. 157

1. a, 2. b, 3. b

Practice 2 p. 157

1. a, 2. c, 3. b

CONCLUDING SENTENCES

Practice 1 pp. 159–160

1. a, 2. b, 3. c, 4. d, 5. b, 6. a, 7. a, 8. c, 9. d

Practice 2 pp. 160–161

1. b, 2. a, 3. c

UNITY

Practice 1 p. 162

1. b, 2. a, 3. a, 4. b, 5. a, 6. a, 7. a, 8. a, 9. a, 10. c

Practice 2 p. 163

Sibling rivalry is a problem which has several solutions. It is common for brothers and sisters to get upset and fight over toys, activities, and adult attention. Some parents punish children for fighting with time-outs, and others resort to spanking. One simple way to reduce sibling rivalry is to actively teach children to share with each other. Often, parents will buy two or three of the same toy for each child to reduce fighting. A second way to decrease rivalry is for each parent to spend individual time with each child. Individual time doing what each child wants can help the child feel accepted and loved for who he or she is. Experts have shown that children who feel more secure about their parents' love don't fight as often with their siblings. In fact, researchers suggest that children who have siblings develop their personalities by being different from their older and younger siblings. It is clear that parents can encourage better relationships between their children by teaching sharing and spending time individually with each child.

COHERENCE

Practice 1 p. 165

New immigrants could be encouraged to improve <u>his</u> English and become active members in American society in several ways. Often, language difficulties and unfamiliar customs can cause newcomers to the United States to move to a neighborhood where other people from their country live. This can provide a great deal of comfort for the newcomers; thus, <u>he or she</u> may not venture far outside. However, the problem is that they never fully integrate <u>himself</u> into American society. It is important to develop programs that encourage newcomers to learn the language and get familiar with <u>them</u>. They provide low-cost or free English classes for immigrants which may help <u>immigrants</u> with the language barrier. Currently, colleges offer classes on campus, but <u>it</u> might be more well-attended if they were offered in immigrant neighborhoods or at workplaces where immigrants are employed. To sum up, language classes can help immigrants feel more connected and less isolated.

Practice 2 p. 165

1. autism
2. Asperger's
3. a person
4. someone
5. autism
6. a person with Asperger's
7. he or she
8. this mild disorder
9. he or she
10. his or her

Essays

INTRODUCTIONS

Practice 1 pp. 166–168

1. c, 2. e, 3. a, 4. d, 5. e, 6. b, 7. d, 8. a, 9. c, 10. e

Practice 2 pp. 168–169

1. e, 2. a, 3. c, 4. d, 5. e, 6. c, 7. a, 8. b, 9. d, 10. e

THESIS STATEMENTS

Practice 1 p. 171

1. A. returning to school
   B. challenges
2. A. success
   B. completing a goal
3. A. Barack Obama and Franklin D. Roosevelt face similar challenges
   B. different approaches

Practice 2 pp. 171–172

1. b, 2. a, 3. b, 4. b, 5. a, 6. b, 7. b, 8. b, 9. a

CONCLUSIONS

Practice 1 pp. 173–174

1. b, 2. c, 3. a, 4. a

Practice 2 pp. 175–176

1. c, 2. a, 3. b, 4. b

ESSAY STRUCTURE

Practice 1 pp. 177–178

1. a, 2. c, 3. b, 4. a, 5. c, 6. c, 7. c, 8. b

Practice 2 pp. 178–179

I.   Introduction

Thesis: [4]

II. Body Paragraphs

A. [5]

1. [7]

2. A reader decodes to recognize words.

B. [8]

1. A reader uses grammar to understand sentences.

2. [2]

C. [3]

1. The ability to switch between decoding and understanding should be automatic.

2. [6]

III. Conclusion

In conclusion, [1]

COHESION

Practice 1 pp. 183–184

1. For this reason
2. First of all
3. Therefore
4. However
5. Secondly
6. Consequently
7. Finally
8. As a result
9. In addition
10. In conclusion

Practice 2 pp. 184–185

1. Therefore
2. because
3. The first step
4. After
5. the next step
6. As a final step
7. Consequently
8. In addition
9. To conclude

Body Paragraphs

LOGICAL DIVISION OF IDEAS

Practice 1 p. 189

1. several simple solutions
2. the most popular solution
3. the main reason
4. furthermore
5. Long-term solutions like
6. simple solutions
7. Some popular distractions
8. another simple solution
9. Either of these deterrents

Practice 2 p. 190

1. advantages
2. First
3. A second advantage

4. Additionally
5. Furthermore
6. Moreover
7. in order to
8. Thus
9. loneliness, self-esteem, and isolation

CHRONOLOGICAL ORDER

Practice 1 p. 192

1. Upon arriving
2. When
3. Eventually
4. After the dinner ends
5. Finally
6. After Gretta finishes
7. Soon after

Practice 2 p. 193

1. the stages of the writing process
2. Before
3. First
4. As soon as
5. As you write
6. The final stage
7. As you receive feedback

COMPARISON SIGNALS

Practice 1 p. 195

1. a number of parallels
2. Both
3. and
4. Similarly
5. share
6. just as deceptive as
7. similar resolutions
8. quite like

Practice 2 p. 196

1. common
2. both
3. Not only
4. but they also
5. as likely as

6. equally

7. similar

8. the same

9. a number of similar geological features

CONTRAST SIGNALS

Practice 1 p. 198

1. but now

2. some of the differences between

3. a better scientific reputation than

4. In contrast

5. a smaller group

6. more heavily

7. as opposed to

8. Another important difference between

9. Unlike conventional medicine

Practice 2 p. 199

1. But in the last few years,

2. But

3. However

4. different from

5. In contrast

6. Despite

7. Nevertheless

8. though

CAUSE AND EFFECT SIGNALS

Practice 1 p. 201

1. can affect anyone

2. caused by combat

3. because the symptoms

4. the effects of

5. As a result

6. as a consequence

7. because of their PTSD

8. In order to avoid

9. as their behavior

10. can be affected in

Practice 2 p. 202

1. the cause

2. effect

3. results in

4. causes

5. One reason

6. because

7. consequences

8. therefore

WRITING ASSIGNMENTS

pp. 203–251 Answers will vary.

POST-TEST

Post-Test 1

GRAMMAR pp. 267–270

1. c, c, 2. b, 3. b, 4. a, a, 5. b, 6. c, 7. b, 8. a, 9. a, 10. a, b, 11. a, 12. b, 13. b, 14. b, 15. a, 16. a, 17. c, 18. a, 19. a

PUNCTUATION AND MECHANICS pp. 270–271

1. a, 2. a, 3. b, 4. a, 5. c, 6. b

SENTENCE STRUCTURE pp. 271–272

1. a, 2. c, 3. b, 4. a, 5. c, 6. b, 7. b, 8. d, 9. b, 10. a, 11. b

PARAGRAPH AND ESSAY ORGANIZATION pp. 272–274

1. b, 2. c, 3. a, 4. a, 5. b, 6. b, 7. b, 8. c, 9. a, 10. c, 11. c

Post-Test 2 p. 275

Answers will vary.